HEINEMANN BOOKS ON SOCIOLOGY

General Editor: Donald Gunn MacRae

Questionnaire Design and Attitude Measurement

QUESTIONNAIRE DESIGN AND ATTITUDE MEASUREMENT

A. N. Oppenheim

Reader in Social Psychology,
London School of Economics and Political Science

HEINEMANN · LONDON

Heinemann Educational Books Ltd
22 Bedford Square, London WC1B 3HH
LONDON EDINBURGH MELBOURNE AUCKLAND
HONG KONG SINGAPORE KUALA LUMPUR NEW DELHI
IBADAN NAIROBI JOHANNESBURG
EXETER (NH) KINGSTON PORT OF SPAIN

ISBN 0 435 82676 X

First published 1966
First published as an HEB paperback 1968
Reprinted 1968, 1970, 1972, 1973, 1976, 1978, 1979

Printed in Great Britain by Morrison & Gibb Ltd.
London and Edinburgh

TO BETWYN

Preface

The world is full of well-meaning people who believe that anyone who can write plain English and has a modicum of common sense can produce a good questionnaire. This book is not for them.

It is intended to help all those who, for one reason or another, have to design a questionnaire. It could serve as a textbook for research students and undergraduates in Social Psychology and Sociology, and for practitioners of market research. It could also help doctors, personnel officers, civil servants, criminologists, social anthropologists, teachers, and many others whose curiosity or need for information may impel them into the quicksands of social research.

Questionnaire design cannot be taught from books; every investigation presents new and different problems. A textbook can only hope to prevent some of the worst pitfalls and to give practical, do-it-yourself kind of information that will point the way out of difficulties. It is not meant to be a work of scholarship, nor is it exhaustive. The number of references has been kept to a minimum, though some annotated readings have been provided with each chapter. Throughout, clarity and basic ease of understanding have been my guidelines; in each case, an attempt has been made to present the main lines of the argument, and while not shirking weaknesses in underlying assumptions, to omit some of the more esoteric controversies.

A short test of statistical knowledge is included (Appendix II), to help the reader to decide whether he may need a refresher course before embarking on a social inquiry.

Inevitably, a choice has had to be made concerning what to include and what to leave out. This book does *not* deal with theory construction and the principles of explanation, with interviewing techniques, group-observation procedures, content analysis, sampling, elementary statistics, observational methods, motivation research, interpretation, or report writing. It *does* deal with question writing, both factual and attitudinal, and with attitude-scaling and projective techniques. In the choice of examples, an attempt has been made to avoid parochialism and to maintain variety; a sprinkling of examples from commercial research is included.

It is a pleasure to acknowledge my indebtedness to Hilde Himmelweit, Graham Kalton, Douglas Price-Williams, Norman Hotopf, Judson Mills, Bridget Dalison, John Raven, Penelope Leach, Eve Tidhar, and to many of my graduate students for helping me to improve the original manuscript. The responsibility for its remaining faults must be mine. Lorna Gadbury did wonders in turning the original draft into a publishable typescript.

January 1966
London

A. N. Oppenheim

Contents

Questionnaire Design and Attitude Measurement

1

Problems of Survey Design

Introduction

A survey is a form of planned collection of data for the purpose of description or prediction as a guide to action or for the purpose of analyzing the relationships between certain variables, such as cancer and smoking. Surveys are usually conducted on a fairly large scale, as contrasted with laboratory experiments, which tend to be more intensive but on a smaller scale. To gather data, social surveys use questionnaires and interviews, attitude scales, projective techniques, and various related methods; small-scale experiments, for instance in the classroom, may also use these.

A social-research study may last from a few months to many years, but most surveys go through the same stages or cycles of stages. We may distinguish the following:

1. Deciding the aims of the study and the hypotheses to be investigated.

2. Reviewing the relevant literature; discussions with informants and interested bodies.

3. Designing the study and making the hypotheses specific to a situation (making the hypotheses operational).

4. Designing or adapting the necessary research methods and techniques; pilot work and revision of the research instruments.

5. The sampling process: selection of the people to be approached.

6. The field-work stage: data-collection and returns.

7. Processing the data, coding the responses, and preparing punch cards.

8. The statistical analysis (simple at first, but becoming more complex); testing for statistical significance.

9. Assembling the results and testing the hypotheses.

10. Writing up the results: relating the findings to other research; drawing conclusions and interpretations.

It is obvious that a survey is an operation of some complexity, and, therefore, a first requirement is the development of a good plan or over-all design, which is the problem that will concern us in this chapter. Succeeding chapters will describe how to create or adapt such research techniques as questionnaires, attitude scales, and so forth that are relevant to our stated aims, and, finally, how to deal with data-processing and -analysis.

There are textbooks available, such as those by Hyman[11] and Moser,[10] that deal with survey methods through all their stages; inevitably, in such books there is less opportunity to take any one stage and consider it extensively. The present volume tries to complement those more general texts. It will *not* deal with sampling or with basic statistics (anyone who feels uncertain about the adequacy of his statistical background should try the test in Appendix II, which requires no calculations), with theory construction and the nature of explanation, with content analysis, or with experiments in group dynamics. It will not deal specifically with the problems of interviewing, interviewer-selection, or interviewer bias. Its main aim is to provide guidance for the design of questionnaires and to discuss various techniques for the measurement of attitudes and their analysis.

The subject of questionnaire design is intimately related to the general plan or design of the survey. A questionnaire is not just a list of questions or a form to be filled out. It is essentially a scientific instrument for measurement and for collection of particular kinds of data. Like all such instruments, it has to be specially designed according to particular specifications and with specific aims in mind, and the data it yields are subject to error.

We cannot judge a questionnaire as good or bad, efficient or inefficient, unless we know what job it was meant to do. This means that we have to think not merely about the wording of particular questions, but, first and foremost, about the design of the investigation as a whole.

The Need for Survey Design

Too often, surveys are carried out on the basis of insufficient design and planning or on the basis of no design at all. "Fact-gathering" can be an exciting and tempting activity to which a questionnaire opens a quick and seemingly easy avenue; the weaknesses in the design are frequently not realized until the results have to be interpreted—if then! Survey literature abounds with portentous conclusions based on faulty inferences from insufficient evidence wrongly assembled and misguidedly collected. Not everyone realizes that the design of a survey, besides requiring a certain amount of technical knowledge, is a prolonged and arduous intellectual exercise, in the course of which we are trying to get our own minds clear about our goals. We often find that, as the early stages of the research take shape, its aim undergoes a number of subtle changes as a consequence of greater clarity in our thinking. Such changes may require a new and better design, which in turn will lead to a better specification for the instrument of measurement, the questionnaire.

Survey design attempts to answer such questions as: Which variables should be measured? What kind of sample will be drawn? Are control groups needed? Who will be questioned, and how often? What scales may have to be built or adapted? And so on. It can be helpful to approach the natural sequence of survey operations in reverse order. First, let us decide exactly what conclusions we wish to be able to draw. Then, we can state what statistical tables and cross-tabulations of results we shall need to permit the drawing of these conclusions or their antitheses. From the tabulations, we can infer the type of questions and their quantification and something fairly precise about the nature of the sample required.

The process of survey design as a whole is aimed at precision, logic-tightness, and efficiency. A poorly designed survey fails to provide accurate answers to the questions at issue; it leaves too many loopholes in the conclusions; it produces much irrelevant information, thereby wasting case material and money.

Some years ago, when television-viewing was rapidly gaining ground in Great Britain, a survey was commissioned to supply answers to two broad questions: (1) What kinds of people were buying television sets? (2) How was the new medium affecting them? The large-scale survey that eventually took place used two samples. The first was intended to be representative of television-owners and was drawn from the lists of television license holders. This sample was bound to be incomplete since it failed to include set-owners who had not applied for a license, but by and large it could give reasonable estimates of the income, family size, social and educational background, religion, consumer habits, and so on of television owners at that time.

The second sample was assembled by asking the interviewers to question the householder in a non-television home adjacent to that of each set-owner in the first sample. It was reasoned that by interviewing the people next door a sample could be obtained, for purposes of comparison, that would be similar to the television-owners in milieu, socioeconomic background, consumer habits, and so forth.

The faults in this design were only realized toward the end of the investigation. Let us consider the logic of it step by step. The research had two purposes. The first was to find out what kinds of people were buying television sets. This implied something more than a purely descriptive study of a representative sample of set-owners, since to state that such families had an average income of X pounds a week or that Y per cent of them had telephones or washing machines would be almost meaningless unless it could be put into some kind of context; in other words, it had to be compared to other figures. It might then become possible to conclude that television-buyers more often came from the lower income levels, or had larger families, were less religious, and so on. For a few points of comparison, data were probably available for the nation as a whole (including the television-owners), but most of the questions had to be asked again. In order to show how television-buyers differed from nonbuyers, the second sample would have to be a representative sample of all the people who had not bought a television set. That a sample of people living next door to set-owners would accurately represent the nonbuying public was clearly too much to hope for, since in any case they had been chosen on the grounds of similarity in milieu and socioeconomic background to the television-owners. As the figures subsequently showed, the second sample, not being representative of the non-television-buyers, was usless for purposes of comparison. Consequently, the accurate figures obtained from the first sample could not be made to reveal any social change or pattern.

And what of the second purpose of the investigation; how was the new medium affecting television-owners? Here there were many difficulties, since it is often hard to disentangle the effects of *one* variable, such as television, from the effects of many others operating at the same time. A comparative study can try to do this by making the control sample as similar as possible to the television sample in every relevant respect, so that we can see what the people in the television sample would have been like if they had not bought television sets. There are still weaknesses even then, because of pre-existing differences, matching problems, and effects of guest-viewing, but the sample design failed to produce sufficient similarity between the two groups. Consequently, there was no way of telling whether or in what way changes had been produced in the television sample.

The second sample, that of the neighbors, turned out to be useless. It was neither a representative sample of non-television-buyers (as required for the first purpose) nor a closely comparable control sample (as required for the second purpose). It should have been realized from the beginning that, since the inquiry had two purposes, two different comparison samples were required. This may seem obvious in retrospect, but the professional survey organization that carried out the research realized too late what had happened. Mistakes like this occur every day and can only be prevented by making every effort to clear our minds before we start.

Cause and Effect

The study we have looked at in the preceding section raises many other interesting problems of design, not the least of which is the problem of causal interpretation. We might have found, for instance, that viewers go to church less often than do their controls. Does this "prove" that television causes people to go to church less often? Clearly not, since it might be shown that the sample of viewers had been going to church less often even before they bought their television sets. (To show this, we would need a longitudinal design of the before-and-after type, interviewing the same sample at least twice, once before and once after buying a television set.) Surveys cannot usually show a causal connection; all that they can do is indicate associations or correlates, and so we must be careful in our interpretation of results. Whereas our results would suggest that A causes B, we must allow for the possibilities that B caused (or at any rate preceded) A or that both A and B are the result of C—a third variable that affects them both. In the above case, a general "materialistic" outlook might produce both the infrequent church-going and the early television acquisition. In social research, we rarely find relations of the type "A causes B"; more often we deal with complex patterns of interacting variables where B is the outcome of a whole range of determinants, each of which accounts for only a small portion of the variance. This means that, in designing our study, we must make allowance for multiple variables in interaction.

In any study of effects or changes, the respondents will probably have their own ideas concerning the nature and degree of such changes, and these ideas may well bias the way they answer our questions. Thus, if we wish to know how television has affected visiting behavior, we should certainly never ask: "Do you find that you go to visit friends less often now that you have a television set?" (which would be a grossly leading question and open to a biased response by the subject, according to whether he did or did not think it had reduced his visiting and regarded this as something to be proud of or to conceal) or even, "Since you have had a television set, do you go to visit friends (1) more often, (2) less often, or (3) about the same as before?" (which is still too open to bias and distortion, though less leading). It might be better, if possible, to conceal the purpose of the research, say, by making it a general inquiry into leisure habits and asking a series of factual questions about the subject's current behavior, comparing the answers to those given by a matched control group without television. However, this problem of concealment raises ethical issues as well as difficulties in design; it also tends to make questionnaires longer, since concealment often takes the form of "burying" the crucial questions among a number of unimportant ones.

In the commercial field, one is often asked to design a survey among the users of Product P. On inquiry, it may turn out that the research has two distinct purposes: first, to expand the market for Product P and, second, to make current users buy Product P more often. A survey among the users may well suggest ways in which they could be persuaded to buy P more frequently, but it is unlikely to help us meet the first purpose, namely, to sell P to nonusers. It now becomes clear that we need two samples and two questionnaires—one for users and one for nonusers; other samples, such as one of ex-users, might be added. Again, it is essential to clear our minds before we start.

Descriptive and Analytic Survey Designs

The function of research design is to help us obtain clear answers to meaningful problems. Depending on the type of problem, we may need to carry out a controlled laboratory experiment, a large-scale survey, or we may find ourselves involved in a "natural experiment." In all three cases, we will have to carry out measurements and collect data.

Experiments and surveys are often contrasted with one another. Those who favor surveys criticize experiments for being unrepresentative and for dealing with artificial situations. Experimentalists are critical of surveys for their reduced ability to control important variables, for following events rather than making them happen, and for their inability to prove causal relationships. Indeed, the survey is sometimes called "the poor man's experiment," but, on the other hand, laboratory experiments often fail to achieve the degree of precision and control that would justify them. Perhaps it would be more helpful to suggest that choosing the best design or the best method is a matter of appropriateness. No single approach is always necessarily superior; it all depends on what we need to find out, on the type of question to which we seek an answer. Indeed, many research inquiries have employed *both* surveys and experiments at different phases, using the results of the one to inform and refine the other, so producing conclusions that are both precise and representative.

It is possible to make a broad distinction between two types of survey: (1) the descriptive, enumerative, census type of survey; (2) the analytic, relational type of survey. The purpose of the descriptive survey is to count. When it cannot count everyone, it counts a representative sample and then makes inferences about the population as a whole. There are several ways of drawing representative samples, and the whole problem of sampling and sampling error is dealt with in a number of excellent textbooks (see, for instance, Moser[10]). The important point to realize is that such surveys chiefly tell us how many members of a population have a certain characteristic or how often certain events occur; they are not designed to "explain" anything or to show relationships between one variable and another.

Descriptive surveys are well known and important. Any form of census falls into this category, as do many public-opinion polls and commercial investigations. These surveys provide governments, manufacturers, economists, and politicians with necessary information for action. The job of such surveys is essentially fact-finding and actuarial—although it should be added that the data thus collected are often used to make predictions, for instance by comparing the results of surveys at different times and producing a trend, by trying to forecast elections or the number of new homes that will be required in ten years' time, and so on. Representativeness (or full enumeration) of a defined population is a first requirement.

There are many questions that actuarial surveys cannot answer or can only answer inadequately, since they were never designed to do so. Such questions usually start as "why"-questions and then proceed to an examination of group differences from which relationships between variables can be inferred. For instance, in comparing the results of election polls, we may find a rise, over a period of time, in the percentage of people choosing a particular party. We may wonder why this is happening and wish to explore the suggestion that, say, this party's policy on old-age provisions makes it very attractive to older voters. We go back to our data and arrange the results according to age to see whether there are marked age-group differences. We could go further and try to find out whether low-income groups, or childless elderly couples, or young couples with elderly dependents are more prone to vote for this party, but clearly, there is a limit to what we can do in this way: we may not have obtained the necessary information about income or elderly dependents; there may not be enough low-income voters above a certain age in our sample; we may not have asked any questions bearing on pensions, and so forth.

It is this kind of analytic, relational survey, set up specifically to explore the relationships between particular variables, that is sometimes referred to as "the poor man's experiment," since its design is quite similar to that of laboratory experiments. It is less oriented toward representativeness and more toward finding associations and explanations, less toward description and more toward prediction, less likely to ask "how many" or "how often" than "why" and "what goes with what." Like experiments in the laboratory, it is usually set up to explore specific hypotheses.

Types of Variables

In designing such a survey, it is helpful to distinguish between different kinds of variable:

1. Experimental variables. These are the factors the effects of which we are trying to study, our "causes" or predictors, sometimes referred to as "independent" or "explanatory" variables. The analytic type of survey, like the experiment in the laboratory, is so set up that these factors can be varied systematically, so

that the results can be observed. We are often interested in several such variables working both in isolation and in various combinations.

2. Dependent variables. These are our results, the effects-variables, the "yield," the predicted outcome. These variables have to be carefully measured and group differences tested for statistical significance.

3. Controlled variables. We are trying to eliminate these as a source of variation in our study in order to fulfill the condition of "other things being equal" when we state the effects or correlates of our experimental variables. We can control variables by excluding them (for example, by having only males in our sample, thus excluding sex as a source of variation); by holding them constant (for instance, by interviewing all respondents on the same day, thus eliminating day-of-the-week effects); or by randomization (for instance, in the case of a multiple-choice question, by systematically randomizing the order in which the alternatives are presented to the respondents, thus eliminating serial effects as a source of variation).

4. Uncontrolled variables. These are "free-floating" variables, and can be of two kinds: a) confounded variables, and b) error. The confounded variables, sometimes called "correlated biases," have influences of unknown size on the results, which are very difficult to disentangle and can lead to serious misinterpretation of the findings (but also can lead to the development of new hypotheses). The error variables are (or are assumed to be) randomly distributed or, at any rate, distributed in such a way as not to affect the results.

In analytic surveys, as in experiments, we always try to make the influence of the uncontrolled variables as small as possible. To study or eliminate the effects of confounded variables, we may need to engage in a large number of cross-tabulations; we may have to match various subgroups; or we can use regression-analyses and other statistical techniques.

An example may help to clarify these terms. Let us assume that we are trying to understand some of the determinants of children's bedtimes. We have decided to study the effects of age, which will be our experimental variable, and the survey will obtain information from a sample of children for every day of the week. Our dependent variable will be the children's bedtime, in all its variations. There are many variables that we will have to control in order to observe the effects of age. For instance, children who have recently been ill may have to go to bed especially early; we will probably control this variable by excluding such children from the sample. Children go to bed later in the summer and on school holidays; we may control these variables by holding them constant, that is, by collecting all our data during one short period in the school term. Children go to bed later if they have older brothers or sisters; we can try to take care of this by randomizing, making sure that children with older siblings are randomly distributed through our sample. There remain a considerable number of uncontrolled variables, some of which are very likely to be confounded. For instance, socioeconomic background is likely to be an important influence on bedtimes; if we realize this in advance, we may be able to control it, but otherwise this factor can easily introduce a bias in our conclusions. It may, for instance, happen that the older children in our sample also come from more well-to-do homes, where bedtimes tend to be earlier; in that case, we may wrongly conclude that increasing age is *not* a good predictor of later bedtimes because, unknown to us, the socioeconomic factor is counteracting the age factor. Again, the child's sex, membership in a youth organization, or a keen liking for television may be important determinants of bedtimes in parts of our sample. Such uncontrolled variables, unless they are known to be randomly distributed, can readily bias the results to an unknown degree. The "ideal" design would contain no uncontrolled variables.

Cross-Sectional Designs

In the preceding example we have compared the bedtimes of different children at different ages, on the assumption that these comparisons could tell us what would happen to children over a period of time. We have not actually taken the *same* group of children and followed them over a number of years. We hoped that the groups of children were comparable and that we could thus in fact observe the relationship between age and bedtimes. This type of design is known as cross-sectional, to distinguish it from longitudinal or "before-and-after" designs.

Suppose that in our example we had obtained a representative sample of children, say, between the ages of five and fifteen. What often happens is that such a sample is collected for a descriptive or actuarial purpose and that a kind of cross-sectional design is imposed on it afterward. First, we obtain the over-all average bedtime. Next, we compare the different age-groups and find that bedtimes get later with increasing age. Then, we decide to compare the sexes, and we find that boys, on the average, go to bed a little later than girls. We go on in this way, comparing bedtimes against a number of variables in turn, such as social class, size of family, urban/rural differences, and so on. Suppose that each time we find a difference in bedtimes. We now want to go further; we want to know, for instance, whether the age-differences still remain if we hold social class constant. This means that for each of our social-class groupings, we have to compare the bedtimes of children in their different age-groups separately. We could go still further and try to study the effects of three variables in combination, say, social class, urban/rural, and size-of-family differences. However, to do this we need to have a sufficient number of cases in each of our combinations or "cells" (unless our predictions refer only to *part* of the sample). Some of these cells will be readily filled, for instance those for children from large families in rural districts with working-class backgrounds. Other cells will be difficult to fill or may remain empty, such as those for children from small working-class families in rural areas. This is because a sample selected to be representative of the child population as a whole will not contain sufficient numbers of these rarer combinations to make comparisons possible. But by now its representativeness has become almost irrelevant and somewhat of an embarrassment, since we no longer ask "How many?" but "What goes with what?" We have moved from a descriptive to an analytic type of survey that tries to answer questions about relationships and determinants, and therefore, we shall need a different type of sample, a sample that is primarily geared to making comparisons.

Upon reexamining the preceding example, we note that our difficulties arose partly from running out of cases to fill the cells representing rare combinations, and partly from the fact that some of our experimental variables were related to one another, as well as to the dependent variable (bedtimes). Thus, in finding differences between children with urban or rural backgrounds, we wondered whether this difference would disappear if we held social class constant, because the proportion of working-class children was much higher among the rural part of our sample. Perhaps, if there had been as many middle-class children as working-class children in both the urban and the rural parts of our sample, the urban/rural differences would have been negligible. This kind of difficulty can sometimes be handled by using a weighted stratified sample, but this requires a modified sampling technique.

Another point we note is that it becomes necessary to plan the comparisons we wish to make in advance and to make them part of our research design; we cannot usually apply this kind of analysis to a sample which has been collected for some other purpose.

Factorial Designs

This kind of thinking has led logically to the development of factorial designs, whose particular function is to disentangle complex sets of interrelationships. They are analogous to the "agricultural plots" type of design, which led to the development of analysis-of-variance techniques (see Fisher,[5] Cochran and Cox,[6] and Maxwell[7] for the statistical analysis of experimental designs). Analysis of variance is, however, chiefly applicable to quantitative variables, whereas surveys deal mostly with qualitative variables, such as percentages.

This type of analytic survey design is one of the ways in which we can approach laboratory conditions. However, in laboratory experimentation we create or introduce our experimental variables and, while controlling for most other variables, observe the concomitant changes in the dependent variable. In survey research we are not normally in a position to impose experimental factors or to manipulate the lives of our respondents, for instance by allocating them at random to an experimental or a control group. Instead, we select respondents who already have the characteristics required by our design and compare them in their groupings.

At the outset, we have to decide which are going to be our experimental variables—we will want to vary these systematically and in combinations with one another. We must aim to control all other variables by exclusion, holding constant, or randomizing. The choice of experimental variables predetermines what we can hope to get out of our study; if we decide, later on, that some other variable should have been chosen, it may not be possible to show its effects except by selecting a new sample. This means that we must have an adequate general idea beforehand of the lay of the land in our particular area, either through previous studies or from the pilot work.

The choice of our experimental variables will be limited by practical considerations. We might start off rather ambitiously by choosing, say, sex, age, class, urban/rural, and size of family in our bedtimes study. Let us assume that we have ten age-divisions, seven socioeconomic grades, and five family-size groupings, while sex and urban/rural are dichotomies. This would give us a design containing $10 \times 7 \times 5 \times 2 \times 2 = 1{,}400$ cells, which, even at no more than ten cases per cell, would require 14,000 children. If this is unacceptable, we can either cut down the number of experimental variables, or make them cruder (for example, by reducing class from a seven-point scale to a dichotomy), or probably both. In this way we can reduce the number of cells and, thus, the number of cases required, to more manageable proportions. Even so, a design with three dozen cells and forty cases per cell would not be at all unusual. Equal (or proportionate) numbers of cases are required in each cell in order to disentangle the experimental variables from one another.

The number of cases per cell will often have to depend on the highest number obtainable in the cell which is most difficult to fill. Another important consideration will be the range of answers in our dependent variable(s). If, say, our dependent variable has ten possible responses, then we must remember that this will split up our cells even further. Suppose we wish to compare two groups of four cells each with respect to one particular answer category and that there are forty cases in each cell. That would give us two groups of 160 cases to compare, which would seem to be quite appreciable numbers; however, if there are ten answer categories, then we may expect each of them to be chosen with a frequency of around 16, on the average. Thus, one sample may give this particular answer 19 times, the other 14 times, but only extreme differences would be statistically significant under such conditions. So, sooner or later, we will either combine larger groups of cells for our comparisons (thus losing some of the benefits of the factorial design), or we will classify our answers more crudely, or both.

Factorial designs are efficient. For the number of cases required they yield more information about relationships than almost any other type of design. They use these cases over and over again to make comparisons for each factor in turn and then for their various combinations and interactions. Also, instead of dealing with just one experimental variable and controlling all others, the factorial design enables us to study several experimental variables in combination. Not only does this provide us with more information, but also with greater confidence in predicting the results under various circumstances.

A disadvantage of the factorial design is the need for careful selection of cases. Sometimes this will mean that a special enumeration stage, using only a short questionnaire, will have to precede the main inquiry (the much larger enumeration sample being used to supply the respondents to fit each cell of the factorial design). At other times, the number of respondents in some cells will unavoidably remain below requirements, and in that case, some method of statistical extrapolation or "randomized replication" will have to be used.

The factorial design makes no pretense of being representative. Indeed, in its final form it is often markedly unrepresentative, due to the need to incorporate equal or proportionate numbers of respondents in each cell, so that very rare combinations of determinants may be encountered as often as the more popular or typical ones. (However, it is usually possible to extrapolate and adjust afterward, so as to make this kind of sample yield population estimates also.) The respondents in each cell should be a representative sample of all those eligible to be in that cell. It should also be remembered that the strength of the relationships shown in a factorial design might not be found to quite the same extent or in quite the same way in other samples. Instead of sampling persons, one could imagine sampling relationships, which might not be present in uniform degree throughout a population.

The factorial design permits us to vary our experimental factors systematically and in combinations of two or more. Needless to say, it also requires us to introduce measures to control the remaining variables and to eliminate as many uncontrolled variables as possible. Some of this can be done, as before, by exclusion, holding constant, and randomization, but inevitably some confounded variables may remain. In the later stages of the analysis, various hypotheses concerning these confounded variables will be explored by means of special cross-tabulations, matching of subsamples (see below), and by regression-analysis. While a confounded variable may turn out to have an unexpected effect on the results, upsetting the regular pattern of the design as planned, it can also be stimulating to further research and the discovery of new relationships.

Longitudinal Designs and Panel Studies

We have already seen that a cross-sectional design cannot tell us anything about cause-and-effect relationships; it can only provide us with information about correlates. In an effort to overcome this, longitudinal or before-and-after designs have been developed. A set of measurements is taken of a group of respondents, who are then subjected to the experimental variable and afterwards measured once again or perhaps several times. At first sight, it may appear that this design will present far fewer problems in terms of controlled and uncontrolled variables, because the respondents in the sample "act as their own controls." They provide the "other-things-being-equal" condition that enables us to draw conclusions about the effects of the experimental variable. Moreover, under these conditions, differences would be more likely to attain statistical significance. (Related t-test becomes applicable.)

We cannot, however, legitimately attribute *all* the before-and-after differences to the effects of the variable we are investigating until we have made sure that without it such changes would not have occurred. Quite likely, with the passage of time and the introduction of new events, *some* differences may occur which cannot be attributed to the experimental variable. If the respondents are aware that they are participating in a survey or experiment, this in itself will produce certain changes. It is therefore necessary to have, in addition to the experimental group, a matched control group. If, for instance, we are investigating a new method of medical treatment for a particular illness, we cannot simply count the number of recoveries and attribute these to the new treatment; we need to know also how many people would have improved anyway, and by subtracting this number from the number of recoveries in the experimental group, we arrive at the net effects of the treatment. Thus, we should have two groups whose "before" results will be subtracted from those found "after"; the difference between these two subtractions will constitute our results.

There are numerous examples in survey literature where this precaution has been neglected, sometimes with very misleading results. In studies of the effects of psychoanalysis, for instance, recovery rates of about two out of three were often reported and attributed to the success of the treatment, until similar but almost untreated samples were shown to have the same rates of improvement ("spontaneous remission"). Again, in early trials of new drugs, the psychological effect of being given a new medicine (the "placebo" effect) is often very positive, making it difficult to evaluate the effects of the drugs themselves; therefore, the control group is given some inert substance (a placebo) and made to feel part of the experiment. In the "double blind" trials, neither patients nor medical staff know who is being given the new drug and who is receiving placebos, in an effort to isolate the effects of the drug from those of other variables. Often, several control groups are needed, to show the effects of varied dosages or other conditions.

The function of the control group is to show us what would have happened to the experimental group if it had not been subjected to the experimental variable. The two groups should, therefore, be closely matched. There are several ways of achieving this. Sometimes, it is possible to draw the two samples in exactly the same way from a larger population or to split the original sample in two in a completely random way. At other times, all we can do is to match for the over-all distributions on a few important variables, for instance making sure that both groups contain the same percentage of women, that their average age is about the same, and that the proportion of people with a university education is the same in both groups. An improvement on this is individual matching; for each respondent in the experimental group, we select another individual just like him to act as control. Since, obviously, we cannot match pairs of individuals on everything, we should match them on those variables which are relevant (likely to be related) to the dependent variable. In a well-studied field we will know on what to match (though even then there may be practical difficulties), but in other areas we have only common sense and a limited amount of pilot experience to guide us. The situation becomes even more difficult when, as often happens in surveys, we have numerous dependent variables. If we are studying, say, the effects of television on children, the dependent variables will cover changed leisure habits, information gains, changes in interests, sleep disturbances, emotional effects, and so on, each of which has a different set of determinants. This would mean that we would need to match on different criteria for each type of effect in turn! In practice, matching is usually only possible on four or five variables together, within fairly crude limits, so that investigators tend to choose those with the widest relevance to the different types of effects to be studied. Inevitably, some variance remains uncontrolled.

William A. Belson[13] has developed a statistical method of matching that makes "before" testing unnecessary. This method involves a preliminary study in which the "stable correlates" of the dependent variable are ascertained with some precision. In the main research, measures are only taken *after* the introduction of the experimental variable. The pre-experimental data are obtained by "prediction" backward in time with the aid of the stable correlates. This approach is probably most suitable where numerous studies involving the same dependent variable have to be made.

How is it possible, outside the laboratory, to introduce an experimental variable and to study groups of people before and after its introduction? Sometimes, volunteers are recruited—though there are dangers in generalizing from them. At other times, a policy-making body will ask for the collaboration of social scientists in introducing and evaluating certain planned changes. Occasionally, an alert social scientist will make use of the emergence of a new social variable in order to do a before-and-after study; such studies are often referred to as "natural experiments." In these studies, in addition to the requirements of matching and control groups, we also have to concern ourselves with whatever caused certain respondents to subject themselves to these new variables in the first place. The problems of self-selection and volunteer bias are particularly intractable because they cannot be overcome by matching. The question to be answered is not, "Has self-selection produced a bias?" but rather, "Is the self-selection bias related to the dependent variables?"

A panel study is a particular kind of longitudinal study that usually involves not merely one "before" and one "after" measurement or interview, but several, sometimes over a considerable period of time. This is, for instance, how a trend or the impact of a political campaign can be evaluated. Panel studies do not aim for great precision and frequently do not have control groups; their function is more often to throw light on processes of slow, informal influence and change or to illustrate the stages through which people go in adapting themselves to a new variable. Panel studies can throw more light on turnover: percentage distributions before and after may be the same (or different), but they do not show how many individuals have changed. Similar overall distributions may be produced by very different turnover rates; even control groups may have unexpectedly high turnover rates. Inevitably, panel studies suffer from the problems of volunteer bias and contracting sample size. It becomes more and more difficult, as each interviewing wave follows the next, to locate panel members and to maintain their interest in the survey, and replacements are only a partial answer to this. Often, too, members of a panel begin to take a special interest in the problems at issue; they become more knowledgeable and more critical and, to that extent, less representative; or members of a panel may change their behavior as a result of the greater awareness produced by repeated questioning. Nevertheless, successful longitudinal studies can make unique contributions. (See Douglas and Blomfield.[19])

Follow-up studies of various kinds also use panels, but many of these, too, are weakened by the absence of a separate control group. Studies in social medicine and epidemiology frequently employ survey methods, the panel-study design among them. We may distinguish prospective and retrospective studies. In a retrospective study we look at people who already suffer from the disease or abnormality and try to find antecedent factors that are linked with it. In a prospective study we take a given population "at risk" and follow it for a given period, comparing those who develop the disease with those who do not in order to uncover possible causes. Studies of the connection between smoking and lung cancer have used both designs. Medical surveys can often point to a previously unsuspected cause by plotting cases of a given disease geographically or by relating them to other variables, such as occupation or diet, which can then be followed up in the laboratory.

Error

All research is involved in the never-ending fight against error. Sometimes it is possible to compare observed differences between groups against "chance errors" by means of statistical tests of significance, for instance, in designs in which respondents have been assigned to one of two or more groups at random. More often, however, our attempts at controlling variables have left a host of possible sources of error unaccounted for, such as:

faults in the design of the survey;

sampling errors;
errors due to nonresponse;
bias due to questionnaire-design and question-wording;
unreliability or lack of validity of various techniques used;
varieties of interviewer bias;
respondent unreliability, ignorance, misunderstanding, reticence, or bias;
bias in recording and coding the responses;
errors in processing and statistical analysis;
faulty interpretation of the results.

Great strides have been made in recent years in the improvement of sampling methods and the assessment of sampling-error limits, but the remaining sources of error are still very much with us, and any of them could easily outweigh the gains from improved sampling techniques. Nor is this all, for each of these sources of error covers a dozen or more types of error, to each of which a chapter could be devoted. (See, for instance, Hyman,[15] Moser,[10] Kahn and Cannell.[16] While this is the case, and so long as questionnaire methodology and technique are built up haphazardly and are themselves so rarely subjected to controlled experimentation, it behooves the research worker to remain severely critical, to search out biases in others and in himself, and to avoid giving the appearance of spurious exactitude.

• *Selected Readings*

SAMPLING METHODS

1. A. Stuart, *Basic Ideas of Scientific Sampling* (London: Griffin, 1962).

   An excellent, nonmathematical account.

2. Isidor Chein, "An Introduction to Sampling," Appendix B in Claire Selltiz, Marie Jahoda, Morton Deutsch, and Stuart W. Cook, eds., *Research Methods in Social Relations* (New York: Holt, 1959).

3. F. Yates, *Sampling Methods for Censuses and Surveys* (London: Griffin, 1949).

4. Morris H. Hansen, William N. Hurwitz, and William G. Mordon, *Sample Survey Methods and Theory* (New York: Wiley, 1953), Vol. I.

   Practical sampling methods applied to surveys.

EXPERIMENTAL DESIGN

5. Ronald A. Fisher, *The Design of Experiments* (Edinburgh: Oliver and Boyd, 1947).

   A classical textbook on experimental design.

6. W. G. Cochran and G. M. Cox, *Experimental Designs* (New York: Wiley, 1950).

7. A. E. Maxwell, *Experimental Design in Psychology and the Medical Sciences* (London: Methuen, 1958).

8. Allen L. Edwards, "Experiments: Their Planning and Execution," in Gardner Lindzey, ed., *Handbook of Social Psychology* (Cambridge, Mass.: Addison-Wesley, 1954).

9. D. R. Cox, *Planning of Experiments* (New York: Wiley, 1961).

SURVEY DESIGN

10. Claus A. Moser, *Survey Methods in Social Investigation* (London: Heinemann, 1958).

    A good general text on survey methods. See especially chapters on sampling and on interviewing.

11. Herbert H. Hyman, *Survey Design and Analysis: Principles, Cases, and Procedures* (Glencoe, Ill.: Free Press, 1955).

    For the advanced student.

12. Robert L. Kahn and Charles F. Cannell, *The Dynamics of Interviewing* (New York: Wiley, 1957).

    A useful textbook on surveys, questionnaire-design, and interviewing.

MATCHING PROBLEMS

13. William A. Belson, "Matching and Prediction on the Principle of Biological Classification," *Applied Statistics*, VIII (1959), 65–75.

    On the uses of the stable-correlates method of matching.

14. W. Z. Billewicz, "Matched Samples in Medical Investigations," *British Journal of Preventive and Social Medicine*, XVIII (1964), 167–173.

INTERVIEWER ERRORS

15. Herbert H. Hyman *et al.*, *Interviewing in Social Research* (Chicago: University of Chicago Press, 1954).

Experimental studies of interviewer bias and the effects of interviewers on respondents.

16. Robert L. Kahn and Charles F. Cannell *The Dynamics of Interviewing* (New York: Wiley, 1957).

See especially the section dealing with interviewer bias.

EPIDEMIOLOGY AND SOCIAL MEDICINE

17. J. N. Morris, *Uses of Epidemiology* (Edinburgh: Livingstone, 1957).

A short basic textbook.

PANEL STUDIES

18. Morris Rosenberg, Wagner Thieleus, and Paul Lazarsfeld, "The Panel Study," in Marie Jahoda, Morton Deutsch, and Stuart W. Cook, eds., *Research Methods in Social Relations* (New York: Dryden Press, 1951), Part II.

19. James W. B. Douglas and J. M. Blomfield, "The Reliability of Longitudinal Surveys," *The Millbank Memorial Fund Quarterly*, XXXIV (1956), 227–252.

2

Problems of Questionnaire Design

From what has gone before, it is clear that questionnaire construction is by no means the first stage in carrying out a survey. Many weeks of planning, reading, design, and exploratory pilot work will be needed before any sort of specification for a questionnaire can be determined. The specification will follow directly from the operational statement of the issues to be investigated and from the design that has been adopted. The questionnaire has a job to do: its function is measurement, and the specification should state the main variables to be measured.

Before actually constructing the questionnaire, we would have formed a rough idea of the pattern that the inquiry is likely to follow. We would know approximate answers to such issues as how large will the sample be? Will we be dealing with children or with adults; with housewives, company directors, relatives of prisoners, or undergraduates; or with a representative sample of the population? Do we intend to approach the same respondents more than once? Are we concerned with seasonal fluctuations? Are we dealing with a short, factual inquiry or with analytic, attitudinal research? And so on. But we still have to make a number of decisions before we can begin to write our first question. These decisions fall into five groups: (1) Decisions con-

cerning the main and auxiliary methods of data-collection, such

as interviews, mail questionnaires, observational techniques, and study of documents; (2) The method of approach to the respondents (after selection through sampling procedures), including sponsorship, stated purpose of the research, confidentiality, and anonymity; (3) The build-up of question sequences and the order of questions and other techniques within the framework of the questionnaire; (4) For each variable, the *order* of questions within each question sequence, such as funneling, quintamensional design, and factual versus attitudinal opening; and (5) The use of precoded versus free-response questions.

Though decisions of this kind can benefit from general considerations such as will be given in this chapter, it is to be emphasized that each survey presents its own problems and difficulties and that expert advice and spurious orthodoxy are no substitutes for well-organized pilot work. The importance of really careful piloting will be stressed over and over again in these pages; pilot work can help us with the actual wording of questions, but also with such procedural matters as the design of a letter of introduction, the ordering of question sequences, and the reduction of nonresponse rates.

Pilot Work

Almost every aspect of a survey inquiry can be made the subject of pilot work, so that obviously a line has to be drawn somewhere. The greatest amount of pilot work will usually be devoted to those problems that are thought to be most difficult at the outset and to those that are most important from the point of view of the survey as a whole. The measurement of the dependent variable will often take pride of place, but very likely we will also have to develop new attitude scales or projective devices, questions about personal habits and attributes, and ways of collecting background data. It is essential that some of the pilot interviewing be done by the research director himself.

The earliest stages of pilot work are likely to be exploratory. They might involve lengthy, unstructured interviews; talks with key informants; or the accumulation of essays written around the subject of the inquiry. Once this has given us a "feel" for the problem, the remainder of the pilot work will have to proceed in organized form. This organization should be somewhat like an assembly line; after intensive work on each subsection, the results should be put together into a coherent whole. Pilot work can proceed piecemeal with advantage and might even be farmed out, but we should never lose sight of the order and sequence of the total structure. Often the "ideal method" developed in part of the pilot work will be too lengthy or cumbersome in relation to the rest of the survey; with the information from the pilot work before us, we are, however, in a much better position to shorten or alter a particular technique than if we had "just jotted down a few questions."

Pilot work can be of the greatest help in devising the actual wording of questions, and it operates as a healthy check, since fatal ambiguities may lurk in the most unexpected quarters. When a question is reworded after pilot work, it must be piloted again; the rewording may have introduced new difficulties or biases. When an "open," free-answer question is turned into a multiple-choice one, it must be repiloted in its new form. Some questions may go through as many as eight revisions before producing satisfactory results, and it is not uncommon to "use up" several hundred respondents in pilot work. Even questions that are "borrowed" from other surveys need to be piloted, to ensure that they will yield satisfactory results with our kind of respondents.

It is probably best, therefore, to start off with a number of question booklets—rather in the manner of subassemblies—each covering a particular variable to be measured. Such subsections can be piloted and developed on their own, without involving the rest of the questionnaire-to-be; this will break up the pilot work into a number of small operations and give us experience in contacting our respondents, explaining the purpose of the survey, timing each operation, and so forth. When ready, several subsections may be piloted together, and eventually we will need to pilot the questionnaire as a whole.

As suggested earlier, question-wording is not the only problem to which pilot work should be devoted. Letters of introduction should be piloted, as should be various ways of reducing nonresponse. We can pilot the color of the paper we use, the effect of the age or sex of our interviewers, the ordinal position of multiple responses (do people tend to pick the first and the last items?), and the timing of each section of the questionnaire (so as to avoid overburdening respondents). If these issues are important, pilot studies of some size and complexity may be needed.

It is important, at this point, to think well ahead toward the analysis stage. For instance, suppose we are doing a survey of the adjustment of foreign students in this country and that we propose, as important variables for assessment, their pattern of friendship choices, their leisure-time activities, and their contacts with home. We will of course be thinking of ways to question students on these points in some detail, but we should repeatedly ask ourselves exactly why we need these answers and what we propose to do with them later on. For instance, with regard to friendship choices, do we want to obtain an estimate of the extent to which respondents chiefly make friends with members of their own nationality? If so, we would have to ask for the nationality of each friend mentioned and compute some kind of ratio. Do we want to investigate in what way various social contacts have influenced their attitude toward this country? If so, we would have to get an assessment of the "satisfactoriness" of these relationships. If we ask them about their leisure-time activities, perhaps these should be compared to their previous leisure patterns in their own country. Have we remembered to ask about those, and is the information in comparable form? Are we, at a later stage, going to want to calculate an over-all "adjustment index" or a "loneliness quotient"? If so, *now* is the time to work out exactly how this should be done.

This kind of thinking ahead does not necessarily mean added questions and greater complexity; sometimes it helps to simplify questions. A well-known example concerns asking female respondents for their age. This can cause a certain amount of embarrassment, and so we must consider what we are going to do with this information. Very likely we will use it in our tabulations in condensed form, such as "over 45" versus "under 45" or in steps of ten or fifteen years at a time. If this is so, then we need not ask respondents for their exact age, they should merely be asked to state whether they are over 45 or under, or whether they are in their twenties, thirties, forties, and so on, thus causing less embarrassment. The purpose of each question must be kept in mind.

In the process, due attention should be given to the methods of statistical analysis to be used. A well-phrased question emerging from careful pilot work may produce responses that are difficult to quantify. The calculation of an index or a scale score may produce computational difficulties. The introduction of probes and of multiple answers to the same question each produce problems of quantification, to which attention should be paid during the pilot stages. (See Chapter 9.) Altogether, there is a limit in any survey to the number of free-answer questions that can be coded.

How do we know whether a question needs rewording? In principle, we always try to see whether the responses tell us what we need to know, but, in addition, there is always the problem of inadvertent biases. A poor question will produce a narrow range of responses or will be misunderstood by part of our sample; it may be too vague in content or ask for information which the respondent does not have or cannot remember; it may be a leading question, which biases the answers, or a question that operates at the wrong level of intimacy for its purpose. A question may be too wide or too narrow in scope; it may require an introductory sentence or a supplementary question; it may be too colloquial or too technical, too intimate or too abstract. Perhaps most typical are questions that seem perfectly reasonable but which produce meaningless answers. For instance: "How do the clothes you wear at home compare to the clothes you wear at work?"—which will produce answers such as "Very well," "Not at all," "Somewhat better," "About the same." These tell us nothing about the cost, type, quality, or degree of formality of either set of clothes and only occasionally indicate which set is regarded as "better."

Probably the best way to assess a question is to make it part of a short questionnaire and administer it to a pilot sample of about fifty people. All answers to each question should then be copied onto sheets of paper, one sheet per question. In this way, one can see quickly whether the question has any of the above faults and whether the answers seem to bear on the issues required. Sometimes it helps to group the questionnaires before copying, in order of the respondents' ages or in terms of socio-economic class or some other experimental variable. Such copied sets of responses are a great help in anticipating the problems of coding and statistical analysis and in devising multiple-choice answer categories. Though pilot samples tend to be small, some of the anticipated group differences should emerge and can be given greater scope and precision.

One of the chief uses of pilot work is to enable us to turn free-answer questions into multiple-choice ones. For instance, suppose we asked people to say what vitamins are. We might find from the pilot work that definitions tend to fall into four or five circumscribed categories, in which case we might gain in speed and in ease of administration if we offered our respondents five alternatives plus one "Other (please specify)" category. On the other hand, the spread of answers might be such that multiple choices would have to be many and lengthy, in which case we might leave the question "open." Or, again, we might have a particular interest in certain *wrong* answers, in which case we might wish to include those in a set of multiple choices. We must note, however, that the multiple choices offered become part of the question and may affect the responses.

On whom should our questions be tried out? Respondents in pilot studies should be as similar as possible to those in the main inquiry. If the main inquiry is meant to highlight certain group differences (for instance, between people who have and people who have not had a surgical operation), then such groups should also be available for comparison in the pilot samples. The practice of habitually trying out questionnaires on university students is to be deprecated most strongly (unless the questionnaire is intended for use with undergraduates), for differences in educational background and literacy may produce very different levels of understanding, misunderstanding, and capacity to respond. In the rare instances in which our total population is very small and highly specific so that we cannot afford to "use up" any part of it for pilot samples, we must seek some alternative samples that should be, above all, comparable in their knowledge and ways of thinking.

Sometimes an organization has to repeat similar surveys many times over the years, for instance, audience research in the mass media. A standard questionnaire technique may be evolved in which only the details are changed to correspond with the relevant day, week, or month. Such a situation is sometimes used for split-ballot type of pilot work. The whole sample is divided at random into two or more equivalent subsamples, and two or more versions of the same questionnaire are produced, for instance on different-colored paper or with a slightly different question order. Comparison of the results will show the effect of these variations in technique, which can then be utilized in similar surveys.

Methods of Data-Collection

There are numerous methods of data-collection in social research, from the lengthy, exploratory pilot interview, with its "hidden agenda," to the impersonal, mailed questionnaire and the analysis of documents. Here we shall concern ourselves only with those methods that use a questionnaire, namely, the standardized, formal interview; the mail questionnaire; and such minor variants as the self-administered questionnaire and the group-administered questionnaire. It is clear from this that we use the term "questionnaire" in its widest sense.

Interview Schedules versus Mail Questionnaires

There are many kinds of interviews, such as the journalistic interview, the employment interview, and the therapeutic interview. Here we are concerned only with the data-gathering or research type of interview. It consists of three interacting variables: the respondent, the interviewer, and the interview schedule or questionnaire. Each of these, as well as the interview situation, can have an important influence on the results.

The art or science of interviewing and the problems of rapport and interviewer bias and selection will not be discussed here. They are obviously of major importance in the process of data-gathering, and the reader is referred to Kahn and Cannell,[1] Hyman,[2] Merton,[3] Sheatsley,[4] Maccoby and Maccoby,[5] and other textbooks. We may just remark here that although every interviewer receives the same questionnaire schedule, and though the interviewing procedure is standardized, there will always remain differences in the way in which questions are put to each respondent; and these may (or may not) have an important influence on the results. Equally, what is understood by the respondent and what is recorded or noted down from the respondent's answer will be selected and possibly biased. Thus, while our primary concern here is with the design of question sequences, we must not imagine that once they go into the field they constitute an absolutely standardized set of stimuli; nor will the responses reach us in "pure" form.

The greatest advantage of the interview in the hands of a skilled interviewer is its flexibility. The interviewer can make sure that the respondent has understood the question and the purpose of the research. We can ask the interviewers to probe further when particular responses are encountered; we can ask them to classify the answers on the spot (field coding); they can show the respondent cards, lists, or pictures, hand out product samples, or self-completion checklists, or diaries, and make ratings or assessments of attitudes, furnishings, dwelling areas, and so forth. Above all, they can build up and maintain rapport, that elusive mctivating force that will keep the respondent interested and responsive to the end of the interview.

The interview situation is, however, fraught with possibilities of bias. The interviewer may give an inkling of her own opinion or expectations by her tone of voice, the way in which she reads the questions, or simply by her appearance, dress, and accent. She may unwittingly influence the respondent by pausing expectantly at certain points, by probing with leading questions, and by agreeing with the respondent in an effort to maintain rapport. Her own expectations and her selective understanding and recording of the answers may produce bias. An interviewer may misunderstand or fail to obey instructions; she may show surprise or boredom in tone or emphasis or in other ways unconsciously communicate her own attitudes and her expectations of the respondent's attitudes. Interviewers differ in age and sex, social background, skin color, dress, speech, and experience. Interviewers react differently to different respondents and carry out their probes with more or less care. Questions concerned with "delicate" issues raise special problems. Some of these biases can be largely eliminated by suitable selection and training and by careful checks and supervision; but other biases may remain and will influence the results to an unknown degree.

Interviews cost money. There are traveling and subsistence expenses to be met, as well as payment to the interviewers—even when the interview is unsuccessful. Interviewers have to be briefed, organized, and assisted, as well as trained, all of which requires a field-work organization that may have to cover many dozens of sampling points all over the country. Interviewers leave or get stale, so that replacement is a continuous problem. The interviewing of selected samples (for instance, all the graduates of a particular college in a particular year, ten years after graduation) may become prohibitively expensive. Unless considerable numbers of interviewers are employed, data-collection may take a long time.

There remains the undisputed advantage that the richness and spontaneity of information collected by interviewers is higher than that which a mailed questionnaire can hope to obtain. The researcher may also feel a sense of security due to the fact that all the data were collected in face-to-face situations, even if biases may have crept in now and then. We know that some interviewers will produce a systematic bias, but that others may only make random errors, which may cancel out in the long run. Many researchers will take a chance on the possibilities of bias for the sake of the richness of information that only the interview can give.

The chief advantage of the *mail questionnaire* is cheapness. Since it does not require a trained staff of field workers (who may also incur considerable travel and maintenance expenditure), virtually all that it requires is the cost of the planning and pilot work, printing or duplicating expenses, sampling, addressing, mailing, and providing stamped, self-addressed envelopes for the returns. The processing and analysis are usually also simpler and cheaper than in the case of interviews. Another advantage is that often a much larger sample can be covered at a modest increase in cost and that the sampling can be more accurate, since an envelope can be addressed to a particular individual, whereas the interviewer has to find people on the street meeting certain criteria or has to try to find the right person at home in a particular household. In one study comparing the results of mail questionnaires with those of interviews 88 per cent agreement between the two methods was obtained on assessment of occupational grade. Mail questionnaires are preferable if information has to be checked against documents or if other informants have to be consulted, for instance in a business firm. The fact that no interviewer is present means that there will be no interviewer bias (though in this case each respondent virtually interviews himself, which may produce other biases), but the absence of the interviewer may also have considerable disadvantages.

First of all, eliminating the interviewer means that the questionnaire has to be much simpler and that no additional explanations can be given and no probes requested. A mail questionnaire cannot hope to cover people of low intelligence or of very limited educational background. It also lacks the personal introduction of the research by the interviewer, though a good covering letter can be of great help. In an interview we have strict control over the order and sequence of the questions, and the respondent does not know what is coming; mail questionnaires are usually perused before being answered, so that respondents often skip questions or come back to them later, all of which may bias the responses. Since the interviewer is not present, we can obtain no interviewer ratings or assessments on such points as social class or quality of furnishings. Also, with the best will in the world people often pass on mail questionnaires to others; thus, if they receive a questionnaire about lawn mowers, and they do not own one, they will pass it on to someone who does, with consequent unsuspected distortions in the sample.

By far the largest disadvantage of mail questionnaires, however, is the fact that they usually produce very poor response rates. For respondents who have no special interest in the subject matter of the questionnaire, figures of 40 per cent to 60 per cent are typical; even in studies of interested groups, 80 per cent is seldom exceeded. The important point about these poor response rates is not the reduced size of the sample, which could easily be overcome by sending out more questionnaires, but the possibility of bias. This is because almost invariably the returns are not representative of the original sample drawn; *nonresponse is not a random process;* it has its own determinants, which vary from survey to survey. We cannot overcome this problem entirely, but we can partly *prevent* it by sending out several suitably worded reminders and partly *allow* for it by ascertaining the nature of the bias. Incidentally, in surveys using face-to-face interviewers, we also have a considerable nonsuccess rate; in such cases, the interviewer can usually at least fill in some of the classifying data, if only approximately, so that the nature of the likely bias can be ascertained or the field-staff headquarters can arrange for a substitute respondent.

To study response bias, we must make sure that we know the return date of every questionnaire, for it has been found that respondents who send in their questionnaire very late are roughly similar to nonrespondents. We have open to us two methods to find out whether and in what way a bias has been introduced: first, by comparing respondents with nonrespondents on the original sampling list (in terms of geographical location, date of birth, first letter of family name, sex, type of qualification, and so on), and second, by comparing early respondents with late respondents (in terms of their answers to the questionnaire). It may be that the nonrespondents have failed to reply because the questionnaire reached them on a busy day or because they were on holidays or in the hospital. It seems unlikely in such cases that the geographical or sex distribution of the returns would show a bias, or that late respondents would differ markedly from early respondents in terms of, say, a questionnaire on vegetarianism or ball-point pens. But if the questionnaire dealt, let us say, with minor foot disorders such as corns, bunions, and athlete's foot, then we might find a geographical bias in the returns favoring, for instance, places often chosen by retired people, and the late returns might report far fewer ailments than the early returns. In this example it would seem that interested people are *more* likely to respond, but the opposite may be the case, say, with a questionnaire dealing with nervous symptoms in children sent to a sample of parents. The more disturbed the child, the less the parent may feel inclined to return the questionnaire.

It is possible to carry out controlled studies to show whether or not a certain method actually improves response rates. Christopher Scott,[6] of the British Government Social Survey, reports, for instance, that stamped self-addressed return envelopes produce a higher response rate than business reply envelopes—so much for those who believe that people often steam off the stamps and throw away the envelopes! He finds that government sponsorship of a survey improves response rates, but that "personalizing" the accompanying letter makes no difference to the return rates. Similarly, an imposing, printed letterhead makes no difference, nor does the use of colored paper; and there seems to be no foundation for the belief that questionnaires that reach respondents over the week-end are more likely to be answered. Any other day of the week makes no difference. Concerning length, much would seem to depend on personal involvement: the more interested people are in the subject of the questionnaire, the more they are likely to fill in and return even quite lengthy questionnaires. Certainly, one cannot be dogmatic about the number of pages that "cannot" be exceeded. Experiments have also been made with inducements of gifts, money, or free samples; small sums of money enclosed with the initial questionnaire can be quite effective.

Thus we see that the problem of nonreturn can be tackled and to some extent overcome, once the nature of the bias (if any) has been ascertained, but we must plan for it. We must expect some people not to return our questionnaires, and we must take steps beforehand so that we can ascertain who they are, send them reminders, and eventually make suitable corrections in our results.

Self-Administered Questionnaires

The self-administered questionnaire is usually presented to the respondents by an interviewer or by someone in an official position, such as a teacher, or a hospital receptionist. The purpose of the inquiry is explained, and then the respondent is left alone to complete the questionnaire, which may be sent in or collected later. This method of data-collection ensures a high response rate, accurate sampling, and a minimum of interviewer bias, while permitting interviewer assessments, providing necessary explanations (but *not* the interpretation of questions), and giving the benefit of a degree of personal contact. Research workers may in this way utilize the help of someone in an official capacity who is not a skilled interviewer. However, the greatest care is needed in briefing such persons or they may, with the best intentions, introduce fatal biases.

Group-Administered Questionnaires

The group-administered questionnaire is also largely self-explanatory and is given to groups of respondents assembled together, such as school children or invited audiences. Depending on the size of the group and its level of literacy, two or more persons will see to the administration of the questionnaires, give help where needed (in a nondirective way), check finished questionnaires for completeness, and so on. Sometimes, variations in procedure may be introduced. For instance, the audience may be provided with empty booklets; some slides or a film may be shown, and then a group of numbered questions might be read aloud, one at a time, while the respondents write their answers in the booklets next to the question numbers. This ensures that all respondents answer the questions in the same order and that they all have the same amount of time to do so. Groups of forty can readily be controlled in this way, but contamination (through copying, talking, or asking questions) is a constant danger.

Anonymity

Data obtained by means of interviews and questionnaires should always be regarded as confidential, in the sense that no responses or findings should ever be published which could be traced back to particular individuals. In enlisting co-operation for the survey, respondents are usually given assurance to this effect and a guarantee of anonymity. This is often crucial in obtaining frank and revealing responses; indeed, anonymous mail questionnaires often produce a greater proportion of socially unacceptable responses than face-to-face interviews. Where possible, therefore, respondents should not be asked for their names or requested to sign their questionnaires; instead they can be given numbers.

Question Sequences and Question Types

Question Sequence

The whole questionnaire will consist of a series of question sequences, and the order of question sequences must first be considered. We may wish to start with some factual questions, followed by attitudinal ones, or the other way around. We may wish to repeat the same questions in different contexts or by the use of different techniques. We must, however, avoid putting ideas into the respondent's mind early in the interview, if we need spontaneous responses on the same points later on. Last but not least, we must make the questionnaire attractive and interesting to the respondent. For instance, we ought to start off the interview with some easy, impersonal questions and not ask for details like age, family, occupation, and so forth until rapport has been well established. We must ask ourselves how this question sequence will strike the respondent. Is it too intimidating? Do the questions seem relevant to our explanation of the purpose of our research? Have we unwittingly made our own attitudes too obvious? Are the questions worded in a friendly way? We are not likely to produce a helpful attitude in the respondent if we start off the interview with some staccato questions such as: "Age," "Occupation," "Marital status," "Income."

We may, in the pilot work, have obtained suitable measures of certain variables by using several different techniques, such as checklists, free-answer questions, and projective material. Looking now at the shape of the questionnaire as a whole, we might decide to put all checklist questions together at the beginning, followed by all free-answer questions, and ending with a variety of projective devices. This may ease the task of the respondent and give the questionnaire a more uniform appearance, but the questions will no longer follow logically one after the other. The context of each question will be changed, so that the respondent will have other preceding questions in mind when answering it. That is why we should also pilot the final questionnaire as a whole, after assembly. The matter of total length and the amount of time and effort that can be requested from the average respondent must also be considered at this stage.

If we have not varied our technique, but are employing, for example, a succession of sets of open and closed questions, each set dealing with a different variable, then we must consider the phrasing of any particular question in relation to its place in such a set of questions. In what sequence can we best approach the relevant issue? The "funnel" approach, with various "filter" questions, is a well-known type of sequence. The funnel approach is so named because it starts off with a very broad question and then progressively narrows down the scope of the questions until it comes to some very specific points.

For instance, suppose we want to know whether some people avoid hard candies because they are said to be harmful to the teeth. It would not do to ask them a question such as, "Do you believe that hard candies are harmful to the teeth?" or, "Do you avoid eating hard candies because you feel that they harm the teeth?" These would be grossly leading questions, and, besides, the respondent may never eat hard candies, or he may avoid them for some other reason. Obviously, it would be valuable if we could get the respondent to say spontaneously that he avoids hard candies because they are damaging to his teeth, before we suggest it to him, and before he becomes aware what the questions are really about. Therefore, we may start off with some very broad questions, such as: "What is your opinion of hard candies?" "What do you think of people who eat hard candies?" Each question provides the respondent with an opportunity to mention the issue of dental decay spontaneously. Next, we might ask more restricted questions, such as: "Do you eat hard candies at all?" "Did you eat hard candies when you were a child?" "Do you allow your children to eat hard candies?" Each should be followed up with "Why?" if the reply is negative, thus providing further opportunities for the dental issue to emerge spontaneously. After that, we may narrow the questions still further: "Do you believe that hard candies can be harmful in any way?" "What would happen if you ate too many hard candies?" "What are some of the disadvantages of eating hard candies?" Note that the dental problem still has not been mentioned directly. Finally, we bring up the problem as nondirectively as possible: "Some people say that eating hard candies is bad for your teeth, but others say that it makes no difference. How do you feel about this?" Or, "Do you believe that eating hard candies is bad for your teeth, or do you think that most people's teeth will not be damaged by eating hard candies?" And so on. By proceeding in this way we not only increase our chances of obtaining what we are seeking through a spontaneous reply, we also place the whole issue of hard candies and tooth decay in the context of some of the other factors that determine the eating of hard candies. This context can be very important; it may well be that other reasons for not eating hard candies are mentioned far more frequently than the possible danger to the teeth.

A filter question is used to exclude a respondent from a particular question sequence if those questions are irrelevant to him. Thus, in the above example, we might wish to ask for some factual information about candy-buying behavior and hard-candy purchases. Obviously, if the respondent never buys these sweets then there is no point in asking him about frequency, weight, type of shop, type of container, color preferences, and so forth. Therefore, our illustrative question sequence will be preceded by a filter question, such as, "Do you buy hard candies from time to time?" or, "Have you bought any hard candies within the past two weeks?" If the answer is negative, the interviewer will be instructed to skip the next few questions and proceed to the beginning of the next question sequence.

Each survey produces its own problems of question order, which makes it difficult to offer general principles. We try, as much as possible, to avoid putting ideas into the respondent's mind or to suggest that he should have attitudes when he has none. Therefore, with regard to any issue, we will want to start with open questions and only introduce more structured or pre-coded questions at a later stage. Gallup[7] has suggested that his "Quintamensional Plan of Question Design" is often useful. In this, we start off with questions designed to find out whether the informant is aware of or has thought about the issue at all. Next, we ask some open questions concerning his general feelings on the issue. Following these, we try to get answers to questions dealing with specific parts of the issue—they will usually be of the multiple-choice type. Then, we ask questions designed to find out the reasons for the respondent's views, and finally, we inquire how strongly such views are held.

Some survey workers prefer to start each question sequence by asking a few factual, multiple-choice questions about the respondent's own habits, background, or experience. Further questions follow naturally about the respondent's attitudes concerning these points and about wider issues. For example, we may ask the respondent how often he goes to church, if at all, whether he went to Sunday school as a child, and then follow these questions with some broader ones on religious issues and attitudes. Other survey workers prefer to start each sequence with wide-open questions, and ask about the respondent's own behavior or experience at the end. In both approaches there is the danger that inconsistencies and contradictions between attitudes and behavior will emerge, which the respondent may try to cover up.

Our final choice of approach and sequence must be determined by our own survey problems and by the results of the pilot work.

Open and Closed Questions

Broadly speaking, all questions are either "open" or "closed." A closed question is one in which the respondent is offered a choice of alternative replies. He may be asked to check or underline his chosen answer(s) in a written questionnaire, or the alternatives may be read aloud or shown to him on a prompt card or a slide. Questions of this kind may offer simple alternatives, such as "Yes" and "No," or the names of five political parties in an election; or they can offer something more complex, such as a choice of ways of keeping order in a classroom or a choice of motives for smoking cigarettes.

Open or free-answer types of question are not followed by any kind of choice, and the answers have to be recorded in full. In the case of a written questionnaire, the amount of space or the number of lines provided for the answer will help to determine the length and fullness of the responses we obtain. Inevitably, some of this richness is lost when the answers are classified later, but it is useful to report a few such answers in full in the final report to give the reader some of the flavor of the replies. Statistical tabulations are important and must remain our first aim, but they make dull reading.

The chief advantage of the open question is the freedom that it gives to the respondent. Once he has understood the intent of the question, he can let his thoughts roam freely, unencumbered by a prepared set of replies. We obtain his ideas in his own language, expressed spontaneously, and this spontaneity is often extremely worthwhile as a basis for new hypotheses. In an interview, however, there is the risk that we will obtain, not so much a rounded and full account of the respondent's feelings, but rather just what happens to be uppermost in his mind at the time. If this is true, then we may still ask whether what comes first to the respondent's mind is not also most important for him and for us.

Free-response questions are often easy to ask, difficult to answer, and still more difficult to analyze. As a rule, we employ a classification process known as "coding" (see Chapter 9), which requires drawing up some system of categories, a coding frame. The composition of such coding frames and the actual coding operation require trained staff and are extremely time-consuming; for this reason survey workers have to curb their desire to have too many open questions.

Sometimes, if the first answer seems a little ambiguous or does not go far enough, we can instruct the interviewer to probe. This often takes the form of asking the respondent to explain further or to give his reasons for something stated earlier; at times, a particular issue may be brought into the discussion deliberately, if the respondent has not already mentioned it. Such probes should be as nondirective as possible, thus: "Could you say a little more about . . . ?" "Why did you say just now that . . . ?" "Now, what about the . . . ?" "And how do you feel about . . . ?" The risk of interviewer bias is probably at its highest whenever probes are employed. They are "safe" only in the hands of the most highly trained and experienced fieldworkers, and many survey organizations avoid probes altogether.

Closed questions can be attitudinal as well as factual. The alternatives offered are, as we have seen, very much part of the question and should be reported as such, for they guide the respondent's answers. Suppose that we ask the question: "Some people in this community have too much power. Who are they?" Left to their own thoughts, some respondents might think in terms of political parties, others in terms of criminals and racketeers, still others in terms of certain professional groups. Consider now the different effects of offering either of the following lists of possible answers:

Negroes	newspaper owners
Jews	landlords
Catholics	the police
Poles	big businessmen

Each of these leads the respondent in a particular direction, which may or may not correspond with his own thoughts. Moreover, he is expected to express an opinion; very few people would insist on a response such as "None of these." Under these conditions, merely to report that X per cent of our sample stated that, say, landlords have too much power, would be grossly misleading unless the other alternatives offered to the respondents were also reported. On the other hand, the fact that we are directing the respondent's thoughts does not of itself make the question invalid or worthless. We may be particularly interested in comparing hostility toward landlords with hostility toward newspaper owners, and the pilot work may have shown us that these two groups are rarely mentioned in a free-answer question.

But we must be aware of what we are doing and make our choice suit the requirements of our research.

Incidentally, if we guide the respondent's thinking along particular lines in this way, it may also influence the answers to subsequent free-response questions.

Closed questions are easier and quicker to answer; they require no writing; and quantification is straightforward. This often means that more questions can be asked within a given length of time and that more can be accomplished with a given sum of money. Disadvantages of closed questions are the loss of spontaneity and expressiveness—we shall never know what the respondent said or thought of his own accord—and perhaps the introduction of bias by "forcing" him to choose between given alternatives and by making him think of alternatives that might not have occurred to him. Closed questions are often cruder and less subtle than open ones, although this is not necessarily so, and we do lose the opportunity to probe. There may also be some loss of rapport, if respondents become irritated because they feel that the choice of answers fails to do justice to their own ideas.

Sometimes, there may be good reasons for asking the same question both in open and closed form. For instance, if we ask, "What are some of the things that make a man move up in the world?" we shall get a pretty clear idea of the way in which the respondent thinks the social system works, and the relative importance to him of several avenues of mobility, such as education, hard work, money, luck. We get a free, spontaneous sketch in the respondent's own language and containing his own ideas. This is most valuable, but it makes it difficult to compare one group of respondents with another. Also, we cannot be sure that such an impromptu sketch really contains all the factors that are important to the respondent. A momentary lapse, a feeling of reticence, or the inability to put ideas into words can cause the omission of significant points. Therefore, later in the interview we may ask the same question again, but this time we will offer him a list that he may be asked to rate or rank (see Chapter 4) or from which he may be asked to choose the three most important factors. Having already obtained the spontaneous responses, there can now be little harm in introducing a set of ideas obtained in the pilot work, even though some of these might not have occurred to our respondent. By using a "closed" approach we ensure that the results of several groups can readily be compared and that all respondents have considered the same universe of content before giving their replies.

Belson[8, 9] and others have shown that when it comes to an enumeration of items of behavior, such as newspapers or magazines read the previous day or programs heard on radio or television, the open type of question produces a lower yield than the prompt-list kind. This is partly due to temporary forgetfulness and partly to the fact that some papers or programs have low memorability. Weeklies and monthlies are not recollected as well as dailies, when open and closed questions are compared. On the other hand, checklist questions are subject to a small degree of spurious inflation; people confuse yesterday with some earlier day or confound the names of programs or publications. (Diary techniques [see Chapter 8] may give the most valid and precise estimates, but they cause some respondents to engage in "duty viewing" or "duty reading.") It is clear, therefore, that caution must be exercised when we compare prompted results with those of free-answer questions.

Field Coding

Closed questions should be distinguished from questions requiring field coding. A closed question is read or shown to the respondent complete with a set of answers; in the case of field coding, a set of possible answers is provided for use by the interviewer, but *only* the question (without the answers) is read aloud. This technique may cause considerable bias and loss of information, though it has its uses. For instance, we may ask the respondent which television programs he saw yesterday, but, although the interviewer will be supplied with a complete list of the relevant programs, this list will not be shown or read to the respondent. The purpose of this would be to test the "memorability" of a particular program, because we have found from experience that respondents may claim to have viewed programs they did not actually see, if shown a list of the previous day's programs. In this case the loss of information will be comparatively small. But suppose that we have asked respondents what they think about keeping pets and have provided the interviewer with a number of prepared categories, such as "Make the house dirty," "Teaches children to take care of others," "Animals are better friends than people," "Too expensive," "Always good company, someone to talk to when lonely," all obtained from the pilot work. When this very general question about pet-keeping is asked, most respondents will offer a considerable amount of comment, and it will be up to the interviewer to select and condense what seems most important, and check or circle or underline the most relevant categories. Even with the best interviewers in the world some bias and some loss of information cannot be avoided.

Loss of Information

The problem of loss of information, of condensation and compression, should be placed in perspective. The question is not how we can avoid loss of information, but rather at what point we can best afford to lose information. At first sight, it may seem as if the open question causes the least loss. All the interviewer has to do is to ask the question and write down the reply. But already some loss of possibly relevant information has occurred: the facial expression and tone of voice of the respondent, the hesitations and reformulations, the little digressions and repetitions, not to mention large parts of a longer answer. All these will not be recorded, for most interviewers cannot use shorthand, and most interview sheets provide only a limited amount of space in which to write. Inevitably, even when attempting to get a complete record of an answer, the interviewer selects, and selection may reflect bias. Sometimes, she only hears what she expects or wants to hear. Nor is the interview situation the only point at which loss or distortion of information may occur. Further loss will take place when the questionnaire reaches the office and is coded, for the number of coding categories cannot be unlimited. At a still later stage, during the statistical analysis, more information loss may occur, if coding categories have to be combined, or when over-all scores or indices are calculated. Therefore, if we allow the respondent a free answer, we must ask ourselves at what stage the inevitable loss of some information will cause the least bias: during the interview itself, by asking for field coding; or later, if we ask for complete answers to be recorded first. The interviewer in the field generally has a better appreciation of what the respondent was trying to say, but the rushed circumstances of an interview may make it more difficult to fit the response immediately into the appropriate category. The coder in the office can ponder more carefully, but by then only the written record is available. The content of the question and the complexity of the answers will largely determine our decision, but the quality of our field force and of our coders will also have to be considered.

A further point in connection with loss of information is the question of relevance. Many surveys, regrettably, contain redundant or irrelevant questions, which have been put in for the sake of "interest" but have no bearing on the problems at issue. Also inevitable are the many open questions that will—due to the freedom they give the respondent—produce a good deal of information that is not really relevant to our inquiry. In such instances, we may eliminate the irrelevant information as early as possible, by means of closed questions or field coding. However, we must be careful not to omit information that may be important as contextual or background material.

These comments about loss of information apply also to the use of closed or multiple-choice questions, with the added problem that the alternatives offered may bias the responses. All closed questions should start their career as open ones, except those where certain alternatives are the only ones possible: the names of the candidates in an election, the daily newspapers on sale, and so on. Careful pilot work is very important here; only by trying out an open question in various forms and attempting to "close" it afterwards, can we gain an appreciation of the loss of information involved. Also, the pilot work will provide us with a set of multiple choices that will really fit the range of answers to be expected and that will reduce, if not eliminate, the loss of information. Whether we choose to put the question in open or closed form will partly be decided by whether it is possible to provide a set of suitable multiple-choice answers. Surprisingly, the pilot work sometimes offers the possibility of closing quite subtle questions, thus avoiding the expense and possible distortion of coding.

• *Selected Readings*

INTERVIEWING

1. Robert L. Kahn and Charles F. Cannell, *The Dynamics of Interviewing* (New York: Wiley, 1957).

   Chapter 6 is a useful introduction to questionnaire design; chapters 7, 8, and 9 deal fully with interviewing skills, sources of bias, and so on.

2. Herbert H. Hyman *et al.*, *Interviewing in Social Research* (Chicago: University of Chicago Press, 1954).

   Experimental studies of interviewer bias and the effects of interviewers on respondents.

3. Robert K. Merton, Marjorie Fiske, and Patricia L. Kendall, *The Focused Interview* (Glencoe, Ill.: The Free Press, 1956).

   A careful and clear analysis with many examples of interviewing problems and procedures.

4. Paul B. Sheatsley, "The Art of Interviewing and a Guide to Interviewer Selection and Training," in Marie Jahoda, Morton Deutsch, and Stuart Cook, eds., *Research Methods in Social Relations* (New York: Dryden Press, 1951), Part II.

   An introduction to the conduct of interviews and the problems of interviewer training.

5. Eleanor E. Maccoby and Nathan Maccoby, "The Interview: A Tool of Social Science," in Gardner Lindzey, ed., *Handbook of Social Psychology* (Cambridge, Mass.: Addison-Wesley, 1954).

   Basic textbook reference on problems of research in interviewing.

MAIL QUESTIONNAIRES

6. Christopher Scott, "Research on Mail Surveys," *Journal of the Royal Statistical Society,* XXIV, Series A (1961), 143–195.

   An excellent contribution to research into mail questionnaires, together with a full review of the literature.

QUESTION SEQUENCE

7. George Gallup, *Qualitative Measurement of Public Opinion: The Quintamensional Plan of Question Design* (Princeton, N.J.: American Institute of Public Opinion, 1947).

QUESTION RELIABILITY

8. William A. Belson and Judith A. Duncan, "A Comparison of the Check-List and the Open Response Questioning Systems," *Applied Statistics,* II (1962), 120–132.

9. William A. Belson, *Studies in Readership* (London: Business Publications Ltd., 1962).

   A carefully conducted follow-up inquiry into the causes of unreliability in a national readership survey.

3

Question-Wording

The function of a question in an interview form or a questionnaire is to elicit a *particular* communication. We hope that our respondent has certain information or attitudes on the subject of our inquiry, and we want to get these from him with a minimum of distortion. If it were possible to do this without asking him any questions and without the respondent having to "respond," that would be so much the better—for the questions we ask, the possible misunderstandings they provoke in the respondent, the mental phrasing of his or her answers, and the recording of them—all have influences on the final result that we could well do without. Some people still design questions as if the process of interviewing or of filling out a questionnaire were rather like unloading a ship, with every item of cargo labeled and with a specific destination, picked out of the hold and set down according to a pattern. In reality, questioning people is more like trying to catch a particularly elusive fish, by hopefully casting different kinds of bait at different depths, without knowing what goes on beneath the surface!

The Process of Responding

Let us assume, for the moment, that our question has been understood by the respondent as intended and that he does have the knowledge, facts, opinions, or attitudes required as a response.

The question has alerted him in a particular direction; he has searched that corner of his mind and has found what we are looking for. Now he begins the process of responding. The attitude or information may be clear and well organized, or it may be diffuse and vague. It may be deep or superficial, latent or held very strongly. What comes to mind first, what is uppermost in the respondent's mind, may not amount to a fair representation of his collected thoughts on the subject. Some process of bringing into awareness has to take place, coupled with a degree of self-analysis, feedback, conceptualization of ideas, generalization from specific points, and so on. The respondent is trying to form a percept of his own ideas. The processes of producing this percept may be affected by wishful thinking, a desire to please the research worker, and the urge to be fair to oneself and to others and will probably be accompanied by a good deal of confusion. Problems of memory and ability to recall will also play their part. However, the respondent can now be said to have some kind of "inner picture" of his response, though he has not yet communicated it. To do this, he must have a certain degree of ability to communicate—he must be able to "put things into words" adequately. He must also have the willingness to communicate—he must have accepted the role of respondent in the situation. He must have found motives that will not only allow him to spend time and effort on responding, but allow him also to communicate private or taboo information, if necessary. His willingness may, however, easily be curbed by various forms of inner censorship, poor rapport, the wish to maintain a social façade, and the response expectations which the question suggests. It is, in other words, difficult enough to obtain a relatively unbiased answer even from a willing and clear-headed respondent, who has correctly understood what we are after, without making our task practically impossible by setting this "train of responding" off on the wrong track through poor question-wording.

In some ways, the problem of question-wording is a sampling problem. We are sampling a particular universe of content in the respondent's mind, for instance his attitude to Mexicans. We are not planning to obtain the whole of this universe of content but only enough of it to enable us to outline its salient features, general direction, depth or intensity, and perhaps the presence or absence of specific items. Our questions must be adequate for this sampling process; they must not be too one-sided, and they must make it easy for the respondent to respond fully. This means, first of all, that their content must be right; second, that the wording must be suitable; and third, that the context, sequence, and response categories (if any), must help the respondent without biasing the answers.

Question Content and Purpose

As we have seen in the preceding chapter, we should have a questionnaire plan or outline giving the sequence of all the major and minor issues with which we are concerned. We must now decide, for each issue in turn, how thoroughly we will "sample" it. Here, for instance, is a question from a survey dealing with dental services:

Have you heard of fluoridation of water supplies?

Yes 1
No 2
Don't know ... 3

If "yes"

How do you feel about fluoridation of water supplies?

Do you approve? 4
Do you disapprove? 5
Are you undecided? 6

Probe all answers

Why do you say this?

There are no other questions concerning fluoridation in the survey. Presumably the research workers concerned regarded this as an interesting but relatively unimportant issue on which they did not propose to spend a great deal of interviewing time. Or perhaps the pilot work had shown that very few people had ever heard about fluoridation. At any rate, the survey team must have made some decisions. First, they decided not to leave out this issue. Second, they decided to sample it only briefly. Third, they decided that one multiple-choice attitude question, preceded by a filter-question, and followed by a "Why"-probe, would suffice. They must have been tempted to ask more questions, perhaps designed to find out what information the respondent had on this subject. They might have considered the possibility of making the questions more specific, for instance, by asking about the fluoridation of "your" water supply. They did not assume that everyone would know what fluoridation is or would have a clearly defined attitude toward it, but they did not find it necessary to offer an explanation of this technical term before asking questions about it. The questions were kept as short as possible, using mostly familiar words.

Do we know why the question was asked at all? Very often problems of question construction make us realize that we are not clear enough in our own minds as to what the questions are about. As Payne[1] puts it: "If we did but realize it, the first half of the battle consists of putting the issue in a form that we can understand ourselves. We need first and foremost to define the issue precisely, regardless of the general understandability of the words." He goes on to suggest that we ask ourselves the newspaper reporter's stock five questions about each issue: Who? Why? When? Where? How? Very likely, for instance, in the example just given, the main interest centered around the reasons against fluoridation. If, instead, the main issue had been the amount of information possessed by respondents about the effects of fluoridation, different questions would have been asked.

Greater precision concerning the purpose of the questions will sometimes make it easier to avoid ambiguity in question-wording. Consider, for instance, the meaning of the word "read" in a factual question such as: "Which magazines have you read in the past seven days?" Should "read" here be regarded as synonymous with "bought"? Or with "bought and also read"? Or with "borrowed but read"? Or could it include "borrowed but only glanced at"? "Picked up in a waiting room"? What about "borrowed in order to read just one article"? What about exchanges of magazines? Annual subscriptions? "Just looked at the pictures?" It is obvious that we must stop thinking of the meaning of words in dictionary terms and instead, ask ourselves what we are trying to find out. What are we going to do with the data when we have collected them? This will make it easier to decide which of many possible meanings of a word we wish to employ. For instance, if we were concerned with magazine sales or with personal expenditure, we might alter the question to: "Which magazines have you bought in the past seven days?" However, if we were concerned with exposure to magazine advertising, a very broad definition of "read" would be appropriate. It all depends on the purpose of the question.

Payne[1] has written an amusing and instructive little book on questionnaire-wording that can be highly recommended. General textbooks such as Kahn and Cannell,[2] Selltiz *et al.*,[3] and Festinger and Katz[4] contain worthwhile sections on question-phrasing with many detailed examples.

Factual Questions

The adjective "factual" is here used to distinguish this type of question from others, thought to be more difficult to design, that may deal with knowledge, motives, or attitudes. However, even factual questions can present the research worker with awkward problems. Consider, for instance, the use of the word "bought" in the preceding discussion. Does this include buying for others? Does it include buying on account? Does it include things paid for by and bought on behalf of someone else? Does it include gifts and presents?

Mealtimes are another example. In England, the word "tea" as in the question: "When do you usually have tea?" refers to a light meal (which may or may not include tea as a beverage) taken at almost any time after about three-thirty in the afternoon. Some families have "tea" in the mid-afternoon. Others refer to the main evening meal as "tea." Some give their children "tea" when they come home from school and then give them "supper" later. In other families the same meal given to children is called "tea" and taken later by adults is called "dinner." Different customs exist in different social classes and in different parts of the country. The institution of Sunday "high tea" further complicates matters. To say, therefore, that something happened "at tea-time," or to hear that product X is always taken with one's tea, requires elucidation. When drawing up a questionnaire we tend to forget how circumscribed our own experience is and we take for granted that whatever the word means to us it will mean to everyone else.

Suppose that, in a written questionnaire to be filled out by schoolchildren, we have to find out the length of time they have been exposed to television. We might start with a simple, factual question such as: "How long have you had a television set?" But what is meant here by "you"? The child obviously does not own a television set himself. We had better change the question: "How long has your family had a television set?" But this, too, produces complications. The family is a very flexible unit. If grandmother has a set, and the children are allowed to look at television every Sunday afternoon, does this count? If a married, older sister has television, does that count? We must try again: "How long has there been a television set in your house?" However, the house may be a unit of apartments with any number of families who have television sets. Or there may be tenants renting the upstairs apartment of a private house who have television. Another rewording: "How long has there been a television set in your home?" This is a little better. Actually, when we pilot this question we will find that it consists, in reality, of two questions. The first tries to attach some date to the time of purchase of the television set. The second requires subtraction, and not all children can subtract accurately. Since this constitutes a potential source of error, why not ask then simply for the time of purchase? "Since when has there been a television set in your home?" Apart from problems of gross inaccuracy if the date is a number of years back, we will get a flood of answers such as: "Since my granny's birthday"; "Since my dad had his win at the races"; "Since my mommy went out to work"; "Since we moved to X Street"; and so on. This is obviously not very helpful. Let us try again: "If there is a television set in your home, when was it bought?" But of course, the set may be the second or third one since television was first introduced into the home, or the family may have rented a set for several years before buying one, or the present set may be rented; and so on.

In a housing survey it was found that many respondents reported fewer bedrooms than their houses actually contained. They simply did not think of a study, a playroom, a sewing room, or a guest room as "bedrooms" in the sense intended by the survey. Similarly, in a survey concerning coffee, many housewives failed to mention powdered or "instant" coffee because they did not think of these products as "coffee." The last two examples point, first of all, to the need for definitions—both for the sake of the research worker and to help the respondent. "Is the child afraid of one or more animals?" we may ask a sample of mothers, and add, "that is, ordinary domestic animals, not lions, tigers, etc." More subtly, both examples also point to differences in frame of reference that may exist between researcher and respondent. A typical problem word might be "family," a term which has widely different meanings depending on one's frame of reference. Or, to give another example, in a study of saving, insurance policies were often not mentioned: people don't think of them as a form of saving.

We must not assume that people have the information that we seek. They may be reluctant to admit that they do not know, or being anxious to please, they may guess. We must avoid giving the impression that respondents ought to know. Such questions as, "What was the name of the author?" (of a recently borrowed library book), and "What brand was it?" (of consumer goods), would be better worded: "Can you remember the author's name?" and "Can you remember what brand it was?" Or we may offer a face-saving phrase, such as: "For many people, life is so hectic nowadays that they often cannot remember small details from one week to the next." If in doubt, and especially if technical terms or difficult words are part of the question, a filter question such as used in the fluoridation example earlier in this chapter can be helpful. Recall is often poor even on quite important issues. For instance, Robbins[6] has shown that parents are quite inaccurate in their memory of details about child-rearing practices and early developmental progress even if their children are only three years old, and the parents were part of a special panel study. In consumer surveys, to go back more than two or three days can be extremely misleading.

It is generally best to keep questions short—preferably not more than twenty words. If more than two or three alternative answers are possible, a card should be offered on which the respondent can read the multiple choices; he should not be asked to keep too much in his mind. Every effort should be made to use familiar words; there are lists of the 1,000 or 3,000 most familiar words in the English language (see Payne[1]). Even so, some of the simplest words can become problem words if they are too vague—words such as: *you, about, all, any, few, government, fair.*

If we offer the respondent a list or a set of multiple-choice answers, we run the risk that these may become subject to ordinal biases. For instance, when asked for a numerical estimate, people tend to choose a figure near the average or near the middle of a series. In a list of opinions or ideas, those at the beginning and those at the end may have a greater drawing power. Even when only two possible answers are offered, there may be a tendency to choose the latter. To overcome these problems, some investigators randomize the order on the cards, so that each interviewer or group of interviewers (or each subsample of respondents in a mail inquiry) has the answers in a different order. Others use the split-ballot technique in pilot work, dividing the sample into two or more equivalent parts and presenting each part with a different answer sequence, which makes it possible to measure the ordinal bias and to make allowance for it. Though such procedures are expensive and demanding, they should certainly be applied to questions which recur from one survey to another; only by drawing general conclusions from split-ballot and similar pretests in many investigations will we be able to arrive at a more precise principle that will enable us to minimize these biases.

The problem of the double-barreled or double-negative question is mentioned by many writers. "Have you suffered from headaches or sickness lately?" (Would a positive answer refer to headaches, to sickness, or to both?) "Would you rather not use a nonmedicated shampoo?" (What does a negative answer mean here?) "Do you know if the deadline has expired yet?" (A negative answer might mean that the respondent does not know or that he knows the deadline has not yet expired.) Obviously, such confusing questions should be avoided.

Moser[5] has pointed out that with recurrent or habitual forms of behavior, most investigators choose one of three types of question: (a) "How often . . . in the last week (two weeks, etc.)?" (b) "How often do you . . . on the average?" (c) "When did you last . . .?" Questions (a) and (c) are subject to seasonal variations and assume that the preceding week or the preceding occasion are "typical." Question (c) relies a little too much on guesswork and is too indefinite about the period covered. In any case, many people tend to answer all three types of question in terms of what they *think* they habitually do or aim to do rather than in terms of facts. If we ask all three questions (suitably spaced!) in the same survey, the results may well be different, and we will have no objective way of choosing between them, unless we have observational data, or diaries, or prompt-list information. Since this problem applies to so many different forms of recurrent behavior, it requires much more research. There is, however, one consolation: although such questions often yield divergent results in terms of absolute frequencies of, say, magazine reading or cinema visiting, they may show similar trends in terms of relative group differences, such as age trends, social-class distinctions, or regional variations.

The classification questions are a special type of factual question that asks about age, sex, marital status, income, education, occupation, family size, and so on. These are of special importance in stratifying the sample and tend to recur from survey to survey; for both these reasons they are worth special attention. As we have already seen, unless there is some special reason to do otherwise (for instance, in quota sampling), such questions should come right at the end of the questionnaire, by which time we can hope to have convinced the respondent that the inquiry is genuine. Even then, we ought to use an introductory phrase, such as: "Now, to help us classify your answers statistically, may I ask you a few questions about yourself and your family?" With these questions, too, we must be particularly rigorous in excluding unnecessary detail. As mentioned before, there is no need to ask for the respondent's exact age, when all we really want to know is whether he or she is over or under forty-five. Or, to take another typical question, do we really need to know whether the respondent is separated, divorced, or widowed? And must we go into quite so much detail with regard to household composition?

One need hardly stress that in gathering this kind of information, in particular, definitions are important, both for the interviewer and for the respondent. There must be clear instructions concerning stepchildren, mortgaged house ownership, part-time occupations, and so forth.

The purpose of asking for the occupation of the main breadwinner is usually in order to grade it on some scale of social class or social prestige (see Appendix I). People often give such vague job identifications as: clerk, engineer, businessman, farmer, secretary, civil servant; these terms require further information before they can be classified. One can ask supplementary questions or probe in various ways, but the information needed for each job is different. We have found, however, that the following two questions keep the "unclassifiables" to well under 10 per cent: (1) "What is the name of your job?" (2) "Please describe as carefully as possible the work that you do." Moreover, even in written questionnaires directed to wives (about their husband's job) or to schoolchildren (about their father's job), enough information will usually be obtained to make classification possible.

It has been suggested that wives and children do not know what their husbands or fathers do for a living. Nowadays, in Western societies, this is very rare and likely to be due to special circumstances, for instance, if the man is "something" with an oil company in the Persian Gulf. (Questions about earnings, though, are apt to be far less successful!) Even children of below-average intelligence can give job descriptions that are very clear and mercifully free of deception. Here are some examples from Himmelweit *et al.*:[8]

> A constable in the Z borough police. My father sees that shop doors are closed at night and gives advice to passing motorists.
>
> Plumber's mate. He does all of the dirty work for the plumber. He works in a shipyard and he has no skilled job as he was in the Army.
>
> Sorter in the Post Office. He sorts letters into one of 68 holes in a wooden frame. There are different frames for every town.
>
> Electrician. He cuts the light off of people who do not pay the bill.

Wives, on the other hand, will sometimes introduce prestige distortion describing the husband as "engineer" when he is a repairman, as "civil servant" when he is a streetcleaner, or as "manager" when he is a small store owner.

Classification questions tend to be predominantly sociological, but for some inquiries a psychological classification would be more relevant, for example, a score on a general-knowledge test, a do-it-yourself score, a romanticism score, a radicalism score, or a frustration-resistance score.

Leading Questions and Loaded Words

Leading questions are so worded that they are not neutral: they suggest what the answer should be or indicate the questioner's own point of view. Examples might be: "You haven't forgotten to brush your teeth today?"; "Do you read a daily newspaper?"; "Most people nowadays believe in racial integration, do you?"; "Are you against giving too much power to the trade unions?" Generally, factual questions are less sensitive to "leading" than attitudinal questions.

A "loaded" word or phrase is one which is emotionally colored and suggests an automatic feeling of approval or disapproval, for instance Nazi, bosses, interference, motherly, starvation, strikebreakers, British, intelligent, Socialist. Respondents are reacting not so much to the issue posed by the question as to the loaded phrase itself. Split-ballot trials will show considerable differences in the distribution of answers to a question using the phrase "bosses" compared to one using "leaders"—both loaded phrases but loaded in different directions. Once we are aware of the problem, we can exercise our ingenuity in trying to find a less loaded term, but the trouble is that we often fail to realize the danger. Words and phrases that are more or less neutral in one context or to one group of people may be highly loaded in another context or to another group, for instance the term birth control. A classical example is contained in a study carried out by *Fortune* magazine in February, 1940,[9] in which a representative sample of Americans were asked to place themselves in one of three classes: "upper class," "middle class," and "lower class." The preference for middle class was overwhelming (79 per cent), even among the lower-income groups, and this was taken by some writers as evidence of the basic "middle-class consciousness" of the American people. However, a later survey carried out by Centers[10] gave people the opportunity to classify themselves as "upper class," "middle class," "working class," or "lower class." Now, only one per cent chose "lower class" but 51 per cent called themselves "working class"—clearly the formulators of the *Fortune* questionnaire failed to realize the negative loading of the term "lower class," thus leading many working-class respondents to describe themselves as middle class.

Here are some items from a questionnaire dealing with various aspects of job choice. Each item consisted of a pair of choices, only one of which could be selected by the respondent; this technique sometimes helps to overcome problems of loading. In the pilot work, strenuous efforts were made to reduce or eliminate loaded phrases:

(1)	A job in which you do a lot of hard thinking	OR	A job where, once you have learned it, you always know how to do it
(2)	Where somebody helps you to decide what is to be done	OR	Where you have to decide for yourself how to do things

(3)	Where the pay is not very high, but you get a pension when you retire	OR	Where the pay is high, but you don't get a pension when you retire
(4)	Where you work with your brain	OR	Where you work with your hands

The results showed that the items were, in fact, fairly evenly balanced in pairs and that the respondents were expressing genuine preferences and were not merely reacting to such loaded words as "routine job," "independence," "security," or "manual job."

Much inadvertent leading comes from a failure to state alternatives. The possible alternatives are merely implied or assumed to be so obvious as not to require stating, for instance, "Do you prefer being examined by a doctor of your own sex?" instead of "Would you rather be examined by a male or by a female doctor, or doesn't it matter which?" However, sometimes a question which is leading because it fails to state alternatives becomes less so when the alternatives are given or read aloud to the respondent as multiple choices, for example, "How much trouble have teeth and gums been to you throughout life?" (This is leading, in that it assumes that the respondent's teeth or gums *have* been troublesome and fails to suggest a negative alternative or to use a neutral filter question.) It is followed by (1) "A lot of trouble." (2) "Some trouble." (3) "Little trouble." (4) "No trouble." One cannot help feeling that the wording of the question still suggests to the respondent that he must have had some dental troubles, but if the four alternative answers were shown or read to him, he might well see that a negative answer was acceptable, which would reduce the leading effects of the question. As we have seen earlier, any multiple-choice answers offered to the respondent become part of the question and should be reported as such.

There is a place, in the hands of skilled investigators, for a deliberately leading question, for instance in the study of socially disapproved attitudes or behavior. Kinsey and his associates[11] made habitual use of the "When-did-you-stop-beating-your-wife?" type of question (which puts the onus of denial on the respondent) in order to make their respondents feel that the behavior in question was common and well known and to counteract the prevailing tendency to conceal. Great care has to be taken, however, in interpreting the results.

Leading bias often creeps in when we are formulating probes and follow-up or "Why"-questions, e.g., "How often do you go to your local supermarket?" followed by "Why don't you go more often?"—which suggests that the respondent ought to go more frequently. If the formulation of probes is left entirely to the interviewer, serious biases may result that will never be brought to light. For instance, a question about voting intent might be followed by the instruction, "Probe for importance of education policy, housing development, and defense program." It is almost impossible to imagine how one could phrase, on the spur of the moment, probes and follow-up questions that would allow the respondent to indicate his awareness of these issues and their bearing on his voting intentions without at the same time leading him. Even if we phrase a neutral "Why"-question it may become a source of bias if different interviewers read it differently. Payne[1] gives as an example: "*Why do you say that?*" in which the stress can be placed on each of the five words it contains with very different effects!

Prestige Bias

We should always be aware that many factual questions are loaded with prestige. Some people will claim that they read more than they do, bathe more often than is strictly true, and fill more pipes from an ounce of tobacco than would seem likely. They claim that they buy new tires for their car when in fact they buy retreads; they deny reading certain Sunday newspapers of dubious repute; the shirts that they buy are expensive; they would seem to brush their teeth with great frequency and to visit museums almost every week! There is no simple answer to this problem, but, in addition to being aware that it exists, there are two general measures that may help: (a) use filter questions, or word the main question in such a way that a low-prestige answer is equally possible; thus, instead of "Have you read any of the following magazines within the last seven days?" perhaps try "Have you had time to read any magazines at all within the past seven days?" The latter creates a more permissive situation for the nonreader; (b) brief our interviewers to impress repeatedly on the respondents that *accuracy* is the prime requirement, and that a negative response is just as good as a positive response.

As we have noted, classification questions such as occupation, income, education, and even age, lend themselves very readily to prestige bias, and we must be particularly on our guard with these. However, not all cases of overclaim are due to prestige factors. In some cases, especially where there is a long list of possible answers, respondents are too eager to please; they want to give the interviewer "something" to put down so as not to disappoint her. Nor is overclaiming the only likely source of error; in respect of the consumption of certain goods, such as alcohol or tobacco, we often find persistent *under*statement.

People are reluctant to admit lack of knowledge. In straightforward knowledge questions we generally get a higher percentage of "Don't know" responses than in opinion questions dealing with the same issues. This is because people are reluctant to admit that they do not really understand the question or are unfamiliar with its contents. We must always keep this possibility in mind (if possible, sift out those people for whom the question is meaningless), and not assume that "everyone" will know and will have an opinion on the subject of our inquiry. Similarly, if we start questions with phrases such as "Doctors say that . . . ," "As you know . . . ," "Many people nowadays . . . ," "Research has shown . . . ," or with the mention of names of well-known personalities, we are inviting prestige bias.

People do not like to think of themselves as fools, and it is best to avoid questions that require the admission of foolish or reprehensible behavior. Not many mothers would, for instance, reply affirmatively to the question "Are there any foods or drinks that your children have that you know are bad for their teeth?" In a survey dealing with oranges, fruitsellers were asked whether customers often requested their advice on which brand to buy. This was followed by the question, "And do they mostly act on your advice?" Not surprisingly, 98 per cent said "Yes." If the question does contain some low-prestige alternatives, we should offer the respondent a respectable "out"—an opportunity to say that he intended to read the prestigeful book mentioned (but had not actually done so), or that he had been too busy to become acquainted with certain political issues.

Embarrassing Questions

A question can be embarrassing for several reasons: because it asks for socially disapproved attitudes or behavior, because it deals with very private matters, or because it requires low-prestige answers. Social investigators sometimes forget how sensitive people can be and rush in where angels fear to tread.

As we have already seen, if we are dealing with socially disapproved behavior (such as sexual perversions, excessive alcohol consumption, breaking the laws or customs of a society), we can perhaps presume that a taboo exists that a nondirective question would fail to penetrate. Kinsey[11] has used what almost amount to police tactics in his investigations, firing rapid leading questions that put the onus of denying a particular sexual practice on the respondent. It remains, however, questionable whether he succeeded in breaking the existing taboos or whether he may not have obtained an overestimate. In milder instances of socially disapproved or private issues, merely offering the respondents a number of prepared categories can be sufficient. If such matters are printed on an official-looking form, respondents realize that they are not alone in engaging in this behavior or in having these problems, and so these matters become more admissible. For instance, few mothers would admit that one of their children was a thief, but such admissions become easier when they are offered the following alternatives: (1) "Never takes anything that belongs to someone else"; (2) "Has helped himself to someone else's things at least once or twice (including taking things belonging to other members of the family)"; (3) "Has stolen things on several occasions." Altogether, the creation of a permissive atmosphere in the questionnaire as a whole, together with a guarantee of anonymity, can do much to overcome this problem.

Maintaining Rapport in Mail Questionnaires

In designing questionnaires it is not merely important for us to look at things from the respondent's point of view, but also to make *him* feel that we are doing so. After we have decided, through pilot work and armchair thinking, what it is we need to know, we try to obtain it in ways that will get the respondent on our side and will not antagonize him. We must also make it easy for him by asking for as little effort and time as possible, by reducing the amount of writing he has to do, by making mail questionnaires look attractive (as unlike a tax return as possible), by not calling on him at times that are bound to be inconvenient, and so on. In other words, we must at all times maintain what Festinger & Katz[4] have called "respondent orientation."

Each question and its response will affect, to some extent, the respondent's motivation to go on answering questions and to give of his best. A question that strikes the respondent as rude or inconsiderate may affect not only his reply to that particular question but also his attitude to the next few questions and to the survey as a whole. We must strive, therefore, to meet the respondent halfway and to give and maintain the general feeling that he is being treated with respect and with consideration. By taking time and trouble to answer our questions the respondent is doing us a favor, and we must never allow ourselves to forget this.

A positive feeling in the respondent can be produced and maintained in many ways. The initial explanation of the survey is most important, together with its sponsorship, and even its name or title. We should tell the respondent how he came to be selected for this particular survey and stress the confidentiality and anonymity of the results. We must try never to put him on the defensive or to make him feel in the wrong. Politeness helps: instead of staccato phrases such as "marital status," "length of service," and so on, we should write out or state the questions in full, not forgetting to say "please," or "would you mind." We must try not to talk down to respondents, nor talk over their heads by using technical terms or abbreviations. Keeping in mind that we will probably be dealing with people of different educational backgrounds, our questions should be clear to the less well-educated while not seeming too vague or silly to the college graduates. The use of slang and colloquialisms and the commission of deliberate grammatical errors in an effort to maintain rapport requires the greatest care if unexpected misunderstandings or unintentional double meanings are to be avoided.

In written questionnaires the layout, printing, choice of paper, spacing, and so forth should all be carefully considered. The method of answering multiple-choice questions should be consistent: either circling, checking, or underlining. Open-ended questions, which require most thought and writing, should be kept to a minimum. Often, the number of lines provided will determine the length of the answer, unless we specify the number of answers or ideas required, for example, "What do you think are the three most important qualities that a teacher should have?" Since reading is so much quicker than writing, every effort should be made to save the respondent time and effort by the use of lines, insets, different type-forms, headings, boxes, and so forth.

With free-answer questions, it is sometimes helpful to have the questions in pairs, asking for the pros and cons of a particular issue. For instance: "Is there something about your dentist, his staff, surgery, or waiting room, that you particularly like?" "Is there, perhaps, also something about dentists, their staff, surgeries, or waiting rooms, that you don't like so much?" Note, by the way, the more impersonal and permissive wording of the second question, which asks for criticism. We often ask people to say what are the good and bad points about a particular job, product, political party, and so forth. If, however, a nondirective opening is wanted, in order to establish the respondent's frame of reference, a "What-do-you-look-for" question may first be asked, such as, "What do you look for when choosing a camera?" Another approach might be to ask respondents to complete a sentence, such as, "A good teacher is one who. . . ." (See Chapter 7 on projective techniques.)

Once the final draft of a questionnaire has been assembled, the general layout and appearance is too often left to a subordinate. Even where this is unavoidable, the research worker in charge should at least check the proofs or stencils himself before printing or duplication commences. He should try to put himself in the place of a typical respondent and smooth any remaining rough edges.

Instructions

Each questionnaire or interview form will contain instructions to the respondent, while recording forms will contain instructions and briefing for the interviewer as well.

Instructions to the respondent will usually be confined to the way an answer should be recorded ("Check the one you prefer") and to procedural directions ("If NO, continue with Question 26"). More rarely, simple definitions will be offered ("In counting the number of rooms in your home, include the kitchen but do not count the bathroom and lavatory"), sometimes as part of a question ("Do you perhaps have some form of denture [removable false teeth or tooth]?"). Some research workers like to include more personalized remarks in mail questionnaires, such as "You are doing very well; now, take off five minutes to do something else, and then return for the remaining questions." The main function of all these instructions is to compensate for the absence of an interviewer. They aim at clarifying questions and procedures and at maintaining rapport.

In the case of interviews, directions on procedure will usually be printed on the form, and these can be quite complex at times. Some definitions will, as above, be included in the wording of a question, but most of them will be given to the interviewers in their briefing. The need for adequate briefing emerges clearly from the following example.

Some time ago, a market-research agency began to doubt some of its own findings. The agency was doing repeated interviews, at set time intervals, concerning the purchase of certain consumer goods, and the results, when suitably multiplied to give national figures, did not tally with production figures supplied by manufacturers over the same period. At first, doubt was cast on the production figures because they involved accumulation of data from many depots and other sources, making allowance for quantities "still in the pipeline" (not yet sold), and because stocktaking involves all kinds of time lags. However, allowing for the probable effects of these various sources of divergence, the figures resulting from the interviews were still widely off the mark. After an investigation of sampling procedures and other variables, the agency came to the conclusion that "memory factors" in the respondents were to blame.

However, a different possibility came to light when some of the agency's interviewers were interviewed themselves. Among other things, they were asked what was meant by the frequently recurring phrase "during the past week." One interviewer said that if she were interviewing, say, on a Thursday morning, then she would ask the respondent to think of all purchases between the previous Thursday morning and the day of the interview. Another interviewer, however, said that this included a Sunday, which was not a shopping day, and so she would ask the respondent to consider the last seven clear shopping days, excluding Sundays and sometimes public holidays as well. A third interviewer suggested that, effectively, the question meant a week from Monday to Saturday; if she were interviewing early in the week, she would ask about the past week from Monday to Saturday, but if she were interviewing late in the week or on the week-end, she would ask about the current week, from Monday until the day of the interview. Yet another view was expressed by a fourth interviewer, who said that for all practical purposes the question related to the last big Saturday shopping expedition and that she would ask about that. Some interviewers excluded purchases made on the day of the interview; others included them only if the interview took place after midday. There was, in other words, a clear failure in briefing.

This example illustrates that simple everyday words like "week" may come to mean widely different things when used in a questionnaire. It may be possible to give them a definition or a specialized meaning for the purpose of our particular inquiry, or such ambiguous words may have to be dropped. It is bad enough when the same word means different things to different respondents, but when even our interviewers cannot agree as to what it means, it is high time to do something about the briefing.

Besides a review of definitions and procedural instructions, the briefing of interviewers will generally contain a number of other specific matters, such as the selection of respondents, callbacks, use of ratings, distribution of free samples, handling of display cards, timing, and recording techniques, as well as the more general instructions about rapport, probing, introduction and purpose of the survey, and so on. Many research organizations do their own interviewer-training and have standard handbooks that cover all routine interviewing problems. Some survey organizations refuse to allow their interviewers to do any probing. Others train their interviewers in particular techniques of recording or in specially developed methods such as the guided recall technique. This is a specialized interviewing technique, which has given accurate results but obviously requires a high level of skill and training. The respondent is taken systematically through the previous day, hour by hour and event by event, and is asked to recall by association whether the radio or the television set was turned on at the time and what the program was.

Validity and Reliability

At the end of Chapter 1 an outline was given of the chief sources of error that arise in the course of a survey. We will not concern ourselves here with errors that arise due to sampling, faulty design, high nonresponse rates, or interviewer bias (see Kahn & Cannell[2]); nor shall we discuss ignorance, misunderstanding or reticence on the part of the respondent, bias in recording or coding of the answers, nor errors in the statistical analysis and final interpretation. We will look primarily at the possibility of bias due to question-wording and at the reliability and validity problems raised by questionnaire techniques. These issues underlie much that is prevalent in social research and deserve careful discussion.

First of all, we should distinguish between reliability and validity. Reliability refers to consistency, to obtaining the same results again. Validity tells us whether the question or item really measures what it is supposed to measure. For instance, a clock is supposed to measure "true" time, and to do so continuously. If it were to show the wrong time, we would say that it was invalid. If it were sometimes slow and sometimes fast, we would call it unreliable. It is possible to have a measure that is highly reliable yet of poor validity, for instance a clock that is precisely eighteen minutes fast consistently. The degree of reliability (consistency) sets limits to the degree of validity possible: validity cannot rise above a certain point if the measure is inconsistent to some degree. On the other hand, if we find that a measure has excellent validity, then it must also be reliable. We often have to face these issues in the development of psychological tests, such as measures of intelligence or personality.

By purifying a test we can make it highly reliable, so that repeated administrations of the test will give very similar results, but how can we be sure that it really does measure what it sets out to measure? In principle, the answer to this question is not so very difficult if a criterion can be obtained. A criterion is an independent measure of the same variable, to which the results of our test or questionnaire can be compared. For instance, if our test is a measure of intelligence, then it ought, at the very least, to discriminate between university students and patients in a hospital for the mentally retarded. If it is a measure of neuroticism, then we may compare it with psychiatric assessments or show that it distinguishes between "normals" and patients under treatment in a mental institution. However, many criteria that might be suggested are themselves unreliable and of doubtful validity, for instance teachers' ratings or psychiatric diagnoses. Moreover, in a great many instances criteria are not available—a "true" answer simply does not exist.

Reliability and Validity of Factual Questions

Let us consider, first of all, the somewhat easier case where some sort of criterion is available or could be obtained. Typically, this is most likely to apply to the realm of "factual" questions. If we ask the respondent: "How often have you been to the movies in the last two weeks?" presumably a "true" answer does exist and could be found, if we were able to take sufficient time and trouble. Therefore, in similar cases, asking the same questions again and again ought to yield consistent results (show high reliability).

To ascertain reliability in the case of factual questions we should plan to have a number of internal checks. So as not to annoy the respondent we will probably refrain from asking the same question repeatedly in the same way, but in spite of variations in technique we expect a co-operative respondent to be consistent in factual matters; an inconsistency would point to faults in question-wording, serial or contextual effects, or other sources of error. For instance, having asked the above question about movie attendance, we might, at a later stage, offer the respondent a list of activities, such as: "Could you tell me if you have visited any of the following within the past two weeks: museum, art gallery, movie, zoo, exhibition?" followed by a question about frequency. Another form of internal check would be the introduction of phony items, such as a nonexistent brand name or radio program; endorsement of such items would suggest guessing or carelessness on the part of the respondents. A more elaborate form of check is the split ballot, which requires that we split our sample into two or more equivalent subsamples and give each of them a slightly different form of wording. The true answer is usually taken to be the average of the subsamples. In some cases, the internal check is a logical one; for instance, if a man claims to have fought in the war, then he must have been of a given age at the time. Some survey workers go out of their way to include a number of such logical tests of consistency in their questionnaires. Occasionally, the interviewers may be instructed to confront the respondent (tactfully!) with an apparent inconsistency[7] as it may reveal an error or an unexpected ambiguity in question-wording. (Without such confrontation the internal checks leave us in a dilemma, for we do not know which of two answers to believe. That, however, is a problem of validity.) In some surveys, it is possible to reinterview respondents, for example in panel studies, but we must be careful not to leave an appreciable time interval between the original question and its repetition, or true changes in behavior may occur in the meantime. It is probably true to say that internal checks would not detect a respondent who was really determined to mislead.

To ascertain the validity of factual questions, a variety of techniques is employed, usually known as cross-checks, where a second, independent source of information is required, though not often available. Sometimes, records can be used to check on certain points of information, for instance military-service records, factory-absenteeism figures, insurance cards (for aggregate weeks of employment over a given period). Sometimes, the total survey results can be compared with census figures, retail audits, or manufacturers' production records, though these may themselves be open to doubt. Occasionally, we may be tempted to use two informants concerning the same facts or events, for instance husband and wife (with regard to marital relations or joint financial transactions), parent and teacher (with regard to a child's behavior habits). However, there are many reasons why two observers or two participants in the same action may yet report differently on it, so that in cases of disagreement one cannot say who is right and whether or not the criterion is more valid. This applies particularly to different observers reporting on the same individual.

Occasionally, some of the respondents to a mail inquiry are interviewed, on the assumption that the interview is more valid. In other studies "quality checks" are made; this means that some of the respondents who have been interviewed in the usual way are reinterviewed by a highly trained group of superior interviewers.[7] This is especially worthwhile where a large number of temporary interviewers has been engaged. The second interviewer is usually allowed more freedom and can often track down a discrepancy, for instance to a simple mistake in recording. In certain instances—in a hospital or supermarket—it is possible to check on the responses with the aid of observations.

Kinsey[11] believed that maximum validity and a guarantee against exaggeration were obtained by looking the individual squarely in the eye and firing questions at him with maximum rapidity. More commonly, the best safeguard is said to be good rapport, so that the respondent becomes willing and eager to give information that is really accurate. It still remains difficult to be sure of reasonable validity even when we are dealing with factual questions, and when we deal with attitudinal questions the difficulties become almost insurmountable.

We have so far considered mainly the type of questions that deal with facts or behavior in the past or present. Our test of validity is to compare the respondent's account with what "actually happened"—assuming that we can verify that by some other means. However, some surveys, such as election polls, are intended to be predictive, and in that case the criterion of validity may be a specified event in the future. This illustrates that a measure can have more than one purpose and thus more than one validity. A preelection poll may be valid in the descriptive sense, if it gives us a true picture of the present political allegiances of the respondents, yet it may show poor validity as a predictor of the popular vote three weeks later. The vote may be affected by any number of variables, such as a press campaign, the weather, a political scandal, or a domestic disagreement, and, therefore, a valid description of the present may not be a good predictor of the future. People are often poor predictors of their own behavior, so that statements of intent often lack validity when compared with subsequent events, though they may well have been valid as statements of hopes, wishes, and aspirations. Altogether, we do not often find a one-to-one relationship between attitudes or opinions, and behavior (see Chapter 6).

Reliability and Validity of Attitude Questions

Since attitudinal questions are more sensitive than factual questions to changes in wording, context, emphasis, and so on, it becomes almost impossible to assess reliability by "asking the same question in another form." It will no longer be the same question. For this reason, we should not rely on single questions when we come to measure those attitudes that are most important to our study; we should have sets of questions or attitude scales (see chapters 5 and 6). Sets of questions are more reliable than single opinion items; they give more consistent results, mainly because vagaries of question wording will probably apply only to particular items (and thus any bias may cancel out), whereas the underlying attitude will be common to all the items in a set or scale. The reliability of a scale can be assessed in the usual way by a split-half correlation coefficient (see Cronbach[13]) without having to ask the same questions twice.

The assumption underlying these procedures is that there is such a thing as a "true" attitude, which is also relatively stable, just as in the case of factual questions there are "true" facts or events. However, since an attitude is more complex than, say, a respondent's method of traveling to work, it is unlikely that a single question will reflect it adequately. Also, the chances are that too much will depend on the actual question form and wording, on context, emphasis, and mood of the moment, so that the results will be a compound of the (relatively stable) attitude and of these other (momentary) determinants—hence the poor reliability of the single-attitude question. By using sets of questions, provided they all relate to the same attitude, we maximize the more stable components while reducing the instability due to particular items, emphasis, mood changes, and so on. None of the previously mentioned internal checks can readily be applied to opinion or attitude questions, but split ballots are sometimes used.

There have also been attempts to introduce logical checks for consistency; for instance, if a respondent has strong left-wing political sympathies, it would be surprising if he showed hostility to trade unions. Needless to say, such inconsistencies frequently exist side by side and can be defended; certainly, they do not necessarily mean that the questions are unreliable.

It may be helpful to introduce a distinction at this point between relative and absolute consistency. If we need to know what percentage of our sample habitually travels to work by car, then this will be an absolute figure, give or take a margin of error. If we ask the question more than once, we can reasonably hope to get a similar and consistent result. However, if we wish to know what percentage of our sample has a positive attitude to saving, a great deal will depend on how the question is phrased. At what point, on a continuum from unfavorable through neutral to favorable, do we begin to include a respondent in the proportion of those with a positive attitude to saving? What kinds of saving do we ask about? How strong is the respondent's attitude? Suppose we have developed four different techniques (say, a free-answer question about the best ways to take care of the future, a checklist, an attitude scale, and a projective device using pictures), and that after due consideration of the results we apply a cut-off point to each technique, with the result that we get four different estimates of the proportion of respondents with a positive attitude to saving. Do we now say that the questions are unreliable? Not necessarily. We have to state, of course, that the answer will depend on how one defines and measures positive attitude to saving, but we may find that all four methods intercorrelate quite well, and that group differences between subsamples are consistent. Thus, we may never be able to say what proportion of our sample has a positive attitude to saving in absolute terms, but we may well be in a position to show that the *relative* differences, such as those between middle class and working class, or between older and younger respondents, are in the same direction irrespective of the technique used and consistently show that older people, or middle-class people, have a more positive attitude to saving. This type of consistency is well worth stressing, especially if it applies to techniques that apparently tap different "levels" (see Chapter 5).

The chief difficulty in assessing the validity of attitude questions is the lack of criteria. What we need are groups of people with known attitude characteristics (criterion groups), so that we can see whether or not our questions can discriminate between them. Occasionally, such groups can be found, for example the adherents of a particular political party or the members of a particular church, but unfortunately people join groups for many different motives, and there is no reason to suppose that group membership as a reflection of an inner attitude is any more valid than a set of attitude questions. At best, there will only be a rough correspondence between the two indicators. We cannot necessarily predict behavior from attitudes; nor are attitudes readily inferred from behavior with any validity, nor is behavior necessarily a more valid expression of an attitude than a verbal statement. The links between attitudes and behavior are complex (see Chapter 6), and group membership may or may not be a valid criterion of a particular attitude.

This rather unsatisfactory situation has led to the concept of construct validity (see Cronbach[13]), as contrasted with pragmatic validity. We must face up to the fact that we are trying to measure something that is beneath the surface, and we are trying to give this "something" a more precise formulation by saying what sub-variables it pulls together and how it must be related to other attitudinal or perceptual variables and to some aspects of behavior. If we happen to find pragmatic validity in respect to a particular criterion, we still need to know *why* it works, in terms of constructs. Such constructs, once obtained, would be expected to enter into relationships with other variables in predictable ways. Validity is inferred from such a predicted network of relationships; this validates both the measure and the theory behind it.

An example of construct validity might be authoritarianism (see Adorno[14]). Here we have a construct which links together many kinds of attitudes that would otherwise seem to be quite unconnected—superstitiousness, lack of insight, rigid role differentiation, racial prejudice, and attitude to power. It has predictable relationships to other attitudes, such as anti-Semitism, political conservatism, and strictness in the upbringing of children. It can also be used to predict certain forms of behavior (voting, methods of discipline, friendship-choice patterns, performance of certain roles), though situational variables may upset these predictions. Needless to say, in order to attain construct validity, a set of measures needs to be developed which is first of all reliable and reasonably stable over time. The more varied the techniques and the better they intercorrelate in the way predicted by the theory, the more support they offer both for the construct and for the measuring instruments.

A different approach to validation of attitudinal questions stresses the value of the candor, depth, and richness of the information obtained. The most valid way to obtain an estimate of a respondent's attitude to, say, capital punishment would be to ask him some free-answer questions and let him take his time and state his views in his own way. This approach stresses the richness of the data and the need to obtain a full and rounded picture of the respondent's attitude on a complex matter. The more involved the respondent becomes in his account and the deeper the level from which his answer springs, the more genuine and valid his responses will be and the better they will predict his future reactions. Certainly, such data have a high degree of "face validity"—much more so than a few checks on an attitudinal scale! However, some investigators have urged the opposite point of view, namely, that the most valid response is likely to be the respondent's snap answer, his first immediate reaction to the question, giving what is uppermost in his mind rather than a carefully considered statement. They claim that, as in association tests, the first quick response is less open to defensive bias and face-saving. We urgently need more evidence on this entire issue; quite possibly these two approaches to the problem of obtaining more valid information are not so contradictory as they at first appear to be.

It is worth considering once more the purpose of measuring attitudes in each particular case. For instance, we may obtain data that are very rich, but are they relevant to the issues in question? What are we going to do with our measures? Do we need finely graded precision (say, in order to carry out correlation studies) or do we merely wish to divide our sample crudely into four or five groups, according to their standing on the attitude continuum? Do we really need to explore "in depth" or, conversely, ought we to "dig deeper"? For that matter, do most of our respondents really have "hidden depths"?

One other approach to validation may be mentioned. Sometimes it is possible to compare our own findings with the results of other studies. This will apply chiefly to areas which are comparatively well explored, such as the area of political attitudes, or to instances where a study is repeated or parallels a similar study carried out elsewhere. If such an external check is corroborative we may justifiably feel that we are on the right track, but if there are serious differences we will not know which set of results is more valid. It sometimes happens that a particular area yields very contradictory results from a number of studies until a new theory or a new concept is developed that suggests a different analysis of the data and so may resolve the contradictions.

Inadequate questionnaire construction is not the only cause of poor validity. Naturally, we must do all we can in the spheres of interviewer selection, training, briefing, and supervision since so much error arises from irregularities of procedure, changes in wording, faulty recording, and the failure to maintain rapport. We can also ask the interviewers to rate the success of each interview and to comment on such matters as interruptions or the respondent's evasiveness. The problem of validity remains one of the most difficult in social research and one to which an adequate solution is not yet in sight.

• *Selected Readings*

QUESTION WORDING

1. S. L. Payne, *The Art of Asking Questions* (Princeton University Press, 1951).

   An amusing but pointed book, full of examples on question phrasing.

2. Robert L. Kahn and Charles F. Cannell, *The Dynamics of Interviewing* (New York: Wiley, 1957).

   A useful textbook dealing with various kinds of interviews. See especially chapter 5, "The Formulation of Questions."

3. Claire Selltiz, Marie Jahoda, Morton Deutsch, and Stuart W. Cook, eds., *Research Methods in Social Relations* (New York: Holt, 1959).

   A basic textbook on social research. See especially chapters 5 and 7.

4. Leon Festinger and David Katz, eds., *Research Methods in the Behavioral Sciences* (New York: Dryden Press, 1953).

   A basic textbook in social research.

5. Claus A. Moser, *Survey Methods in Social Investigation* (London: Heinemann, 1958).

PROBLEMS OF RECALL

6. Lillian C. Robbins, "The Accuracy of Parental Recall of Aspects of Child Development and of Child-Rearing Practices," *Journal of Abnormal and Social Psychology,* LXVI (1963), 261–270.

7. William A. Belson, *Studies in Readership* (London: Business Publications Ltd., 1962).

   A carefully conducted follow-up inquiry into the causes of unreliability in a national readership survey.

OCCUPATIONAL GRADING

8. Hilde T. Himmelweit, A. N. Oppenheim, and P. Vince, *Television and the Child* (London: Oxford University Press, 1958).

   See pp. 82–84 for problems of obtaining father's job information from school children.

9. Fortune Surveys, *The People of the United States—a Self-Portrait* (*Fortune,* February, 1950, Vol. 21).

10. Richard Centers, *The Psychology of Social Classes* (Princeton: Princeton University Press, 1949).

EMBARRASSING QUESTIONS

11. Alfred C. Kinsey, W. B. Pomeroy, and C. E. Martin, *Sexual Behavior in the Human Male* (Philadelphia and London: W. B. Saunders, 1948).

    See especially pp. 35–82 on interviewing techniques.

12. Allen J. Barton, "Asking the Embarrassing Question," *Public Opinion Quarterly,* XXII (1958), 67–68.

    A humorous set of suggestions for wording embarrassing questions.

RELIABILITY AND VALIDITY

13. Lee J. Cronbach, *Essentials of Psychological Testing* (New York: Harper, 1960).

A useful textbook on tests and their uses. See especially chapter 5 on validity, and pp. 126–142 on reliability.

14. T. W. Adorno, Else Frenkel-Brunswik, D. J. Levinson, and R. N. Sanford, *The Authoritarian Personality* (New York: Harper, 1950).

4

Checklists, Rating Scales, and Inventories

This chapter gives brief accounts of various techniques that are elaborations of the "closed" type of question. Their main feature is that they do not ask the respondent to write anything, although they may require a certain amount of reading and thought; the response consists of a check or some other indication of choice, and it is usually possible to calculate some kind of score. These techniques are suitable for mail and group-administered questionnaires and can be used in door-to-door interviewing. In the latter case, it is often helpful if a card or form with the questions on it can be handed to the respondent.

As a general background to this chapter, the reader might wish to familiarize himself with the basic principles of psychological measurement and test construction. (See references.)

Checklists

Checklists contain terms which the respondent understands and which more briefly and succinctly express his views than answers to open-ended questions. The example shown in Table 4–1 is taken from a questionnaire designed for female university students as part of a study of their marriage aspirations.

Table 4–1.

Would you please give your opinion on the following attributes of a prospective husband:

	Very important	Important	Indifferent	Undesirable
1. Good looks				
2. Kindness				
3. Money				
4. Dependability				
5. Sense of humor				
6. Ambition				
7. Moral character				
8. Domesticity				
9. Intelligence				
10. Good health				

Checklists are inevitably crude devices, but careful pilot work and assembly can make them less so. They are at their best when they are constructed and used to test specific hypotheses rather than as exploratory tools. Though it is possible to disguise their intent somewhat, such devices operate at the conscious and overt level and run the risk that the respondent will grasp the hypothesis and will try to "help" by making the results come out the way he thinks they should.

This raises the general problem of the interpretation of the results. Often, such techniques look impressive and "scientific" in a questionnaire, but we must maintain a critical attitude and ask ourselves what this set of questions is trying to achieve, and how the results will be used. Many such devices have been hurriedly put together and suffer from lack of pilot work, poor coverage, and doubtful validity. The fact that they have somehow been made to yield a numerical score should not blind us to their possible shortcomings. In the above example, for instance, how do we know that these and not other or fewer attributes are of chief concern to our respondents? What does a check in any of these columns really mean? Will it predict actual behavior some time in the future? Does it reflect certain attitudes in the present? Is the respondent merely trying to please or to conform? How has she interpreted the various terms we have used?

Only careful pilot work can show us whether our selection of items adequately reflects the way in which young university women think about the men they hope to marry. Pilot work is also needed to ensure that we use terms that are like those the respondents use themselves and that have roughly similar meanings to most of them—and to us. Up to a point, the pilot work can also help us to interpret the "level" of the responses. Strictly speaking, all we know is that a given respondent has placed checks in certain columns; why she has done so is, as with most answers to questions, a matter for interpretation. It depends on what we need to find out. We might report, say, social-class differences among groups of university women in the way they answer this inventory—and perhaps that is all we need to know. Or we might have to go further and state that these questions and answers reflect certain genuine attitudes among our respondents and that these attitudes show class differences. We might deduce from these answers that these respondents have certain needs that lead them to respond in different ways, or that they interpret the questions differently and, hence, show different class patterns. Or that the respondents know themselves well enough to predict their own behavior in future situations in this way. Or that the responses reflect varying degrees of past experience. Perhaps the respondents are trying to create a favorable impression of themselves by checking those qualities that they regard as socially desirable—and social classes differ in what they hold desirable. With so many different possibilities of answering and levels of interpretation, it is obvious that we must do our best in the pilot work to find out what use can validly be made of these responses. The danger of overinterpretation is ever present.

Ratings

Rating gives a numerical value to some kind of judgment. Familiar examples are school marks or grades and proficiency reports on personnel in industry, which attempt to give an objective assessment of an individual's performance. Usually, a set of assumptions is made about equality of the intervals on a rating scale.

We may apply ratings to almost anything—to individuals, to objects, to abstractions, and to ourselves. The task is usually to give "so many marks out of so many," or some percentage-equivalent. Sometimes, graphic-rating scales are used, in which the response consists in making a mark on a line running between two extremes.

The use of ratings invites the gravest dangers and possible errors, and in untutored hands the procedure is useless. Worse, it has a spurious air of accuracy, which misleads the uninitiated into regarding the results as hard data. For instance, hospital nurses are often rated by their ward supervisors, after a certain period, on such attributes as practical ability, appearance, neatness, cleanliness, emotional stability, professional deportment, conscientiousness, reliability, punctuality, self-reliance, common sense, physical stamina, and so on. The ratings may run from 1–5, or from 1–10, or any other intervals. These ratings are taken into account when matters arise concerning promotion and transfer or the provision of references. Yet in a typical investigation, if the same supervisor rates the same nurses on two occasions, the correlations between the first and second rating will be very low and will only occasionally reach statistical significance. The correlations with assessment of these nurses by other supervisors and with examination results will be similarly low. The procedure here is, in fact, meaningless; it assumes that we know which traits are important, that these traits are unitary and not complex entities, that the trait names or labels mean the same things to different people at different times, or to one person on repeated occasions, and that the raters have the necessary information. This type of rating tends to be of doubtful validity and suffers from gross unreliability.

Perhaps the chief danger of ratings lies in the ease with which they can be influenced, often by variables of which the rater is unaware. For instance, suppose we asked a child's mother and his teacher to rate him on various attributes such as irritability, shyness, obedience, and so forth. We would probably find differences between the two sets of ratings, not only because the child may behave differently at school and at home, but also because the teacher compares him with other children of the same age and sex, whereas his mother probably compares him with the others in the family and with a few children in the neighborhood. In other words, the two raters have different frames of reference. This is a problem that affects our perceptions and evaluations all the time and can lead to much misunderstanding. It is most important, therefore, when we ask for a set of ratings to indicate the frame of reference that the raters are expected to use. The label or title of the set of ratings will have an influence, too; in the preceding example, a title such as "Neuroticism Scale" would probably yield quite different ratings from a title like "Child Development Scale." It should be recognized that the respondent is also influenced by what he thinks is the purpose of the rating procedure; if we do not tell him what the purpose is (by offering a title or a frame of reference), then he will try to guess what the purpose might be, and since different respondents may guess very differently, their ratings will diverge more than they might have done otherwise.

Another danger is the halo effect: instead of giving his attention separately to each item, the respondent lets himself be influenced by an over-all feeling of like or dislike. Thus, if he decides that he likes a particular make of car, he will give it high marks for performance, comfort, braking efficiency, and so forth; but if he does not like it, he will stress its shortcomings. In neither case has he assessed each item on its merits. A different form of the halo effect expresses itself in a response set. If the rating scales are arranged one underneath the other and always with the "good" (socially desirable) end on the left-hand side and the "bad" end on the right, then the respondent—having once made up his mind that he is favorably disposed toward the object of the ratings—may run down the page always checking a position on the left, or vice versa, without actually reading the items or giving each of them separate thought. To counteract this, we try to randomize the direction of the scales, so that the socially most desirable end falls sometimes on the left and sometimes on the right. It further helps if we put each rating scale on a separate page.

Having the rating scales on separate pages further helps to offset the halo effect and is also useful in combating the logical error, the tendency to give an object or a person similar ratings on two attributes that are thought to be correlated, such as intelligence and emotional stability, or price and quality. We must also make sure that our raters have the necessary information; we should not ask them to rate Greek grammar or the work of an electroencephalographer if they have no relevant knowledge.

Ratings can be used in various ways: (1) as objective assessments; for instance, a rating of the quality of fixtures and furnishings in a home during or after an interview; (2) in a subjective, projective way, to tell us something about the rater, his percepts and his attitudes; (3) as self-ratings, of personality traits or attitudes. Each of these types of rating scales requires a somewhat distinct interpretation, and different aspects have to be stressed in their design and quantification.

In constructing a projective rating scale, perhaps the first step is to define the dimension that is being rated. It should be possible to describe it so that it will have approximately the same meaning to all the raters involved in the investigation. This may be relatively easy when a food product is being rated on "Sweetness," but it becomes more difficult when, say, we want to rate a family on the "extent to which the family supports the child in conflicts with the outside world."

The number of steps in a rating scale tends to vary from three or five to perhaps ten. It will usually be found that raters are unable, in most instances, to make discriminations that are finer than ten points or so. Many research workers favor an uneven number of steps, especially when there are only three or five, in order to have a neutral category or midpoint, to one side of which lie the favorable categories and to the other side the unfavorable ones. This is also because raters are a little afraid of using the extreme categories—a phenomenon known as the error of central tendency. We can try to make our extreme categories sound less extreme, so as to encourage their use, or we may reconcile ourselves to the inevitable and decide afterwards to combine, say, the two or three extreme categories at each end—in which case something like a ten-point scale would seem desirable. Although steps on a rating scale are often used as if they had numerical values and as if the intervals were equal, we usually lack the evidence to justify such assumptions.

Next, after deciding the number of steps in our scale, we have to define the extremes, or better still, define each step. If we have, say, a seven-point scale on "Punctuality" then we must say when or by what criteria a person is to be rated five, or one, or three, and so on. Is a person who is frequently late by a few minutes to get the same rating as someone who is never late, as a rule, but who has been very late on a single occasion? Is earliness rated the same way as lateness? On what occasions is punctuality to be assessed? Over what period? These and many other questions have to be given unambiguous answers, and we have to give all raters full and clear instructions. Unless we do this, two raters rating the same person or object will have conflicting results.

By way of illustration, an excerpt from the Fels[5] scales for the assessment of childrearing by means of home visits is reproduced in Table 4–2. Note that each step, as well as the general dimension, has been described in some detail. When objective assessments are wanted, it is dangerous to give such labels as "frequently," "moderately," "often," "occasionally," and so on to the different grades, since they can be interpreted differently by the various raters. Guilford[4] has given an excellent exposition of the steps to be heeded in the use of ratings and the construction of rating scales.

We often use rating scales when an attitude or a personal impression is wanted in subjective rather than objective terms. For instance, suppose we wished to employ an actress in a thirty-second advertising film concerning baby foods. Our choice may have been narrowed down to three or four candidates whose photographs (with babies on their laps) may be shown to an audience of housewives. To find out how the audience perceives these "mothers" we might ask a group of housewives to fill out the graphic rating scales that are shown in Table 4–3.

Table 4–2.

Fels Parent-Behavior Rating Scale No. 3.15

Democracy of Regulation and Enforcement Policy (Democratic-Dictatorial)

Rate the parent's tendency to share with the child the formulation of regulations for the child's conduct. Does the parent give the child a voice in determining what the policy shall be? Or does the parent hand down the established policy from above?

Disregard immediate issues not covered by policy. Rate independent of justification of policy to child, and independent of restrictiveness of regulations. Include both overt consulting with child and considering child's expressed wishes. Dictatorial policies may be wise or foolish, benevolent or selfish.

☐ Endures much inconvenience and some risk to child's welfare in giving child large share in policy forming. Consults with child in formulating policies whenever possible.

☐ Attempts to adjust policies to child's wishes wherever practicable. Often consults child.

☐ Deliberately democratic in certain safe or trivial matters, but dictates when there is a sharp conflict between child's wishes and other essential requirements.

☐ Neither democratic nor dictatorial, deliberately. Follows most practical or easiest course in most cases.

☐ Tends to be rather dictatorial, but usually gives benevolent consideration to child's desires. Seldom consults child.

☐ Dictatorial in most matters, but accedes to child's wishes occasionally when they do not conflict with own convenience or standards.

☐ Dictates policies without regard to child's wishes. Never consults child when setting up regulations.

Here, where only a rough, personal impression is required and where the differences between the candidates are more important than the absolute figures, only the extremes of each

Table 4–3.

How would you rate the mother on these scales?
(Check appropriate space on each scale)

Warmhearted	⊢—+—+—+—+—+—+—⊣	Coldhearted
Overprotective toward her children	⊢—+—+—+—+—+—+—⊣	Takes good care of her children
Unselfish	⊢—+—+—+—+—+—+—⊣	Selfish
Patient	⊢—+—+—+—+—+—+—⊣	Impatient
Competent mother	⊢—+—+—+—+—+—+—⊣	Incompetent mother
Gay	⊢—+—+—+—+—+—+—⊣	Quiet
Very like myself	⊢—+—+—+—+—+—+—⊣	Not at all like myself
Scatterbrained	⊢—+—+—+—+—+—+—⊣	Sensible
Self-assured	⊢—+—+—+—+—+—+—⊣	Always worried
Unhappy by nature	⊢—+—+—+—+—+—+—⊣	Happy by nature
Bad at housekeeping	⊢—+—+—+—+—+—+—⊣	Good at housekeeping
Takes good care of her children	⊢—+—+—+—+—+—+—⊣	Pampers her children
Would like to have as a friend	⊢—+—+—+—+—+—+—⊣	Would not like to have as a friend

scale have been indicated. Note, however, that the "favorable" extreme is sometimes on the right and sometimes on the left, to try to counteract response set and halo effect. The scales are deliberately contrived to encourage guessing, so as to obtain attitudes and first impressions. We must be very clear in our own minds that we are not getting an "objective" assessment, but rather a snap judgment and sometimes a wild guess—for our present purpose, that is what is required.

Sometimes, rating scales are used to tell us something about the rater, rather than about the object of the ratings. The work of Osgood[6] on the semantic differential is important, particularly in the clinical field. For instance, suppose we take again the set

Table 4–4.

Here are some reasons European students give for dissatisfaction with their conditions in this country. Please indicate how important each has been for *you.*

	Of very great importance	Of great importance	Of some importance	Of no importance
1. Absence of parents, family				
2. Absence of close friends				
3. Separation from wife, husband, children				
4. Missing your own language, books, magazines, etc.				
5. Missing the festivals, celebrations, social functions, etc.				
6. Food difficulties				
7. Discomforts of working in a household				
8. Long period of absence from home				
9. Boredom and monotony of present life				
10. General sense of psychological (emotional) depression				
11. Other reasons (please specify):				

of mother-rating scales discussed earlier and ask a woman to rate herself, her own mother, and also the "ideal" mother on each of the scales. From the results, we might be able to see how she perceives her own mother, how far she looks upon herself as similar to her mother, to what extent her image of her mother and the "ideal mother" overlap, and where she feels that she herself falls short of the ideal. For such an investigation we would no doubt wish to add other variables and change some of the existing ones. (See Chapter 8.)

Table 4–4 gives a simple set of self-assessment ratings, from an inquiry by Postlethwaite[7] into the problems of continental students living in Great Britain.

Table 4–4 really is a scale of subjective importance applied to each item in turn, and each respondent supplies his or her own frame of reference. Such scales of subjective importance can be applied to all kinds of persons, objects, and hypothetical or actual situations. They yield attitudes rather than objective assessments. Table 4–5 is a further example taken from the study of attitudes of unmarried, female university students quoted at the beginning of this chapter.

Table 4–5.

Assuming that you have found the man of your choice, how important would it be for you to have the following conditions fulfilled on or before your marriage date?

	Not important	Fairly important	Very important	Not having this would cause me to postpone marriage
1. Have obtained a degree yourself				
2. Husband to have his training completed				
3. Have earned own living				
4. Have left parents' home				

	Not important	Fairly important	Very important	Not having this would cause me to postpone marriage
5. Have obtained parents' permission to the proposed marriage				
6. Have husband's parents' permission				
7. Have a formal engagement				
8. Have a "white" wedding				
9. Have a joint income of not less than $1,400 per annum				
10. Have reached a specific age (say, 25)				
11. Have had sexual relations yourself				
12. Husband to have had sexual relations				
13. Have joint savings of not less than $600				
14. Have same religious beliefs				
15. Have same political convictions				
16. Have a honeymoon				
17. Have found a suitable flat or house				
18. Have had a "good time"				
19. Other (please specify):				

Ranking

Ranking means arranging in order, with regard to some common aspect. We can rank children in terms of their school performance, soldiers in terms of their leadership potential, lettuces in terms of freshness, or paintings in order of merit. There are practical limitations to the number of rankings most people can be expected to carry out; under normal survey conditions, to put ten objects in rank-order is probably as much as can be asked. Ranking tells us nothing about the differences between ranks; the "distance" between ranks two and three may be very large, but between five and six it may be minute—ranking tells us the order or sequence, but the size of the rank-intervals is unknown and unlikely to be equal. This has led to the development of Spearman's Rho and Kendall's Tau (the special correlation coefficients for two rank orders) and to numerous other statistical devices (see Kendall[9]), none of which requires any knowledge of the size of the rank-intervals. Indeed, we would not use the ranking technique if such knowledge were available (or if suitable assumptions could be made about equality of scale-intervals); we would use some form of rating or scaling, instead.

One must be very clear in one's own mind about the results needed, before setting a ranking task. For instance, to rank paintings in order of "merit" may produce very confusing findings, because merit is a very vague term compounded of a liking for the subject matter, colors, expressiveness, evaluation of technical skill, size, fame of the painter, and so on. But everything depends on the purpose to which the rankings will be put. Sometimes, a fairly vague ranking can be useful, such as to rank jobs in order of "prestige." Also, a ranking on a vague dimension may be used as a first step in an exploratory sequence of questions; when we follow it up with various probes and "Why"-questions we obtain a clearer idea of the criteria used by the respondent in assigning ranks. But these are exceptions; mostly, we should state as clearly as possible on what basis the ranking is to be carried out.

Ranking is a very common process in our society. Among familiar forms of ranking are those by teachers of their pupils. We commonly rank the finishers in a sporting event or in any other competition. We rank many goods in terms of quality and price. We grade farm produce, coffee, and tobacco. We rank books and phonograph records according to their sales. The idea of ranking is familiar, but the basis for ranking in any particular case is not always clear.

For ranking of large numbers of objects we sometimes use classed ranks. We place together all those to whom we assign the first rank, then all those to whom we assign the second rank, and so on. This procedure resembles rating, but it differs from rating in that no statements or assumptions are made about the intervals between classes or ranks—ranking is less precise. The commonly used prestige rankings of occupations are of this kind (see Appendix I).

Mention should be made of paired comparisons. Here, the objects to be ranked are presented two at a time, and the respondent has to choose between them. To obtain a rank order from this procedure, all possible combinations of pairs have to be presented, preferably in random order. For ten objects this requires forty-five paired comparisons ($\frac{1}{2}N(N-1)$), and the number of comparisons rises very steeply when the number of objects is increased. For this reason, paired comparisons are not used much in social research; the method comes more into its own in the laboratory.[4]

Ranking can be used projectively in a useful and revealing way, to tell us something about the respondent rather than about the objects being ranked. Teachers, for instance, may reveal a social-class bias when ranking pupils on "popularity." Nurses may identify themselves so closely with doctors that they tend to upgrade their own job compared to the way nursing is ranked by the general population.

Inventories

An inventory is essentially a list that the respondent is asked to mark or check in a particular way. It may consist of a list of interests, and the task may be to "check those things that interest you a lot." It may be a list of small social misdemeanors, and the respondent is asked to check various columns to say "how bad" each is. It may be a list of personality traits or emotional feelings, and people are asked to check which of these apply to them. It may be a list of spare-time activities, in which one has to check the activity engaged in most often, and so on.

Inventories resemble subjective rating scales, except that they are designed to yield two or more scores. The items—though commonly presented in random order—can be grouped in specified ways, and scores can be computed for each respondent on a number of such groups of items, or on the inventory as a whole. In the better types of inventory, in particular those that can be properly described as personality tests (see Vernon[11] and Messick,[12]) the items are selected after careful pilot work, and the grouping into areas is done on a statistical basis by means of correlations, so that those items that are scored together really belong together. However, since there are always problems for which no inventory has been devised, many people construct inventories and group items together largely on an *a priori* basis. In this way, they obtain a quick, relatively crude but useful set of measures, with reasonable reliability because of the use of area scores rather than single questions.

Here is one set of items, from an inventory dealing with the (perceived) effects of television. The items refer to "stimulation of activities":

(a) I have copied the way people dress on television.
(b) I have tried to cook something after it has been shown on television.
(c) I have made things after they have been shown on television.
(d) I have tried to read a book after it has been talked about on television.
(e) I have gone to a museum or art gallery after seeing it on television.

The items are checked "true" or "untrue," and in the actual inventory they were mixed up with many other items. Note that the item referring to cooking is likely to inflate the total area score for women; depending on the purpose of the inventory, the relative belance of the items in each area should be kept in mind.

Inventories have a wide variety of uses; they can be constructed with various purposes in mind or to test particular hypotheses. Taboo items, inadmissible problems, or antisocial forms of behavior can readily be inserted; respondents who see such items in print often respond to them more readily than to an open question. Table 4–6 is a set of nine items from an inventory of "worries" used with schoolchildren. This particular area covers feelings of rejection by other children; it could be used, for instance, to explore the feelings of colored youngsters going to a racially mixed school.

Table 4–6.

Almost everyone at one time or another is worried about some things. Different people are worried about different things. Read through the list and for each thing check to show whether it worries you a lot, a little, or does not worry you.

Check what is right for you.

	Worries me *a lot*	Worries me *a little*	*Hardly ever* worries me
Not getting along well with other children			
Not being popular			
Feeling that some children would not like to come to my home			
Feeling left out of things			
Other children making fun of me			
Being called names			
Feeling that some children look down on me			

The scoring is 3–2–1, or 2–1–0, or some other arbitrary scores, and the items are given equal weight. Note the careful wording of the instructions.

Inventories can sometimes be made to perform at a fairly subtle level. In a study of the attitudes of psychiatric nurses, a successful attempt was made to discriminate between those with rather autocratic and repressive tendencies and those with a more psychotherapeutic orientation. Table 4–7 is part of the inventory that was used.

Table 4–7. How bad is it? How good is it?

How good or bad would it be, in your opinion, if a psychiatric nurse like yourself on your present ward did any of the following things? (Please put a check in the right column)

How bad is it if you *How good is it if you*	Very bad	Bad	Would not matter	Fairly good	Very good	It would depend
Spend a good deal of time talking to patients?						
Let some patients remain untidy?						
Sometimes show that you are in a bad mood yourself?						
Appear to the patients to be very busy and efficient?						
Forget to put on a clean uniform?						
Avoid discussion of personal problems of a patient with him because you feel that the doctor should do this?						
Take special pride in having patients who are quiet and do as they are told?						
Talk about a patient when the patient is present, acting as though the patient was not there?						
Get deeply involved with what happens to particular patients?						
Find that you have to be very firm with some patients?						

Note the permissive way in which some of the items have been worded ("Find that you have to be firm . . ." instead of "Be firm with . . ."). Also note the category "It would depend," which was hardly ever used by the more autocratic kind of nurse. However, psychiatrists, who were also given this inventory to fill out, made frequent use of "It would depend," partly because they were less aware of the nursing "ethos."

As already mentioned, there are many personality tests which take the form of inventories. They use self-descriptive phrases such as: I make strong demands on myself; I often feel humiliated; I doubt my sexual powers; I usually like people; I usually feel driven; my hardest battles are with myself. There is voluminous literature (see references at the end of this chapter) covering the better clinical devices; these depend for their effectiveness on the full co-operation of the respondent. They tend to suffer from the fact that their purpose is too obvious and, for that reason, are rarely used in social research.

Slightly different from inventories are the adjective checklists. These are commonly used to elicit stereotypes about groups of people or nations (see Chapter 8), though they may be adapted to other purposes. They consist of a list of adjectives, and the respondent is asked to underline the ones that apply. For instance:

Practical	Honest
Talkative	Boastful
Stupid	Imaginative
Aggressive	Stolid
Artistic	Lazy

The adjectives may be grouped and area scores computed. Careful thought and a good deal of pilot work have to go into the preparation and balance of such lists, and of course, not every respondent is willing to apply such adjectives to whole groups of people.

Grids

A grid is an elaboration of the usual type of inventory—almost a two-way inventory. (See Table 4–8.) It is a very simple and straightforward means by which one can quickly collect information without having to ask a great many questions, and the data can be analyzed in several different ways. Particular hypotheses can be explored in a way that does not make them obvious to the respondent.

Table 4–8.

Here are some well-known remedies that can be used to give relief with different types of complaints and illnesses. For each of these illnesses or complaints, please check those remedies that you think are best:

	Nose Drops	Chest Rub	Gargle	Inhalants	Throat Sprays	Syrup	Throat Candy	Throat Tablets	Cough Medicine
Chest cough									
Dry cough									
Smoker's cough									
Severe cough									
Sinus pains									
Common cold									
Sore throat									
Infected tonsils									
Dry throat									
Catarrh									
For a lost voice									
Bad taste in mouth									
Help to sleep									
Indigestion									
Bronchitis									
Asthma									

The over-all frequency tabulation will immediately show which is the preferred method of treatment for, say, a dry throat. It will also show under what circumstances a particular remedy, such as a syrup, will be applied. Next, the maladies can be grouped—comparing, for instance, all the types of coughs with all the various throat disorders. Or we may wish to make a detailed comparison of the profile shown by throat candy with that shown by throat tablets. We can group respondents by age, or sex, or in some other way, to show whether older people are more inclined toward the "traditional" remedies or whether there is a sex difference in preference for chest rubs, and so on. Quite likely the grid has some items in it that are aimed at particular hypotheses; for instance, will harsher remedies be advocated for a smoker's cough, because it is "your own fault"?

Indices

An index is very similar to an inventory except that it usually consists of just one area. A number of (dichotomous) questions are scored together, on the assumption that they have something in common. For instance, we could make a list of all the usual symptoms of indigestion, stomach ulcers, and so on, and make these into an index of gastric symptoms. Or we could enumerate the usual consumer durables—a car, a refrigerator, a washing machine, a lawn mower—and make these into an index of acquisitiveness, or something like that. We may, likewise, decide to calculate an index of social adjustment by adding together the results of a question about number of friends, a question on relations with the opposite sex, on work relationships, on group leisure activities, and so on. Often, the index is not made up until after the survey has been completed, by drawing together a number of separate questions that probably relate to the same thing.

We are on shaky ground here, because pilot work tends to be skimped, so that the balance of the items is often poor, and in the end we have nothing but a few rather doubtful assumptions to sustain us. We assume that the items are related; we assume that we have made a representative selection of items to be included in the index; we assume that it will measure what we want it to measure and that it will do so reliably. We hope that the name or label that we give it will not be misleading.

About the best that can be said of an index constructed *ad hoc* is that it is probably better than having to rely on a single question. This applies particularly when we have to divide our sample rather crudely into a few major groupings with regard to some important variable. Suppose, for instance, that we wish to study the differences between women who like everything ready-made, who therefore rely on craftsmen and specialists, and women who like to do things for themselves. We might try to construct an index of "do-it-yourself-mindedness" for women, as follows:

> Have you, during the past year, done any of the following?
>
> made a dress
> knitted a garment for an adult
> made some children's clothes
> dyed something at home
> shampooed a carpet
> mended a fuse
> fixed a broken lock
> put a new washer on a faucet
> cooked a new recipe
> done some wallpapering
> done some painting
> hung some new curtains
> made some chair covers
> had a home permanent
> given yourself a facial treatment

Or suppose that we are studying people's attitudes to self-medication and the use of proprietary medicines. How would we distinguish between people with high and low self-medication readiness? An index might help:

> Do you usually have any of the following in the house?
>
> vitamin tablets — painkilling tablets
> stomach remedies — sleeping pills
> laxatives — nose drops
> cough medicine — throat tablets
> pep pills — ointments

In the exploration of some psychoanalytic hypothesis, we might need to pick out those people who get much pleasure through habitual use of the mouth; some kind of "orality" index might be useful here:

Do you like to do any of the following?

bite your nails
suck a cherry pit or a plum pit
suck hard candies
suck a pencil or pen
bite an empty pipe (men only)
prepare and eat some special delicacy
take an alcoholic drink regularly
use chewing gum
drink soft drinks through a straw
gargle when you brush your teeth
hum or whistle to yourself while doing something

If in doubt about the inclusion of a particular item in an index, it is perhaps best to calculate the index without it, then correlate the doubtful item with the index as a whole and include it (which means recalculation of the index) if the correlation is satisfactory.

There is, in principle, no reason why indexes cannot be constructed during the pilot work, with appropriate statistical checks to verify some of the assumptions mentioned above. In that case, they become more useful and can be applied in subsequent studies. But, as we have observed, the idea for an index often does not arise until after the survey has been completed, or else the resources available do not permit the necessary preliminary work. Also, the construction of an *ad hoc* index is sometimes the only way out of a tantalizing research problem, the kind of problem that requires measures or techniques that do not yet exist. It may boil down to a straight choice: either we make up an index without the necessary pilot work, or we drop the problem or the hypothesis. In such a case, ingenuity would seem more justifiable than caution, for an index can always be refined and improved subsequently, once the first attempt has been made.

• *Selected Readings*

PSYCHOLOGICAL MEASUREMENT

1. Harold Gulliksen, *Theory of Mental Tests* (New York: Wiley, 1950).

   A basic textbook on test-construction theory.

2. L. L. Thurstone, *The Measurement of Values* (Chicago: University of Chicago Press, 1959).

   This volume brings together some of Thurstone's early papers; see especially Chapter 7 on paired comparisons.

3. S. S. Stevens, "Mathematics, Measurement, and Psychophysics," in S. S. Stevens, ed., *Handbook of Experimental Psychology* (New York: Wiley, 1951).

   An excellent introduction to different types of measurement in psychology.

RATING

4. J. P. Guilford, *Psychometric Methods* (New York: McGraw-Hill, 1954).

   See especially Chapter 11 on rating scales, and Chapter 7 on paired comparisons.

5. Alford L. Balwin, Joan Kalhorn, and Fay H. Breese, "The Appraisal of Parent Behavior," *Psychological Monographs*, LXIII, No. 299 (1949).

6. Charles E. Osgood, George J. Suci, and Percy H. Tannenbaum, *The Measurement of Meaning* (Urbana: University of Illinois Press, 1957).

   The main source book for the semantic differential technique and its various applications. See especially pp. 85–97.

7. Political & Economic Planning Foundation, *Young Europeans in England* (London: P. E. P., 1962).

8. Hans J. Eysenck, *The Structure of Human Personality* (London: Methuen, 1953).

See especially chapters 2 and 3 on ratings, questionnaires, and inventories.

9. M. G. Kendall, *Rank Correlation Methods* (London: Griffin, 1948).

PERSONALITY INVENTORIES

10. L. J. Cronbach, *Essentials of Psychological Testing* (New York: Harper, 1960).
11. Philip E. Vernon, *Personality Tests and Assessments* (London: Methuen, 1962).
12. Samuel Messick and John Ross, eds., *Measurement in Personality and Cognition* (New York: Wiley, 1962).

    See Part I for the design of questionnaire measures of personality variables.
13. Anne Anastasi, *Psychological Testing* (New York: Macmillan, 1963).

5

Attitude Statements

••

Of all the tasks or purposes of interviews and questionnaires, that of attitude measurement has undergone the greatest amount of technical development. There are a great many ways of assessing people's attitudes, the more sophisticated of which are known as attitude scales. We shall not approach the problem of attitude scaling at once, as some textbooks do. This is because, in the past, much attention has been paid to the technical and statistical problems of scaling and not enough to the psychological problem of what was being scaled. The most advanced scaling techniques and the most error-free procedures will not produce an attitude scale worth having unless there has first been a good deal of careful thought and exploration, and unless the ingredients of the scale (the attitude statements) have been written and rewritten with the necessary care. This chapter is devoted to these preliminary procedures, and the next chapter will deal with the construction of attitude scales.

What Is an Attitude?

Most definitions seem to agree that an attitude is a state of readiness, a tendency to act or react in a certain manner when confronted with certain stimuli. Thus, the individual's attitudes are present but dormant most of the time; they become expressed in speech or other behavior only when the object of the attitude is perceived. A person may have strong attitudes for or against foreign travel but these become aroused and expressed only when some issue connected with travel abroad arises—or when confronted with an attitude questionnaire! Attitudes are reinforced by beliefs (the cognitive component) and often attract strong feelings (the emotional component) that will lead to particular forms of behavior (the action tendency component). For further discussion of the nature of attitudes see Katz & Stotland[2] or Krech and Crutchfield.[1]

Attitudes, like many other components of behavior, are abstractions—though they are real enough to the individual who holds them. While most of us have many attitudes in common, some may have attitudes which few other people have; failure to realize this has led to some wasteful and misleading research. We must always, therefore, make allowance for the possibility that the attitude that we wish to study is simply not present in part of our sample.

There is no limit to the topics about which people may have attitudes, from war and peace, God and eternity, to toy trains, sore throats, or frozen peas. It would be possible to argue persuasively that in the final analysis everything in life depends on people's attitudes; be that as it may, attitudes are so important in fields like politics, marriage, religion, food habits, social change, education, fashion, childrearing, racial prejudice, communication, and many others, that it is not surprising that social psychologists have devoted much time and ingenuity to finding ways of measuring them. We become particularly aware of the strength and pervasiveness of attitudes when we try to change them—through the processes of communication, advertising, education, conversion, propaganda, military drill, alcohol, brainwashing, etc.

Most attitudes are labeled by their object—peacemindedness, religious fervor, anti-Mexican sentiment, authoritarianism—though there are exceptions to this, such as radicalism, strictness, vegetarianism, and others. In our own work and in the critical evaluation of the work of others, we must regard labels with caution, because it is of vital importance to know what the attitude scale is supposed to be about. This is more easily said than done, for it brings us up against the problems of attitude units. It is only too easy to impose a preconceived framework (which may or may not be misguided) on an attitude, but this could result in unintentionally measuring the wrong attitude, or only part of an attitude, or too many attitudes all at once. For instance, in measuring attitudes toward women's suffrage, are we dealing with one unitary field, with a multitude of different fields depending on the various political roles of women, or with merely a subfield of such larger attitude-complexes as radicalism and people's attitudes to women generally? Often, one cannot be sure about this merely from reading the attitude statements, for there are hidden components and underlying factors that may determine answers to such statements in quite unexpected ways. We must also know something about the interrelationships of the different statements, and again, we cannot always infer these with certainty merely by looking for logical consistencies. There is no logical reason why people who are against women's suffrage should also believe in corporal punishment for certain crimes, yet research has shown that these two go together; they are part of a much wider, underlying attitude to many social problems.

Our thinking on the nature of attitudes has been rather primitive. Most of the time we tend to perceive them as straight lines, running from positive, through neutral, to negative feelings about the object or issue in question. Our attempts at measurement then concentrate on trying to place a person's attitude on the straight line or linear continuum, in such a way that he can be described as mildly positive, strongly negative, and so on—preferably in terms of a numerical score or else by means of ranking. There is no proof, however, that this model of a linear continuum is necessarily correct, though it does make things easier for measurement purposes. For all we know, attitudes may be shaped more like concentric circles or overlapping ellipses or three-dimensional cloud formations.

The model of the linear continuum or dimension is not always easy or appropriate. For instance, the positive part and the negative part may or may not be linear extensions of one another. In studying the attitudes of mothers to their children we have found that rejection is not the exact opposite of acceptance (as measured by two separate attitude scales); apparently, a variety of other components enter into the attitude of a rejecting mother that are not present in a loving and accepting mother. Moreover, it is possible for some respondents to be ambivalent and to score highly both on acceptance and on rejection. It would clearly have been a mistake to assess these attitudes by means of a single acceptance–rejection continuum. Again, the degree of differentiation at one end of an attitude continuum may be very different from that at the other end; thus, if we considered how we felt about peace, we would find it easy to deal with the negative end —statements about the benefits of war, courage and the will to fight, and national unity—but at the positive end we would very soon run short; there is not all that much that one can say about love for peace. Does this mean that the units or intervals will be smaller, or more numerous, at one end of the scale than at the other? One is tempted to divide the dimension into units of some kind. Such units, while not strictly "legitimate," may help us to compare groups of people with one another, but they are not comparable from one scale to another.

Attitudes have many attributes. So far, we have talked mainly about their content—what the attitude is about. An attitude, however, also has intensity. It may be held with greater or lesser vehemence. To one person, cruelty to animals may be but of passing interest or concern, whereas to another it may be of great importance and propel him to a leading position in animal protection societies. We might expect the latter to agree or disagree more strongly than the former would to a series of statements dealing with the treatment of animals. This attribute of intensity can be very important in understanding attitudes and in predicting behavior.

It has been found that there is a U-shaped relationship between the attributes of intensity and of content. This means that the more extreme attitudes (either positive or negative) are usually held with much vehemence, whereas the more neutral position may be defended with far less intensity. This finding has, in turn, led to the suggestion that to find the neutral point on a scale one must look for the point of minimum strength or intensity.[4]

Some attitudes are more enduring than others. For instance, a man's political beliefs may be fairly stable throughout his lifetime, whereas his attitudes to automobiles or to gambling may undergo multiple changes. Similarly, some attitudes go much deeper than others and touch upon one's fundamental philosophy of life, while others are relatively superficial. Again, some attitudes seem to be more embracing than others; they lie at the base of more limited or specific attitudes and beliefs, thus predisposing the individual in a certain way toward new attitudes and experiences that may come his way. For ease of understanding, social psychologists make a rough distinction among these different levels, calling the most superficial one beliefs, the next one attitudes, a deeper level, values or basic attitudes, and a still deeper level, personality. These rather vague distinctions among different levels of belief must be thought of as more, versus less, enduring; deeper, versus more superficial; relatively stable versus relatively changeable; and more general versus more specific. Nor is this all. For these levels must not merely be thought of as the different layers of a cake; there are relationships and patterns of connection among these layers[3] rather like what is sometimes called the tree model. (See Figure 5–1.)

This diagram should not be taken too literally. Its chief function is to warn against treating opinions and attitudes too much as isolated units and to illustrate the problems we face in trying to bring about a change in anyone's attitudes. At the most specific level, that of beliefs, change is relatively easy to bring about so long as the underlying attitude is not involved. Thus, it may not be too difficult to convince a man with strong anti-Mexican views that he is wrong in his belief that Mexicans have a high crime rate; but his underlying anti-Mexican attitude remains unaltered, and he will soon find some other belief with which to bolster his hostile attitude.

No doubt it is possible to find examples of opinions which are more or less isolated and "free-floating" within the individual and are seemingly unconnected to any other aspect or level of the person. However, the following example illustrates a much more common case. Suppose we are having dinner with a friend in a restaurant and suggest to him that he might like pork chops, which are on the menu. Our friend declines. At this point, we

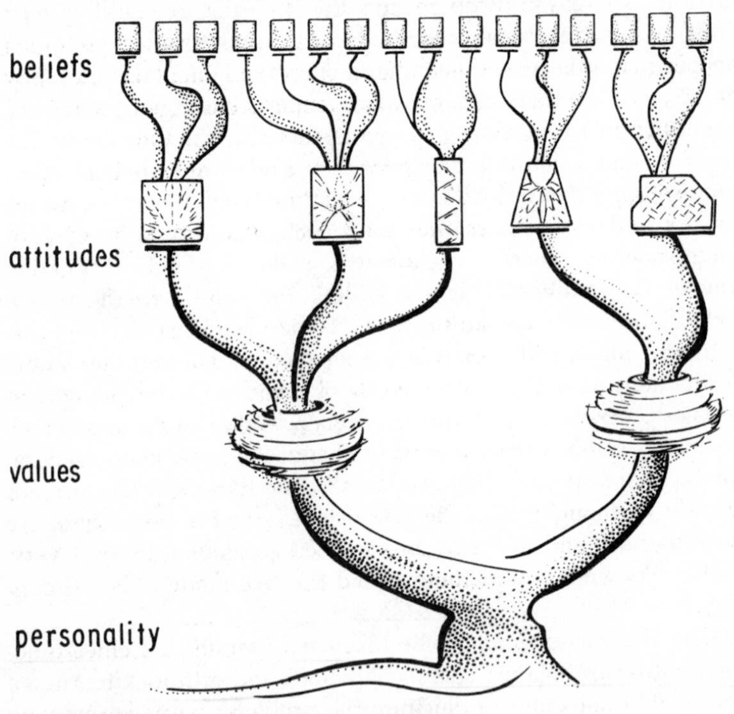

Figure 5–1.

might say to ourselves that we are dealing with a belief, with a relatively superficial and not immutable food preference of the moment. However, suppose we started questioning our friend. We might find that he is a vegetarian, a Jew, or a Muslim, and that his refusal to eat pork chops has to do with a more general and deeper underlying attitude to pigs and other animals as food. This in turn may be linked to an underlying value system that has to do with the role of man vis-à-vis his fellow creatures, with religious proscriptions concerning "clean" and "unclean" animals, or possibly with other taboos. An apparently simple matter of food preference may in fact be a key to the individual's fundamental philosophy of life.

So far, we have talked about relationships in depth. However, attitudes are also related to one another "across," at the same level. Some of the most interesting research contributions in social psychology have concerned themselves with such interrelationships. We find, for instance, that racial prejudice against one minority group is usually associated with prejudice against several other groups and with chauvinistic glorification of one's own group. The word "ethnocentrism" has been coined[5] to reflect such an underlying predisposition, which in turn is part of a personality syndrome known as authoritarianism and which contains many other attitudes besides ethnocentrism. We are dealing here with the difficult problem of isolating one attitude from a considerable number of others to which it is linked and correlated and which, in their turn, may also be part of underlying value systems and personality syndromes. It is difficult to know where to draw the line. On the one hand, exploratory work suggests all kinds of interesting links and patterns with neighboring and underlying fields, but on the other hand, we need, for measuring purposes, a scale covering some relatively well-demarcated area.

Interrelations such as these follow no logic except the "psycho-logic," the logic of feelings and emotions. It is most important to realize that attitudes are only very rarely the product of a balanced conclusion after a careful assembly of evidence; as a rule, attitudes are acquired or modified by absorbing, or reacting to, the attitudes of other people. We like to maintain the fiction of rationality and impartiality in reaching our conclusions, but, in fact, attitudinal predispositions play a very considerable part. One must remember always that attitudes are highly emotional, both in the sense of irrational or illogical and in the sense of arousing powerful needs and ego defenses. When we ask a highland Peruvian to boil his drinking-water[6] so as to kill the germs of disease, we are, in his eyes, also asking him to adopt the white man's magic, to betray his ancestors, and to make a fool and a renegade of himself in his village. To us this may not seem very reasonable at first, but this is where research can help—by showing the underlying attitude links, with their strong emotional connections.[7]

Measurement Problems

From the point of view of measurement, there are a number of lessons to be drawn from the foregoing discussion. Perhaps the most important one is, as we have stressed before, that there is no substitute for careful pilot work. In the early stages, after having covered the literature on the subject, the pilot work will consist of free interviews, also called depth-interviews, the essential purpose of which is two-fold: (1) to explore the origins, complexities, and ramifications of the attitude areas in question, in order to decide more precisely what it is we wish to measure; (2) to get vivid expressions of such attitudes from the respondent, in a form that might make them suitable for use as statements in an attitude scale. (For this reason, if for no other, such interviews should always be recorded on tape.)

Suppose we are asked to construct a scale to measure people's attitudes toward vitamins. We may well find, in pilot interviews, that almost everyone is favorably disposed toward them, so that a pro–con scale concerning vitamins would show little differentiation. This often happens: the pilot work causes a change in the aim of the scale, and possibly in the aim of the investigation. Next, we propose to build a scale dealing with "vitamin-consciousness" or "vitamin-salience," that is to say, dealing with the extent to which considerations of vitamin content enter into people's minds when they shop, cook, medicate, and so on. At first, it would seem that this is directly related to people's knowledge about vitamins; and we shall find it comparatively easy to differentiate between the more knowledgable and the less knowledgeable on the basis of a few well-chosen factual questions. Further exploration may show, however, that many people with little correct knowledge about vitamins nevertheless are very interested in them and are influenced by advertising claims concerning vitamin content. We begin to find various links; health-consciousness is one, of which vitamin-consciousness may be a part, though a rather unruly one. Child care may be another link, associated especially with women and with small babies. Modernity may be a further link, covering various other wishes to be modern and advanced. A general tendency toward self-medication, toward taking pills and tablets of all kinds, may represent yet another connection. Striving for independence may form a link with vitamin-consciousness, in that members of the present generation want to emancipate themselves from the ways of the older generation. And one could go on. This is a part of social psychology where clinical acumen, intuition, and a capacity for "listening with the third ear" are invaluable and where chair-bound, preconceived frameworks may constitute a positive hindrance.

We must next decide, after doing perhaps thirty or forty preliminary interviews, what it is we wish to measure, and we will then be in a position to draw up a rough sketch of the attitude clusters in question, with their likely linkages and possible undercurrents. We should also have some idea of the function that our scale is to play within the context of the research as a whole. This may tell us how general or specific and how deep or superficial our scale should be, and what sub-areas it should include or leave out. As a rule, the more aspects of a particular attitude one can include, the more one is likely to get scores that will mean something in terms of that underlying attitude, rather than in terms of one or two particular aspects of it. But let us remember that the same attitude may express itself in different ways in different people, while some people may have no such attitude at all.

Writing Attitude Statements

Having decided on the general pattern which our attitude scale should have, we now must compose the item pool, the collection of attitude statements from which the scale will be built. Perhaps the best guide to the writing of attitude statements is to say that they should be meaningful and interesting, even exciting, to the respondents. There are many attitude scales which falter because the items have been composed in the office according to some theoretical plan and fail to arouse much interest in the respondents.

How can we tell whether or not we are producing useful attitude statements? We are on the wrong path when many of our respondents start to quibble or want to change the items or add to them; when there are many "Uncertain" or "Don't know" responses; when items are skipped or crossed out; when respondents do not seem interested in discussing the scale or, if they want to discuss it, do so chiefly in order to explain how it fails to cater to their own attitudes. We are on the right path when respondents seem to recognize the statements ("I'll bet you got that from my brother-in-law; he's always saying things like that"); when they make free use of the "strongly agree" or "strongly disagree" response categories; when they seem excited or angered by some of the statements that they disagree with, or show signs of satisfaction that their own views are well represented; when they seem eager to provide us with more examples or more information along the lines of certain statements; and, of course, when there are few signs that they reject the items by making amendments or deletions, skipping, giving "Don't know" responses, and so on.

Remembering that attitudes are emotional, we should try to avoid the stilted, rational approach in writing attitude statements and select from the tapes the more contentiously worded statements of opinion; we must not be afraid to use phrases relating to feelings and emotions, hopes and wishes, hates, fears, and happiness.

In dealing with the attitudes of hospital patients to nurses, for example, we might start out with: "Nurses are too busy to pay attention to the needs of individual patients." Respondents might quibble over this statement or wish to alter it. We might get better results by writing: "Somehow I often feel unwanted here."

In making up items dealing with readers' attitudes to a library, a first attempt might read: "The catalogue system is too difficult for most readers to master." This is, perhaps, too "rational" and may reflect too little personal feeling; an improved version might be: "I can never find the books I want."

In approaching emotionally loaded or taboo issues, respondents who cannot freely discuss such matters will yet respond to an attitude statement if the phrasing is direct and uses colloquialisms that they might use themselves. For instance: "A mother should try to get her baby to use the potty from birth."

It goes without saying that attitude statements should avoid double negatives and should be short and uncomplicated rather than long and garlanded with subordinate clauses. A poor example might be: "No-one but a fool would deny that, in the history of Great Britain, those members of the aristocracy who have been called to high office have, with few exceptions, acquitted themselves with greater distinction than the commoners with whom they shared a government." Edwards,[8] among others, has offered some criteria for editing attitude statements.

As a rule, the beginner is also advised to avoid double-barreled statements, such as: "The Foreign Secretary is a good speaker, but no leader of men." Difficulties arise for the respondent who agrees with one part of the statement but not with the other. Also, in the interpretation of results, it will not be clear what a disagreement-score means—disagreement with the first part, with the second part, or with both? In fairness, however, it should be added that once in a while an occasion may arise where the desire to have an agreement-score to a combination of two or more points may outweigh other considerations.

Proverbs and well-known sayings are also best avoided. Not everyone understands what they mean, and they tend to produce unthinking acquiescence. Attitude statements are better when they have a certain freshness forcing the respondent to think and take a stand.

Paradoxically, however, it does not always pay to make the statements too clear and unambiguous, or to ask the respondent to think very hard. Often, a statement that is, strictly speaking, almost meaningless, works very well because pilot work has shown that respondents cloak it, in their own way, with the meaning that our context requires. For example, the statement "If you're not firm, children will try to get away with anything" is far from exact or unambiguous; yet it works very well with parents and correlates acceptably with other indicators of strictness. Another illustration might be: "Africans can't be expected to behave any better toward the rest of the world than the rest of the world behaves toward them."

As to careful thought, of course we want respondents to be attentive, but we want them to think and express themselves as they do habitually; we don't want them to think out a new philosophy of life on the spot or to start ruminative doubts with every item. This is one more reason for clothing the attitude statements in language that will be familiar to them.

We may not always want the purpose of our inquiry to be obvious. There are many ways of accomplishing this, one of which is to avoid statements that are too direct, in favor of more indirect or oblique statements. An example may make this clearer. Suppose, once again, that we are trying to measure the feelings of readers toward a library. A very direct statement might be: "I hate going to the library," whereas a more indirect statement would be: "I often wish the library did not have so many silly rules and regulations." Research has shown that the two statements correlate well with one another; they express the same underlying dislike for the library but in the second case a little more subtly, so that a respondent can agree with it without fully realizing what he is saying. Or again, instead of: "I don't always trust the doctors in this hospital," try: "I wish my own doctor could look after me here." Of course, one cannot tell in advance whether a more oblique approach will work; only careful item-analysis and correlation studies can show when and where it is justified.

All this illustrates that the writing of successful attitude statements demands careful pilot work, experience, intuition, and a certain amount of flair. Later on, the scaling procedures will separate the wheat from the chaff.

One way of looking at the composition of an item pool is to regard it as a sampling process. Out of the total number of sub-areas within the attitude cluster we wish to measure, only a limited number can be represented in our scale; and within each sub-area the actual statements we compose will represent but a fraction of the almost unlimited number of hypothetical statements that might have been written. Since we do not yet know which sub-areas will have the most powerful correlations with the remainder of the attitude cluster and which others are more peripheral, it would be wise to include items dealing with most of them. In other words, without being too rigid about it, we must try to keep the item pool reasonably balanced. We will want to have roughly equal numbers of items dealing with each main aspect of the attitude; we will want items covering the attitude from one extreme to the other, but we won't want too many extremes; and we need roughly equal proportions of positive and negative items. As we will see, this balancing of the item pool is particularly important in the case of the Likert scaling procedure (see Chapter 6). If we wish to include some long shots—items which, though seemingly unrelated, may correlate well as indirect measures—we must be particularly careful that they do not upset or unbalance the rest of the pool. Finally, before we use them, the items have to be scrambled, by putting them more or less in random order; we might also put a few innocuous items at the beginning, to get the respondents used to the answering procedure.

Response Sets

A few words should be added here concerning different response sets, the tendency to reply to attitude-scale items in a particular way, almost independent of content. One such set has been identified[9] as "social desirability"; this is the tendency to reply "Agree" to items that the respondent believes reflect socially desirable attitudes, so as to show himself in a better light. Another response set has been described[12, 13] as "acquiescence," a general tendency toward assent rather than dissent, especially when the statements are in the form of plausible generalities. Some aspects of rigidity, dogmatism, and authoritarianism may also lead to certain response tendencies. The incorporation of both positively and negatively worded items dealing with the same issue does not really overcome these problems, since response sets are largely independent of content; but such self-contradictory responses (to reversed scales as well as to reversed items) constitute one indication of the presence of such response sets and a way of measuring them. More research is needed in response styles, since they affect some scales and some kinds of respondents more than others, and there seems to be no easy way either of detecting their influence or of neutralizing it.

• *Selected Readings*

ATTITUDE THEORY

1. David Krech, Richard S. Crutchfield, and Egerton L. Ballachey, *Individual in Society* (New York: McGraw-Hill, 1962).

   See Chapter 5, "The Nature and Measurement of Attitudes," for the characteristics of attitudes and attitude systems, an exposition of scaling methods and types of survey questions.

2. D. Katz and E. Stotland, "A Preliminary Statement to a Theory of Attitude Structure and Change," in S. Koch, ed., *Psychology: A Study of a Science,* Vol. 3: *Formulations of the Person and the Social Context* (New York: McGraw-Hill, 1959).

   A wide-ranging essay on attitude theory.

3. Hans J. Eysenck, *The Psychology of Politics* (London: Routledge & Kegan Paul, 1954).

   See especially Chapter 4 on the organization of social attitudes.

4. Edward A. Suchman, "The Intensity Component in Attitude and Opinion Research," in Samuel A. Stouffer, ed., *Measurement and Prediction* (Princeton, N.J.: Princeton University Press, 1950).

5. T. W. Adorno, Else Frenkel-Brunswik, D. J. Levinson, and R. N. Sanford, *The Authoritarian Personality* (New York: Harper, 1950).

   A classic study of prejudice, showing the relationships between different kinds of prejudice and the development of the concepts of ethnocentrism and authoritarianism.

6. E. Wellin, "Water Boiling in a Peruvian Town," in B. D. Paul, ed., *Health, Culture and Community* (New York: Russell Sage Foundation, 1955).

7. Bernard M. Kramer, "Dimensions of Prejudice," *Journal of Psychology,* XXVII (1949), 389–451.

WRITING ATTITUDE STATEMENTS

8. Allen L. Edwards, *Techniques of Attitude Scale Construction* (New York: Appleton-Century-Crofts, 1957).

   See in particular p. 13 showing how to edit attitude statements.

RESPONSE SETS

9. A. L. Edwards, *The Social Desirability Variable in Personality Assessment and Research* (New York: The Dryden Press, 1957).

10. Lee J. Cronbach, "Response Set and Test Validity," *Educational and Psychological Measurement,* VI (1946), 475–494.

11. Samuel Messick and John Ross, eds., *Measurement in Personality and Cognition* (New York: Wiley, 1962).

    See Part I for the design of questionnaire measures of personality variables and Part II for various response sets.

12. Hans J. Eysenck, "Response Set, Authoritarianism, and Personality Questionnaires," *British Journal of Social and Clinical Psychology,* I (1962), 20–24.

13. John Martin, "Acquiescence—Measurement and Theory," *British Journal of Social and Clinical Psychology,* III (1964), 216–225.

    An attempt to discriminate between sets for acquiescence and for social desirability and a suggested response-style theory.

14. J. B. Knowles, "Acquiescence Response Set and the Questionnaire Measurement of Personality," *British Journal of Social and Clinical Psychology,* II (1963), 131–137.

    Argues against the use of "balanced" scales to counteract acquiescent tendencies.

6

Attitude-Scaling Methods

Attitude scales consist of from half-a-dozen to two dozen or more attitude statements, with which the respondent is asked to agree or disagree. Since so much depends on the way the issue is put into words, a single item or a single question is often unreliable and, because it usually approaches an attitude from one particular direction only, may give rather one-sided results. Thus, agreement with the statement "Divorce should be made easier" can hardly, by itself, be a reliable index of a broader attitude, such as the respondent's radicalism, since his agreement may, in any case, be due to personal circumstances; but by having many items we can reduce the effects of one-sided responses. However, more important than the number of attitude statements used is the fact that they have been scaled: they have been selected and put together from a much larger number of attitude statements according to certain statistical procedures. Because of this, we must not judge the relatively small number of attitude statements in a finished scale at their face value; they are the outcome of a process of complicated sifting and, in addition, represent all the preliminary work and thought described in Chapter 5.

Public-opinion polls frequently use a single question to obtain a rough guide to people's attitudes. While this is commonly excused on the grounds of expediency, such questions are the outcome of much trial and error, and, since they are used repeatedly in various surveys, a good deal is known about their correlates.

Attitude scales are relatively crude measuring instruments, and we must not expect too much from them. Their chief function is to divide people roughly into a number of broad groups, with regard to a particular attitude. Such scales cannot, by themselves, be expected to provide us with subtle insights in an individual case. They are techniques for placing people on a continuum in relation to one another, in relative and not in absolute terms.

Principles of Measurement

Let us examine, for a moment, what is involved in the construction and evaluation of any measurement tool. We shall take as our example an ordinary ruler.

1. Unidimensionability or homogeneity. This means that the scale should be about one thing at a time, as purely as possible. Thus, the ruler should measure length, not temperature or viscosity. In the case of attitude scales, problems arise because the manifest contents of the items may be a poor guide to what the items actually measure. We need correlation techniques to find out how the items "hang together" and which of them are "purest."

2. Linearity and equal intervals or equal-appearing intervals. This means that the scale should follow the straight-line model and that some sort of scoring system should be devised, preferably one based on interchangeable units. Such units are convenient to handle statistically, though they may be psychologically dubious. With a ruler, it is relatively easy to make sure that it is straight rather than bent and that it is marked off in equal units of inches or centimeters. Attitude scales assume the straight-line model (though this may not be adequate), but the creation of scoring units is difficult, and they are, at best, of doubtful interchangeability. An inch is an inch, whether it lies at one end of a ruler or at the other, but numerically similar attitude-scale differences may represent very different psychological distinctions. Also, how can we ensure comparability of units from one

attitude to another? For both these reasons, ranking is often preferable when constant scale units are hard to come by.

3. Reliability. This is the indispensable attribute of consistency. If the same measure were applied to the same object today and next week, the results should be near-identical (unless a real change in the object has meanwhile taken place). A ruler can be applied, say, to the leg of a table and the results, for all practical purposes, will be quite consistent over time. The greater length and diversity of attitude scales make them more reliable than single questions, but even so, complete consistency is difficult to achieve; people are bound to react somewhat differently to a scale when they are confronted by it a second time. Nevertheless, reliability coefficients of .80 or higher are quite common. (For a more detailed discussion see Cronbach[10].)

4. Validity. This tells us whether the scale measures what it is supposed to measure. We may have obtained unidimensionality by keeping only those items which intercorrelate highly, yet the scale may not measure what we want it to measure. Instead of measuring authoritarianism, for instance, it may just be a measure of acquiescence. Sometimes, it is possible to correlate the new scale with an older, well-established one. At other times, it may be possible to use criterion groups, such as membership in religious congregations or political parties, between which the scale should be able to distinguish; but behavior is often not a simple manifestation of an underlying attitude, and so there are dangers and pitfalls in this approach. At present, there is no way of making sure that an attitude scale is valid. (See Chapter 3 and the final section in this chapter.)

5. Reproducibility. When we say that a man weighs 150 pounds, we mean that the pointer on the scales will move from 0 to 150, but will cover none of the remainder; in other words, the figure of 150 refers, not to just any odd 150 pound units, but to the first 150 pounds on the scale. From the "score" of 150, we can reproduce exactly which units on the scale were covered and which were not. This is not an essential requirement when we are dealing with constant and interchangeable units, such as pounds or inches; but if we were dealing, say, with the symptoms of the different stages of an illness, it would be helpful if they

could be ordered or scaled in terms of their degree of seriousness in such a way that the presence of symptom D would mean that the patient also must have symptoms A, B, and C. Similarly, a score on an attitude scale might show us, by means of a single figure, which statements the respondent agreed with and which he disagreed with, thus telling us his place on the attitude continuum. This is a requirement that in practice is difficult to achieve, for many attitude pools are not amenable to this kind of cumulative or progressive scaling—partly because they may not be unidimensional.

Apart from these main requirements, there may be others. For instance, it is helpful to have norms or standards derived from the scores of large numbers of respondents, so that we can compare an individual's score with those of others and interpret its meaning.

In the sections that follow we will discuss the four best-known methods of attitude scaling. One might well ask why we need more than one method. This has come about because, over the past three decades, different research workers have developed methods of scale-building in which they have laid particular stress on one or another of the above requirements and have paid less attention to the others. One method has concentrated on unidimensionality, another on finding equivalent scale units, a third on obtaining reproducibility, and so on. There does not seem to be a method that combines the advantages of all of them, and it is therefore very important that we understand their respective aims and the differences between them.

It follows that, for the present, it is impossible to say which method is best. Each has important desirable features, but each of them is also open to criticism. For our own inquiry, the best method is the one which is most appropriate to our particular problem. If we wish to study attitude-patterning or explore theories of attitudes, then probably the Likert procedure will be the most relevant. If we wish to study attitude change, or the hierarchical structure of an attitude, then Guttman's method might be preferable. If we are studying group differences, then we'll probably elect to use the Thurstone procedures, and so on. Each type of scale does one thing rather well, and, if this is what our research needs, then this is the type of scale we will want to use.

Social-Distance Scales

In 1925, Bogardus[11] brought out a social-distance scale, subsequently revised,[12] that has been widely used and illustrates some of the problems in scale construction. (See Table 6–1.)

Table 6–1.

Directions: According to my first feeling-reactions, I would willingly admit members of each race (as a class, and not the best I have known, nor the worst members), to one or more of the classifications which I have circled.

	To close kinship by marriage	To my club as personal chums	To my street as neighbors	To employment in my occupation	To citizenship in my country	As visitors only to my country	Would exclude from my country
Canadians	1	2	3	4	5	6	7
Chinese	1	2	3	4	5	6	7
English	1	2	3	4	5	6	7
French	1	2	3	4	5	6	7
Germans	1	2	3	4	5	6	7
Hindus	1	2	3	4	5	6	7
etc.							

Apart from the rather complicated instructions, at first sight there seems little to criticize in this scale. The idea of expressing ethnic prejudice as "social distance" seems reasonable, and by analogy we may think of a straight road with the seven classifications as milestones along it. Early large-scale investigations did show a fairly regular progression in the proportions of Americans endorsing each position. Usually, there is a "hump" somewhere in the middle—suggesting neither extreme hostility nor complete acceptance, depending on the race or nationality in question.

How well does this scale satisfy the five desiderata outlined above? Concerning unidimensionality, we have little evidence. It is quite possible that, underlying these various categories, there is a single, pure attitude, but then again, such categories as "marriage," "neighbors," "exclude," and others may bring in many extraneous influences. Criticism has been directed against the scale's questionable linearity and its unequal intervals. For some respondents, admission to occupational membership signifies a greater degree of closeness than "to my street as neighbors," and so on. This would require a different (or perhaps nonlinear) ordering of the steps—though in large samples this might only apply to a minority. As for equality of intervals, there is no evidence that the social distance between, say, 2 and 3 is in any way equivalent to the distance between 5 and 6, and so on. The scoring is thus completely arbitrary. Reliability of the scale has reached beyond .90 and must be regarded as satisfactory. There is, at least, some positive evidence of the validity of the scale in comparison with other types of scale. Until lately, the question of reproducibility had not been raised, but a more recent inquiry[13] indicated that this can be surprisingly good.

If we disregard the scoring and consider the results merely as a way of ordering individuals or groups with regard to their ethnic attitudes, then useful comparisons can be made, but a good deal of caution is required in the interpretation of such results. Bogardus himself has, in later years, brought out an improved version of his scale, and the whole concept of social-distance measurement has been further examined by Kirsch.[14]

Thurstone Scales

Thurstone's[15] chief preoccupation was with the problem of equal or, rather, equal-appearing intervals. Part of his reasoning stemmed from experiments in psychophysics, where various methods have been developed to scale the judgments of individuals with regard to various physical properties, such as weight. The smaller the (true) difference in weight between two objects, the fewer people will be able to distinguish correctly between them. (See Guilford[9] for an exposition of various psychophysical methods.) In much the same way, Thurstone attempted to devise attitude scales by getting people to compare attitude statements two at a time and judging which of each pair was the more positive (or the more negative).

This method, known as the paired-comparisons technique, becomes very cumbersome when more than fifteen or twenty items are involved, as is frequently the case. (See ranking, Chapter 4.) A somewhat less precise, but also less laborious method, was therefore proposed by Thurstone, known as the method of equal-appearing intervals.

The first step in this and every other scaling procedure is to design and collect a pool of items (see Chapter 5) from the literature and from pilot interviews. After that, we need a group of "judges." While in the past university students have often been used as judges, it is preferable to have the judgments made by people who are similar to those to whom the finished scale will be applied. To give some rough idea of numbers: one might have 100–150 statements and 40–60 judges, though as many as 300 judges have been used.

Next, the items are reproduced on cards or slips of paper, and each judge is given one complete set of items in random order. The judges are told what the scale is "about," and a hypothetical scale is set up, running from "most favorable" through a neutral point to "least favorable." This is divided into a fixed number of sections, usually eleven, and it will be the task of the judges to consider each item and to place it in one of these eleven sections or piles. In pile No. 1 should go only the extremely favorable items, in pile No. 2 the slightly less favorable ones, and so on through pile No. 6, which should contain only neutral items. Slightly unfavorable items go into pile No. 7, and so forth; the extremely unfavorable items will go into pile No. 11. The intervals between the categories should be regarded as subjectively equal. It is most important that the judge ignore his own agreement or disagreement with the item; his job is merely to place the item in a particular category according to its meaning. Irrelevant, ambiguous, or poorly worded items will have been eliminated beforehand. At the end of the judging process, each judge will record on each statement the number of the pile in which he has placed it.

Next, we assemble all the judgments for each statement. If we consider a hypothetical statement No. 95, we will no doubt find that most judges have placed it in, say, category 8, while some have placed it in 7 or 9, and a few in 6, 10, or 11. We are now going to consider the distribution of judgments for each item in order to select, from our total pool of items, those two dozen or so that will form a scale.

First of all, we consider the spread of judgments. Obviously, the wider the spread, the more ambiguous the item is. Ambiguous items will cause unreliability and have no place in our scale; we therefore wish to eliminate them. Almost any measure of spread (range, variance, standard deviation, semi-interquartile range) will do, but the last is probably the simplest and quickest, and at the same time it allows us to read off the median.

We need the medians in order to examine item position or scale value. After eliminating the items with excessive spread, we will probably still have a considerable number of statements left, and their medians or scale values will be unevenly distributed along the hypothetical continuum of our scale, so that we may get medians reading 1.7, 1.8, 2.2, 2.2, 2.9, 3.0, 3.1, 3.1, 3.2, 3.2, 3.4, 3.5, and so on. (Medians are used because in psychophysics a "just noticeable difference" between two stimuli has traditionally been defined as one that could be distinguished by 50 per cent of the respondents. Thus, for example, if the median calculated for one statement is 4.0 and for another 3.0, then the two statements may be said to lie one just noticeable difference apart on a psychological continuum.) We have to decide how long our scale is going to be and how many items we need to select. Twenty or twenty-two items would be common practice, but longer and also much shorter scales exist; or we may decide to build two parallel forms of the scale, if the available items permit this.

The detailed steps of the Thurstone scaling procedure are as follows:

SAMPLE INSTRUCTIONS TO JUDGES

1. On the enclosed paper slips you will find a set of statements concerning ______. The statements are in no particular order, but they range from extremely favorable to extremely unfavorable. Before starting the judgment process, read through all the items carefully.

2. Note that there is only one item on each slip, that the item number is on the left, and that the space for recording your judgment is on the right.

3. Sort out the items into eleven piles. In pile No. 1, you should put those items that, in your opinion, would reflect the most favorable attitude to ______. In pile No. 2 will be those items that you would regard as slightly less favorable to ______. Thus each successive group of statements should be slightly less favorable than the preceding one, until you reach pile No. 6, which should contain those statements that show a neutral attitude. In pile No. 7 would go those items which you regard as slightly unfavorable, and so on until you reach pile No. 11, which should contain only the most rejecting and hostile items in the pool. Your own agreement or disagreement with these items must be disregarded.

4. Write on each item slip, in the space provided, the number of the pile in which you put it.

5. Feel free to use any of the eleven points on the scale, but do not attempt to get the same number of slips in each pile.

6. After recording your judgments, put all the slips together into an envelope.

INSTRUCTIONS FOR CALCULATION OF MEDIANS AND Q'S

1. The median and the semi-interquartile range will not be calculated but will be "read off" from a cumulative-frequency graph.

2. Sort all the items returned by the judges according to their item numbers. Take a group of item slips all bearing the same number on the left-hand side. Eliminate items that do not belong.

3. Sort the item slips into piles, according to the written judgments recorded on the right-hand side. You will find most often that you will need from four to six piles, sometimes more, but never more than eleven piles.

4. Draw up a frequency distribution by writing down the pile numbers from 1 to 11 and recording the number of slips in each pile. If there are no slips for some pile numbers (categories), record a zero.

5. Add up the total number of frequencies, the total number of slips you have for this item. Convert the frequencies into percentages of this total.

6. The distribution may now be made cumulative, by adding the percentages successively to one another. When the last percentage has been added, the cumulative percentage frequency should read 100. Table 6–2 may clarify this process.

Table 6–2.

Pile No.	Frequency	Percentage	Cumulative percentages
1	0	—	—
2	0	—	—
3	0	—	—
4	0	—	—
5	0	—	—
6	2	4%	4%
7	2	4%	8%
8	10	20%	28%
9	11	22%	50%
10	15	30%	80%
11	10	20%	100%
	50	100%	

7. Draw up a cumulative graph for the cumulative percentage frequencies. The eleven categories are placed along the bottom line, while the percentages are indicated along the side. Find the approximate point directly above each category *value* that

corresponds to the correct cumulative percentage for that category. Draw lines to connect these percentage points. This will give a steeply rising curve of cumulative-percentage frequencies.

8. Lines should be drawn across the page for the median (50 per cent of the total frequencies) and the two quartiles (25 per cent and 75 per cent respectively). Their corresponding scale values may be read off by noting the points at which these lines cross the cumulative-percentage curve and dropping perpendiculars to the base-line at those three points. (See Figure 6–1.)

9. Record the median, from the value of the central perpendicular. Calculate Q = the semi-interquartile range as follows: record the scale value of the third perpendicular; subtract from it the value of the first perpendicular; halve this difference to obtain Q.

10. For the example in Table 6–2, the following values have been found:

$$\text{median} = 9.0$$
$$Q = \tfrac{1}{2}(9.8 - 7.8) = 1.0$$

The actual selection of the items will be in terms of the intervals between them. This might be one whole scale point, or half a point, or any other distance. If we decide, for instance, that we want about twenty items, then we may want to choose those items whose medians are nearest to scale points 1.5, 2.0, 2.5, 3.0, 3.5, 4.0, and so on. In this way we build up a scale with equal-appearing intervals. In exceptional cases, we may wish for finer discrimination on a particular part of the scale than on the remainder, and we may choose items which lie closer together on that section.

Our scale is now ready for administration. The statements will be printed in random order, without their scale values. Respondents will only be asked either to agree or to disagree with each statement. Subsequently, we look up the scale value of each agreed statement, and the median of these constitutes the respondent's score. If all goes according to plan, our respondent should only agree with a very few statements. If, let us say, he

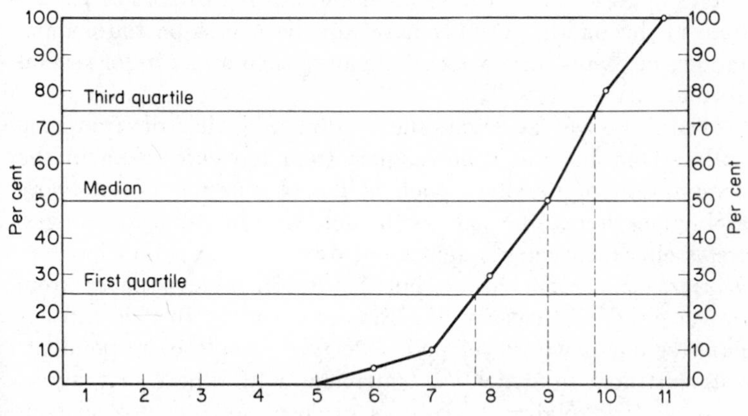

Figure 6–1. Cumulative-frequency graph for item no. ——
median =
Q = ½ (third quartile minus first quartile) =

is mildly positive in his attitude, then he should disagree with items that are strongly positive, neutral, or negative. In fact, ideally, he should agree only with the one or two items that best reflect his particular attitude.

Although, as we have seen, Thurstone's procedure is primarily concerned with locating items at points on a hypothetical scale, we must be careful when treating these scale values as actual numbers, as units that are additive and interchangeable on a linear continuum. We are dealing not with equal, but with equal-*appearing* intervals, with psychological rather than numerical units, which may or may not be equal. Moreover, the division of the continuum into eleven units is arbitrary, so that we should not think of a score of eight as numerically twice as high as a score of four, and so on. In any case, in scale construction one often feels that one would like more units on one side of the neutral point than on the other; some attitudes seem more differentiated at one end of the scale, or go further or deeper, and judges often make finer discriminations at the extremes of a scale than in the middle. Doubts have also been cast on the comparability of scores from one scale to another in a battery of several attitude scales.

What can we say about the unidimensionality of Thurstone scales? Our first guide here, apart from the care taken in the composition of the item pool, is the elimination of the more ambiguous items, the ones with high semi-interquartile ranges. Items on which general agreement exists among judges have an *a priori* claim for inclusion, but this is still quite removed from proven unidimensionality. We can, however, go further and administer our newly developed scale to a sample of respondents with instructions to tick the statements with which they agree. Next, we can analyze the results to check on the internal consistency of the items. If respondents who agree with one particular statement also check other statements with widely differing scale values, the statement has to be rejected since it obviously contains large elements that are irrelevant to the attitude that the scale should measure; if only statements with roughly similar scale values have been checked, the statement can be retained. (See also discussion of factorial scales later in this chapter.)

The reliability of Thurstone scales tends to be adequate, and they have the additional advantage that often a parallel form emerges from the item analysis; this is particularly useful when studying attitude *change.* Reproducibility (in the technical sense) would, presumably, be good in the ideal case where a respondent endorses only a single item, but since this happens very rarely the scales may be criticized on this account. The validity of these scales has occasionally been demonstrated with the aid of criterion groups whose attitudes were allegedly known (because of their membership in certain organizations, their comments in an interview, or their responses to essay-type questions), but since these other measures may be less reliable than the scale that is being validated or may refer to different attitude facets, doubts do remain.

One may well wonder whether different groups of judges produce the same scale values. For instance, would Negro judges produce the same scale values as white judges on a scale of color prejudice? By and large, experimental investigations[16] have shown that the scale values obtained from such widely differing groups of judges correlate highly with one another so long as judges with extreme views are excluded. Judges with strong pro- or anti-feelings concerning the particular attitude in question tend to bunch the items toward the opposite end of the scale; thus, judges with strong pro-Negro attitudes tend to displace items toward the anti-Negro end of the scale and to place few items in the middle (neutral) categories. In practice, judges who place more than one-third of the items in the same category should be excluded; inevitably, all judges will be influenced by their own attitudes, but in most cases the effect will be small and will barely affect the order of the items.

By and large, it remains advisable to use as judges people similar to the respondents in our research sample; the practice of using university students as judges should be deprecated (unless, of course, the scale is to be applied to a student sample). Caution is also required when scales are applied cross-culturally and when some of the older scales are reapplied today—issues, words, and stereotypes sometimes undergo subtle changes.

Likert Scales

The construction of a Thurstone scale always means a lot of work, and it is often difficult to obtain an adequate group of judges. The Likert procedure[16] may have its disadvantages, but it is certainly less laborious, and this—together with the discovery that Likert scales correlate well with Thurstone scales[18]—has helped to make it more popular.

Likert's primary concern was with unidimensionality—making sure that all the items would measure the same thing. He also wanted to eliminate the need for judges by getting subjects in a trial sample to *place themselves* on an attitude continuum for each statement—running from "strongly agree" to "agree," "uncertain," "disagree," and "strongly disagree." These five positions were given simple weights of 5, 4, 3, 2, and 1 for scoring purposes (or sometimes 4–0), after more complex scoring methods had been shown to possess no advantage.

To produce a Likert scale we proceed as follows: First, as usual, we compose an item pool. However, for the Likert procedure it is best not to have many neutral items nor many extreme items at either end of the continuum. Next, we need a sample of respondents on whom to try the items—the entire pool of items together. Probably 100 respondents would suffice for most purposes, but numbers of the order of 250 or 300 are not unusual. Each respondent will be asked, not merely whether he agrees or disagrees with each statement, but to check one of the five positions given above. Respondents should be similar to those on whom the scale will be used.

Next, we score the record of each respondent. To do this, we must decide whether we want a high scale score to mean a favorable or an unfavorable attitude. It does not matter what we decide, but from then on we must be consistent. If we decide that a high score on the scale will mean a favorable attitude, then favorable statements must be scored 5 for "strongly agree," down to 1 for "strongly disagree"—and unfavorable statements must be scored 1 for "strongly agree," up to 5 for "strongly disagree." If we decide that a high score will mean an *un*favorable attitude, then the opposite system of scoring will apply. It helps, therefore, if we have few neutral items, so that we can readily tell from the wording of the statement whether it is positive or negative. But if we feel uncertain about some statements, we can score them arbitrarily from 1–5 or from 5–1; the correlations will subsequently show us whether we are right. Research workers often get into difficulties over this problem of scoring reversals, so it is important to be meticulous about it from the start.

Having scored each item from 1–5 or from 5–1, we next add up the item scores to obtain a total score. For instance, if we have 132 items in our pool, then the possible range of total scores will be from 132 to 660 (5 × 132) for each subject. Table 6–3 illustrates some items from a scale for mothers, dealing with acceptance or rejection of children. It becomes obvious, on reading through the items, that some of them express greater or lesser acceptance, others express degrees of hostility or rejection, and one or two may not fit on this particular dimension. Thus, agreement with statement (2) "It is fun showing

Table 6–3.

	Strongly agree	Agree	Uncertain	Disagree	Strongly disagree
	5	4	3	2	1
(1) Children bring a husband and wife closer to each other.			√		
(2) It is fun showing children how to do things.		√			
(3) Children need some of their natural meanness taken out of them.					√
(4) A mother with young children badly misses adult company and conversation.	√				
(5) On balance, children are more of a blessing than a burden.		√			
(6) It is often difficult to keep one's temper with a child.				√	
(7) Looking after children really demands too much of me.				√	
(8) If we could afford to do so, we would prefer to send our children to a boarding school.			√		
(9) When things are difficult, children are often a great source of courage and inspiration.				√	
(10) If I had my life to live over again, I should again want to have children.	√				

children how to do things" would seem to imply positive feelings for children; agreement with statement (3) "Children need some of their natural meanness taken out of them" would seem to indicate hostility to children on the part of the respondent; while the implications of statement (8) "If we could afford to do so, we would prefer to send our children to a boarding school" are a little unclear: agreement might signify rejection of the children, or it might mean the desire to lavish money on them in order to give them a better education (which could, however, be a form of overcompensation for unconscious feelings of rejection).

We now come to the problem of scoring. If we decide that a high scale score is going to mean a positive attitude to children, then agreement with the statements that imply love of children should be scored 4 or 5, and agreement with statements that imply rejection of children should be scored 1 or 2—in other words, the scoring of these latter statements is reversed. If, on the other hand, we decide that a high scale score will mean a negative attitude to children, then the scoring on the items that imply positive feelings toward children (items 1, 2, 5, 9, and 10) should be reversed. The important thing is to be consistent; likewise, we must make sure that we write our scoring instructions correctly and that in the case of punch-card analysis of each statement we know whether the respondents' checks were punched as they stood or were reversed before punching, where necessary.

In our example we have given but ten items, and we have shown the responses of one particular individual. Just glancing at her responses we get the impression of a mother with a mildly positive attitude toward children (items 2, 5, 7, and 10) who is able to express some moderately negative feelings (items 4 and 9) but shies away from extreme hostility (item 3) or inspired love (item 9). She also expresses some doubts (items 1 and 8); this may be because she is uncertain of her feelings or uncertain of the implications of the items. Perhaps these items do not belong in this scale because they contain other powerful attitude components (to marriage, to social class, to private boarding schools, to separation) besides acceptance or rejection of children. Item-analysis would show us whether these items should be retained.

How should this mother's responses be scored? Let us assume that we have decided that a high scale score shall mean a positive attitude to children. In that case, all the positive items can be scored as they stand:

5 = strongly agree
4 = agree
3 = uncertain
2 = disagree
1 = strongly disagree.

The scoring for items 3, 4, 6, 7, and 8 will, however, have to be reversed, as follows:

1 = strongly agree
2 = agree
3 = uncertain
4 = disagree
5 = strongly disagree.

Note, by the way, that the scoring of "uncertain" is the same (namely 3) in both cases. We can now give a numerical score to each check (in large-scale scoring operations it may be best to write such scores on the scale itself next to each check or in the margin) and calculate a total score, as follows:

item 1 =	3
2 =	4
3 =	5
4 =	1
5 =	4
6 =	4
7 =	4
8 =	3
9 =	2
10 =	5
total score	35

Since there are ten items, we have a maximum possible score of $5 \times 10 = 50$, and a necessary minimum score of $1 \times 10 = 10$. A score of 35 is thus a little above the midway point toward the positive end of the scale—which confirms our earlier impression of someone with mildly positive attitudes toward children.

Now we shall want to carry out an item-analysis to decide which are the best statements for our scale. To do this, something like an act of faith is required. Ideally, the item-analysis should take place by correlating each item with some reliable outside criterion of the attitude that it is supposed to measure and retaining only the items with the highest correlations. Such external criteria are, however, almost never available. It would not be safe to infer from the fact that a woman has children that she necessarily loves them; nor can we be sure that people who vote for a certain political party necessarily occupy a given position on a political spectrum; or that professional military men are necessarily more war-minded; in other words, it is dangerous to infer a person's attitudes from his behavior or from his group membership. We must therefore say to ourselves that, for the moment at least, the best available measure of the attitude concerned is the total item pool that we have so carefully constructed. By purifying this, the items will at least be consistent and homogeneous—they will all be measuring the same thing—and the scale may possibly also be valid. It is rather like trying to pull ourselves up by our own bootstraps!

However, this kind of procedure is not uncommon in the field of mental measurement and, if we are prepared to make this assumption, then the rest is plain sailing. We simply work out correlation coefficients for each item with the total score and retain those with the highest correlations. This is known as the internal-consistency method of item-analysis, since no external criterion is available. There is, however, one practical snag: we should really use, not the total score, but the total score minus the score for the item in question. This means that, for each item in turn, we will have a slightly different set of total scores. However, since we will probably group the total scores to work out the correlations, this subtraction procedure will not often make much difference, especially if the item pool is at all large; many research workers do not bother with it.

Here is an example. Suppose we are concerned with the analysis of item 5 from our previous item pool. We have the scores of ten respondents on the pool as a whole, on item 5, and on the pool as a whole minus their score on item 5 (see Table 6–4).

Table 6–4.

Respondent	Total score	Score on item 5	Total score minus item 5
A	45	5	40
B	42	5	37
C	35	4	31
D	35	4	31
E	20	1	19
F	39	4	35
G	33	3	30
H	40	4	36
I	22	1	21
J	27	2	25

We can set up a scattergram (see Table 6–5) to show the relationship.

Table 6–5.

	Total score minus item score			
Item score	10–19	20–29	30–39	40–50
1	1	1	—	—
2	—	1	—	—
3	—	—	1	—
4	—	—	4	—
5	—	—	1	1

This relationship is very strong ($r = .96$), and we should probably wish to retain this item if such results had been obtained on the basis of a much larger sample and a large item pool.

Our final scale will consist of, let us say, eighteen items. They have no scale values, such as we find in the Thurstone procedure; all the items carry equal weight. The respondents, as before, are asked to indicate their degree of agreement, and these responses are subsequently scored 1–5, remembering that scoring for some of the items may have to be reversed. After that, the eighteen item scores are added up to a total score, and that is the respondent's score on our scale.

Some investigators have used a seven-point degree-of-agreement score rather than the more usual five points. Others prefer to use some index of item discrimination[1] rather than correlation coefficients for item selection. Guilford[9] outlines a score of methods of item-analysis, many of which could be applied to attitude-scaling.

Reliability of Likert scales tends to be good and, partly because of the greater range of answers permitted to respondents, is often higher than that of corresponding Thurstone scales; a reliability coefficient of .85 is often achieved. The scale makes no pretence at equal-appearing intervals but by using the internal-consistency method of item selection it approaches unidimensionality in many cases. The number of items in a Likert scale is arbitrary, but is sometimes very small.

The most serious criticism leveled against this type of scale is its lack of reproducibility (in the technical sense): the same total score may be obtained in many different ways. This being so, it has been argued that such a score has little meaning or else that two or more identical scores may have totally different meanings. Often, for this reason, the pattern of responses becomes more interesting than the total score.

Another criticism has been that the scale offers no metric or interval measures, and it lacks a neutral point, so that one does not know where scores in the middle ranges change from mildly positive to mildly negative. As against this, it should be pointed out that percentile norms or standard-deviation norms can be calculated if a sample of sufficient size is available[10]; certainly, Likert scales will split up people within the same group. With regard to the neutral point on the scale, we must agree that this is not necessarily the midpoint between the two extreme scale scores; moreover, scores in the middle region could be due to lukewarm response, lack of knowledge, or lack of attitude in the respondent (leading to many "uncertain" responses), or to the presence of both strongly positive and strongly negative responses, which would more or less balance each other, suggesting that the scale is not unidimensional. Clearly, with such different possibilities, the neutral point would be difficult to locate and even more difficult to interpret. Where this problem is of particular importance, we can, as Guttman and Suchman[19] have suggested, ascertain for each scale item the "degree of intensity" or certainty with which it is endorsed or rejected, and then plot the average intensity against the scale scores, both converted into percentile units. Since this relationship is usually U-shaped, so that the lowest intensity is felt about the least extreme items, this technique can be used to locate the neutral point, namely the region nearest the low-point on the intensity curve. Since, to ascertain intensity for each item, the number of questions has to be doubled, this approach is only used where exceptional importance is attached to the location of the neutral point.

In practice, if we remember that equal score intervals do not permit us to make assertions about the equality of underlying attitude differences and that identical scores may have very different meanings, the Likert scales tend to perform very well when it comes to a reliable, rough ordering of people with regard to a particular attitude. Apart from their relative ease of construction, these scales have two other advantages: first, they provide more precise information about the respondent's degree of agreement or disagreement, and respondents usually prefer this to a simple agree/disagree score. Second, it becomes possible to include items whose manifest content is not obviously related to the attitude in question, so that the subtler and deeper ramifications of an attitude can be explored. These "long shots," such as the item about sending children to boarding schools in our earlier example, which are unlikely to be included in the Thurstone procedure, enable us to make use of the links that an attitude may have with neighboring areas and to uncover the strands and interconnections of its various components.

Factorial Scales

Internal-consistency methods of item-analysis provide some safeguard against the inclusion of unrelated items in a scale, but clearly a better way of ensuring unidimensionality would be through the use of factor-analysis.[22] This is a statistical technique, based on intercorrelating all the items with one another, which enables us to abstract one or more "factors" that the items, or some of them, have in common. The procedure is widely used in the field of mental testing; a typical battery of tests of ability will probably have one general factor underlying all the tests (which might be equated with intelligence) and some group factors, such as mechanical ability or verbal ability, which underlie some tests, but not others. In the case of a set of attitude items or statements, when we are looking for a single score to express an individual's position on an attitude continuum, we will want to use factor-analysis in order to eliminate items that do not belong and to keep items that have high "loadings" on the factor (attitude) that we want to measure. Sometimes, however, we can use factor-analysis to show how a seemingly unified attitude complex in fact "breaks up" into several independent factors. A person's political orientation, for instance, has been shown by Eysenck[23] to consist not merely of a left-wing/right-wing dimension, but of two independent dimensions. Parental childrearing attitudes have likewise been shown to have at least two independent components.[25]

Since factor-analysis is a laborious technique unless one has a computer available, this approach has its limitations. For instance a factor-analysis of a pool of only twenty items would require, as a first step, the computation of 190 correlation coefficients. Work on item pools of over a hundred items would clearly be out of the question for most researchers. Often, therefore, we find factor-analysis applied not to the original item pool but to finished scales. When applied to a single scale, it can throw light on its unidimensionality after all the individual items have been intercorrelated. When applied to a battery of scales all given to the same respondents, it can reveal similarities and differences between the scales, as well as some of the underlying attitudes or value systems. Factor-analysis then becomes a tool for theoretical investigation and new discoveries. In this connection, the problem of rotation and naming of factors remains a source of difficulties.

Factor-analysis opens the way to other possibilities. In the rare instances where an external criterion is available, validation and purification will obviously lead to a very high-quality scale. More refined scoring might sometimes be useful, by weighting the items according to their factor loadings. Sometimes, certain items or subscales have loadings on two factors, with differently weighted or even reversed scoring, so that we can obtain two different measures from the same group of items. Factor-analysis, even more than the original Likert scaling procedure, enables us to show the common attitudinal basis for some widely divergent issues; for instance, Eysenck[23] has shown that opinions on sovereignty, abortion law, corporal punishment, and religious education have the same underlying attitude structure.

The factor-analysis of attitude scales also opens the way to cross-national comparisons. As a rule, these present problems because of the difficulties of translation and "equivalent meaning," and because one never knows whether the attitude concerned is structured in the same way in another country. However, if scales are translated and factor-analyzed in several countries and continue to produce similar factor pictures,[24] then this strongly suggests similarity of attitude structure and opens the way toward cross-national comparisons.

Scalogram-Analysis

The chief concerns of the method of scalogram-analysis, developed by Guttman[26] and his associates, are the twin problems of unidimensionality and reproducibility. The method enables us, from a respondent's score, to know exactly which items he has endorsed, with not more than 10 per cent error for the sample as a whole. This is, of course, in marked contrast to the Likert scale scores, which can be arrived at in a number of different ways. The method can be used with items other than attitude statements, such as neurotic symptoms or the possession of consumer durables.

The items in a Guttman scale have the properties of being ordinal and cumulative. For instance: lead, glass, and diamond are ordered according to their cumulative degree of hardness; addition, multiplication, and the extraction of square roots are arithmetical operations ordered according to their cumulative degree of difficulty (it is highly likely that anyone who can multiply can also add and that anyone who can extract square roots can both add and multiply). If we think of a dozen or more degrees of hardness or difficulty, ranked in order, then many respondents will endorse the early ones—indicating that they know how to add, subtract, multiply, and so on—but, sooner or later, they will "cross over" and fail to endorse such remaining items as solving differential equations or carrying out integrations. This cross-over point is their individual score. From it, we know precisely which items they must have endorsed.

Another illustration might be a social-distance scale. If it has been constructed with the aid of scalogram-analysis, then the individual's score will tell us which items he has endorsed, since the score tells us at what point he has crossed over to a negative attitude. Research on courting practices and sexual behavior among college students[27] has shown that this area will scale; endorsement of a more intimate form of sexual behavior almost invariably means the endorsement also of all the less intimate items on the scale. There are also scales for measuring women's neighborliness,[28] economic liberalism/conservatism, childhood maladjustment, and so on.

Guttman sets great store by the property of reproducibility, which, as we have seen, is a useful but by no means necessary attribute for most scales. The procedures of scalogram-analysis are designed to test a given universe of content or, at any rate, a group of items for "scalability" by seeing whether it will yield a scale with a satisfactory coefficient of reproducibility (in practice, a coefficient of .90 or over is accepted). Of course, not all areas of content will scale, especially not if they are rather wide and heterogeneous, and one cannot know beforehand whether the attempt at scale construction will be successful. The procedure has been criticized for this and for a tendency to produce scales covering a very narrow universe of content (because wider areas often do not scale).

The procedure of scalogram-analysis is designed to enable us to see how far our items, and people's responses to them, deviate from the ideal scale pattern. Suppose that we start out with a set of social-distance items and that we have given these (as yet unscaled) items to several hundred respondents. A tabulation of the results for the first fifteen cases might look like Table 6–6.

Table 6–6.

Respondent	Item 1	Item 2	Item 3	Item 4	Item 5	Item 6	Item 7	Item 8	*Score*
1	yes	yes	yes	yes	yes	—	yes	—	6
2	yes	—	—	—	yes	—	yes	yes	4
3	yes	yes	—	—	yes	—	yes	yes	5
4	—	—	—	—	yes	—	yes	—	2
5	yes	—	—	—	yes	—	yes	—	3
6	yes	—	—	—	yes	—	yes	yes	4
7	yes	yes	—	yes	yes	yes	yes	yes	7
8	yes	—	—	yes	yes	—	yes	—	4
9	yes	yes	—	yes	yes	yes	yes	yes	7
10	yes	yes	—	yes	yes	—	yes	yes	6
11	—	—	—	—	—	—	—	yes	1
12	—	—	—	—	—	—	yes	—	1
13	yes	yes	—	yes	yes	—	yes	yes	6
14	yes	—	—	—	yes	—	yes	yes	4
15	yes	—	—	—	yes	—	yes	—	3

Note that we have given each respondent a score equal to the number of yes-answers he has given. Let us now rearrange the table, by placing the *rows* (respondents) in order of their scale score. The result is shown in Table 6–7.

Table 6–7.

Respondent	Item 1	Item 2	Item 3	Item 4	Item 5	Item 6	Item 7	Item 8	*Score*
7	yes	yes	—	yes	yes	Yes	yes	yes	7
9	yes	yes	—	yes	yes	Yes	yes	yes	7
10	yes	yes	—	yes	yes	—	yes	yes	6
1	yes	yes	yes	yes	yes	—	yes	—	6
13	yes	yes	—	yes	yes	—	yes	yes	6
3	yes	yes	—	—	yes	—	yes	yes	5
2	yes	—	—	—	yes	—	yes	yes	4
6	yes	—	—	—	yes	—	yes	yes	4
8	yes	—	—	yes	yes	—	yes	—	4
14	yes	—	—	—	yes	—	yes	yes	4
5	yes	—	—	—	yes	—	yes	—	3
15	yes	—	—	—	yes	—	yes	—	3
4	—	—	—	—	yes	—	yes	—	2
11	—	—	—	—	—	—	—	yes	1
12	—	—	—	—	—	—	yes	—	1
	12	6	1	6	13	2	14	9	

Next, let us rearrange the *columns* (items) in the table, by putting them in order of the number of yes-answers given to each item, as shown in Table 6–8.

We have now produced a scalogram pattern that is very nearly perfect and has very high reproducibility. A score of 3 clearly means a yes-response to items 7, 5, and 1 (and not to *any* three items, as would be the case in a Likert scale); a score of 6 means a yes-response to items 7, 5, 1, 8, 2, and 4; and so on. The lowest item on the scale is item 7, to which nearly everyone agrees; the highest or, in this case, most intimate one is item 3, to which almost no one agrees. Note the triangular pattern of the responses—this is the pattern that scalogram-analysis aims to produce. Item intercorrelations may be quite low in a Guttman scale but typically have one zero cell (see Table 6–9).

We should observe several further points. First of all, Table 6–9 is a "rigged" example for demonstration purposes; in practice we may have to rearrange the order of items and of respondents not once or twice, but many times, until we have ob-

Table 6–8.

Respondent	Item 7	Item 5	Item 1	Item 8	Item 2	Item 4	Item 6	Item 3	*Score*
7	yes	yes	yes	yes	yes	Yes	yes	—	7
9	yes	yes	yes	yes	yes	yes	yes	—	7
10	yes	yes	yes	yes	yes	yes	—	—	6
1	yes	yes	yes	—	yes	yes	—	yes	6
13	yes	yes	yes	yes	yes	yes	—	—	6
3	yes	yes	yes	yes	yes	—	—	—	5
2	yes	yes	yes	yes	—	—	—	—	4
6	yes	yes	yes	yes	—	—	—	—	4
8	yes	yes	yes	—	—	yes	—	—	4
14	yes	yes	yes	yes	—	—	—	—	4
5	yes	yes	yes	—	—	—	—	—	3
15	yes	yes	yes	—	—	—	—	—	3
4	yes	yes	—	—	—	—	—	—	2
11	—	—	—	yes	—	—	—	—	1
12	yes	—	—	—	—	—	—	—	1

tained the nearest approximation to a scalogram pattern. This procedure becomes very tedious and fraught with errors, especially if we deal, not with fifteen respondents, but with a hundred or more, and with dozens of items instead of a mere eight. This has led to the development of scalogram boards by Guttman and by others; these are mechanical devices that enable us to move whole rows or whole columns of responses in one operation, without needing to rewrite the whole matrix.[29, 30] Nowadays,

Table 6–9.

		STATEMENT X agree	STATEMENT X disagree	
STATEMENT Y	agree	35	25	60
	disagree	—	40	40
		35	65	100

many research workers prefer to use punch-card procedures. (See pages 149–150.)

Looking again at Table 6–8, we note that it is not absolutely regular. For instance, respondent 8 has given a yes-response to item 4 instead of to item 8. Likewise, respondents 1 and 11 show slight deviations from the perfect scale pattern, and to this extent they make reproducibility less certain. Such deviations are called "errors" in this context. The formula for calculating the reproducibility coefficient is as follows:

$$R = 1 - \frac{\text{no. of errors}}{\text{no. of responses}}$$

(The number of responses is the number of items multiplied by the number of respondents.) If reproducibility is below 0.9 then the scale is considered unsatisfactory. In that case, we might have to give up the scaling attempt altogether, or we might—as with the other scaling procedures—get rid of a number of items and then rescore and rescale the remaining responses and recalculate the coefficient of reproducibility. In the above example, for instance, we might wish to drop item 8 (which contains one error, and has two gaps caused by other errors), and item 3 (which is so extreme that it fails to differentiate and also because it contains one error).

Customarily, scalogram-analysis is carried out on one or more samples of a hundred cases each. The number of items might initially be several dozen that, after repeated attempts at scaling, might be whittled down to perhaps eight or ten items that form a scale. Such a scale might sometimes be much narrower in content than the original item pool; at other times, seemingly unrelated items are unexpectedly easy to scale—there is no way of forecasting the outcome. If we have many respondents, it would be advisable to repeat the scaling operation on several samples of one hundred, to reduce the possibility that a scale pattern is produced by a combination of chance variables. We must also guard against spuriously high estimates of reproducibility, by omitting all items to which almost everyone or almost no one agrees; usually, therefore, items with less than 20 per cent or more than 80 per cent endorsement are omitted from a scalogram-analysis at the start.

So far, we have assumed all the items to be dichotomous. However, we might have items with multiple responses, such as degrees of agreement, or frequency of a symptom. Many investigators would probably fix a cut-off point for each item, and turn them into dichotomies. However, the place of the cut-off point will affect the scale position of the item, and a certain amount of trial and error may be necessary before we find the cut-off point that produces the least number of scale errors. It is also possible to treat each of the multiple responses as a single dichotomous item; thus, if we had two items, one with three response positions and another with five response positions, we might treat these as eight separate items and try to scale them as before. Or we might wish to group the response positions by turning, say, five responses into three. Obviously, this kind of analysis will increase the amount of work involved in the scaling operation, and the investigator will need to bear this in mind when making his decisions.

Several research workers have published punch-card procedures for scalogram-analysis.[31, 32] Essentially the aim is to produce the nearest approximation to the triangular pattern of responses, by concentrating the highest-scoring individuals and the most frequently endorsed items in one corner of the table. To achieve this we need a card punch, a card sorter, and a simple tabulator. First, we select one hundred cases (cards) at random from our sample; on each card will be the responses of one individual, at the rate of one item per column. It is probably easiest if all the items are dichotomized, and the cards repunched so that a positive response is coded "1," and a negative response is left blank, but other scoring procedures are possible. We must now sort on each column, in order to eliminate items with more than 80 per cent or less than 20 per cent positive responses. Next, we print out the entire pack of one hundred cards on all remaining columns (items), together with the case number of each respondent. We print the columns in order of the number of responses per column, so that the column with the highest number of positive responses is printed down the left-hand side, and so on across the page to the column with the lowest number of positive responses. On this first tabulation we score each case by adding up, across the rows, the numbers of positive responses. Next, with the aid of the case numbers, we re-sort the pack in order of the individual total scores, in such a way that the highest scoring respondents come first, and so on down to those who score lowest. We now obtain a second tabulation. This will be our first approximation to the desired triangular pattern.

From here on, an element of judgment enters into the situation. We must examine the pattern of "errors" and try to reduce their number by eliminating a number of columns and perhaps also by changing the sequence of some of the others across the page. Each time we do this, we will have to rescore each case and obtain another print-out. When little more is to be gained by eliminating further columns, we must calculate the coefficient of reproducibility. To do this, it is helpful to draw stepwise lines on our tabulation, as shown on Table 6–8. We count as "errors" all those responses that fall outside the elongated triangular pattern (gaps inside the triangular pattern are not counted, since each error is only counted once), divide those by the total number of responses (100 multiplied by the remaining number of items), and subtract the quotient from unity. Reproducibility coefficients below 0.9 are usually taken to indicate that the pattern is not strong enough to form an adequate scale.

With more sophisticated computing facilities some of these steps can be carried out electronically, rather than by hand. If the items cannot be dichotomized, we can treat each response category as a separate item, punched on a separate column, and proceed as before; we can also experiment with answer combinations and with varying cut-off points. If sufficient cases are available, it is advisable to carry out more than one scale-building operation on groups of one hundred cases each, to ensure reliability.

The use of scalogram boards has been described in detail by Suchman[30] and by Trenaman.[29]

Guttman has been criticized for his insistence on reproducibility and for regarding cumulative reproducibility as the chief criterion for a "true" scale; other writers have felt that these are valuable but not essential properties. He has also been criticized for the somewhat arbitrary standards that he sets, such as the lower limit of 0.9 for coefficients of reproducibility. His procedures are laborious, and there is no certainty that, in the end, a usable scale will result. On the other hand, scalogram-analysis will prevent us from building a single scale for a universe of content that really demands two or more separate scales; in other words, it offers the important safeguard of unidimensionality. Guttman scales are very useful when we wish to examine small shifts or changes in attitudes, perhaps in response to only a single item. Scalogram-analysis can produce some short yet highly effective scales. The problem of validation remains and depends largely on the manifest content of the items; also, the scales do not have equal or equal-appearing intervals, but they are highly reliable, as a rule.

The work of Guttman and his colleagues has led to a number of interesting theoretical developments, which will not be discussed here. For excellent textbook references see Green[1] and Lazarsfeld.[35]

The Problem of Validation

In Chapter 3 we discussed the problems of validity, and we remarked then on the difference between factual and attitudinal measures and the greater difficulty of validating the latter because of their abstract and indirect nature and because of the absence of suitable criteria. Attitude scales share this problem with other forms of mental measurement. The literature contains but a small number of attempts at direct validation against a criterion, and we may well ask whether the measures employed as criteria were themselves valid. Such attempts have included the use of essay-type questions, experts' judgments, membership in groups with known policies or interests, pictorial material, interviews and case studies, judgments by friends or co-workers, self-ratings, political votes, and such overt behavior as church attendance. New scales are often correlated with older, well-known scales which, however, may themselves be of questionable validity.

Scales are often given names or labels that help to create a spuriously high impression of validity. The very fact that they look like tests and can be scored may create expectations of validity and exactitude that may not be fulfilled.

It may be helpful to remind ourselves of the different approaches to the problem of validity. We have repeatedly pointed out the weaknesses in the criterion-group approach, sometimes known as pragmatic validation. As we saw in Chapter 3, for more theoretically oriented research the concept of construct validity has been developed, which hinges on the relationship of our scale with other measures. We also saw that much depends on the quality of the attitude statements and the feelings that they arouse in the respondents; in this sense, validity depends on the respondents' candor and willingness to cooperate and the absence of stereotyped answers or "façade" responses. Some investigators simply state that what the scale measures is indicated by the manifest content of the items; others rely on groups of judges for ascertaining what the items measure. Of particular importance is predictive validity, usually in the sense of predicting some future aspect of behavior. We can see from this that a great deal depends on our purpose in building a scale. It is one thing to require a purely descriptive device, which can roughly divide our sample into several groups with regard to a given attitude, but quite another to ask for a technique that will predict people's actions at some time in the future. Speaking very generally, many of our scales will probably do quite an adequate descriptive job, as long as not too much precision is required of them, but the problems of predictive validity are a long way from being solved.

To illustrate the lack of correspondence that is found at times between verbal attitudes and behavior (predictive validity), the classic demonstration of LaPiere[36] is often cited. In 1934, he traveled through the United States in the company of a Chinese couple. When he later questioned the managers of hotels and restaurants that had served them, over 90 per cent said that they would not accept Chinese guests! Kutner, Wilkins, and Yarrow[37] carried out a study in 1952, similarly showing that ethnic prejudice may not necessarily express itself in discriminatory behavior in a face-to-face situation. Wilkins,[38] on the other hand, found it possible to predict the demand for British campaign stars and medals after World War II with considerable accuracy from an attitude questionnaire.

Can attitude scales, then, predict behavior? As we have seen, behavior does not have a simple one-to-one relationship with one type of inner determinant such as an attitude. The relationship is complex and will involve both other attitudes and character traits and environmental determinants.

A well-known formula for the analysis of any form of behavior may help us here:[39]

$$B = f\,(P, E)$$

In words: behavior is a function of the interaction between P (all the person's inner determinants, such as temperament, attitudes, or character traits) and E (all the environmental factors, *as perceived* by the individual). When we have full knowledge of all but one part of the formula, we can predict the variable that is not known.

Several points should become clear from this. First of all, B (behavior) has a complex relationship with its various inner determinants because of the influence of environmental factors (which may be differently perceived by different individuals). Therefore, we cannot use it as a measure or index of such inner determinants, and we cannot accurately infer attitudes from behavior unless we have full knowledge of the effects of environmental determinants also.

Furthermore, for the same reasons, we cannot expect a direct prediction of overt behavior merely from knowledge of one inner determinant, such as a score on an attitude scale. Other inner determinants (including conflicting attitudes) may play a part, but above all we need full knowledge of the effects of the (perceived) environment. An attitude scale may indicate inclinations toward cheating, but the respondent will probably act honestly if he thinks he will be found out. Behavior is a compromise, a resultant of the interaction of multiple forces.

We may conclude, therefore, that failure to predict a particular action does not constitute proof that the attitude scale was invalid. The scale may well have given valid and accurate measures of a given attitude and correctly described the individual's response tendencies. These may, however, have been offset or nullified by other tendencies (which have gone unmeasured) and by his perception of the environment at that time (which, likewise, has not been taken into account). The attitude-scale score constitutes too small a part of our equation to carry the full burden of prediction. However, we may expect better prediction of overt behavior from attitude scales under conditions of "other things being equal," where the perceived environmental determinants can be held constant or near-constant for all respondents (for example, in laboratory experiments) and also when predicting behavior which is itself verbal, as in voting, writing letters to the newspapers, applying for campaign stars, signing petitions or membership applications, and so on.[41]

More research is needed on internal conflict between contradictory attitudes or between attitudes and other aspects of personality: we have some measures of these variables in isolation, but we do not know how conflicts between them are resolved within the individual. We also need to make a serious start with the measurement of the perceived environment,[40] such as threats, role expectations, and conformity needs. Not until we have arrived at a fuller measurement and understanding of all the components in the behavioral equation and their interaction will we be able to make valid predictions.

• *Selected Readings*

GENERAL REFERENCES TO SCALING

1. Bert F. Green, "Attitude Measurement," in Gardner Lindzey, ed., *Handbook of Social Psychology* (Cambridge, Mass.: Addison-Wesley Publishing, 1954).

   An advanced and comprehensive textbook reference.

2. David Krech, Richard S. Crutchfield, and Egerton L. Ballachey, *Individual in Society* (New York: McGraw-Hill, 1962).

   A basic textbook in social psychology. See in particular pp. 147–169.

3. Quinn McNemar, "Opinion-Attitude Methodology," *Psychological Bulletin,* XLIII (1946), 289–374.

A classic postwar review article, critical but fair and still of great relevance. See in particular Section II, "Attitudes by Scaling Techniques," and Section III, "Single-Question Opinion Gauging."

4. S. S. Stevens, "Mathematics, Measurement, and Psychophysics," in S. S. Stevens, ed., *Handbook of Experimental Psychology* (New York: Wiley, 1951).

On general measurement theory.

5. A. L. Edwards, *Techniques of Attitude-Scale Construction* (New York: Appleton-Century-Crofts, 1957).

6. Matilda W. Riley, J. W. Riley Jr., and J. Toby, *Sociological Studies in Scale Analysis* (New Brunswick, N.J.: Rutgers University Press, 1954).

7. W. S. Torgerson, *Theory and Methods of Scaling* (New York: Wiley, 1958).

For the advanced student.

8. Leonard W. Ferguson, *Personality Measurement* (New York: McGraw-Hill, 1952).

See chapter 4 on attitude measurement.

9. J. P. Guilford, *Psychometric Methods* (New York: McGraw-Hill, 1954).

See especially chapter 16 on factor-analysis, chapter 4–7 on psychophysical methods, and chapter 15 on item-analysis.

10. Lee J. Cronbach, *Essentials of Psychological Testing* (New York: Harper, 1960).

A useful textbook on tests and their uses. See especially chapter 5 on validity and chapter 9 on factor-analysis. Percentiles are discussed on pp. 75–78; standard scores on pp. 78–87; calculating correlations on pp. 110–125; problems of reliability on pp. 126–142.

SOCIAL-DISTANCE SCALES

11. E. S. Bogardus, "Measuring Social Distance," *Journal of Applied Sociology,* IX (1925), 299–308.

12. E. S. Bogardus, "A Social-Distance Scale," *Sociological and Social Research,* XVII (1933), 265–271.

13. Harry C. Triandis and Leigh M. Triandis, "Race, Social Class, Religion, and Nationality as Determinants of Social Distance," *Journal of Abnormal and Social Psychology,* LXI (1960), 110–118.

    Use of a revised version of social-distance scale, developed with the aid of the Thurstone successive-interval procedure and checked for linearity, unidimensionality, reliability, and reproducibility.

14. Arthur D. Kirsch, "Social Distance and Some Related Variables in Voting Behavior," in H. H. Remmers, ed., *Anti-Democratic Attitudes in American Schools* (Evanston, Ill.: Northwestern University Press, 1963).

THURSTONE SCALES

15. L. L. Thurstone and E. J. Chave, *The Measurement of Attitudes* (Chicago: University of Chicago Press, 1929).

    Source book for Thurstone scales.

16. Carl I. Hovland and M. Sherif, "Judgmental Phenomena and Scales of Attitude Measurement: Item Displacement in Thurstone Scales," *The Journal of Abnormal and Social Psychology,* XLVII (1952), 822–832.

    A well-known investigation showing the influence of the judge's own opinions on his placement of items in the Thurstone scaling procedure.

LIKERT SCALES

17. Rensis Likert, "A Technique for the Measurement of Attitudes," *Archives of Psychology,* No. 140 (1932).

    Source book for the Likert scaling method.

18. A. L. Edwards and K. C. Kenney, "A Comparison of the Thurstone and Likert Techniques of Attitude Scale Construction," *Journal of Applied Psychology,* XXX (1946), 72–83.

19. Louis Guttman and E. A. Suchman, "Intensity and a Zero Point for Attitude Analysis," *American Sociological Review,* XII (1947), 57–67.

20. Uriel G. Foa, "Scale and Intensity Analysis in Opinion Research," *International Journal of Opinion and Attitude Research,* IV (1950), 192–208.

    An exposition of the use of the intensity component in relation to Guttman scales.

21. H. P. Kuang, "A Critical Evaluation of the Relative Efficiency of Three Techniques in Item Analysis," *Educational and Psychological Measurement,* XII (1952), 248–266.

FACTORIAL SCALES

22. Raymond B. Cattell, *Factor Analysis* (New York: Harper, 1952).

23. Hans J. Eysenck, *The Psychology of Politics* (London: Routledge & Kegan Paul, 1954).

    See especially chapter 3 on scaling procedures and validation and chapters 4 and 5 on factor-analysis applied to attitudes and their clustering.

24. Hans J. Eysenck, "Primary Social Attitudes: A Comparison of Attitude Patterns in England, Germany, and Sweden," *Journal of Abnormal and Social Psychology,* XLVIII (1953), 563–568.

    A cross-national comparison of attitude structures with the aid of factor-analysis.

25. Earl S. Schaefer, "Converging Conceptual Models for Maternal Behavior and for Child Behavior," in John C. Glidewell, ed., *Parental Attitudes and Child Behavior* (Springfield, Ill.: Charles C. Thomas, 1961).

    A presentation of the two main components of maternal attitudes, in terms of factor-analysis.

SCALOGRAM-ANALYSIS

26. Louis Guttman, "The Basis for Scalogram Analysis," in Samuel A. Stouffer, ed., *Measurement and Prediction* (Princeton, N.J.: Princeton University Press, 1950).

    The main source book for the Guttman scaling technique and its theoretical background.

27. L. Podell and J. C. Perkins, "A Guttman Scale for Sexual Experience—a Methodological Note," *Journal of Abnormal Psychology*, LIV (1957), 420–422.

28. Paul Wallin, "A Guttman Scale for Measuring Women's Neighborliness," *The American Journal of Sociology*, LIX (1953), 243–246.

29. Joseph Trenaman, "Guttman's Scalogram Analysis of Attitudes," in *Attitude Scaling* (London: The Market Research Society, 1960).

    A useful and critical exposition of the scalogram-board technique.

30. E. A. Suchman, "The Scalogram Board Technique," in Samuel A. Stouffer, ed., *Measurement and Prediction* (Princeton, N.J.: Princeton University Press, 1950).

31. R. N. Ford, "A Rapid Scoring Procedure for Scaling Attitude Questions," in Matilda W. Riley *et al.*, eds., *Sociological Studies in Scale Analysis* (New Brunswick, N.J.: Rutgers University Press, 1954).

32. L. A. Kahn and A. J. Bodine, "Guttman Scale Analysis by Means of I.B.M. Equipment," *Educational and Psychological Measurement*, XI (1951), 298–314.

33. Kenneth E. Clark and Philip H. Kreidt, "An Application of Guttman's New Scaling Techniques to an Attitude Questionnaire," *Educational and Psychological Measurement*, VIII (1948), 215–223.

    A critical paper.

34. Hans J. Eysenck, "Measurement and Prediction. A Discussion of Volume IV of Studies in Social Psychology in World

War II: I. Review. II. (by Louis Guttman) Scale Analysis, Factor Analysis, and Dr. Eysenck." *International Journal of Opinion and Attitude Research,* V (1951), 95–120.

Eysenck's critical review of the Guttman procedures and Guttman's reply bring out some of the major issues.

35. Paul F. Lazarsfeld, "Latent Structure Analysis," in Sigmund Koch, ed., *Psychology: A Study of a Science* (New York: McGraw-Hill, 1959), Vol. 3.

For the advanced student.

VALIDATION

36. Richard T. LaPiere, "Attitudes versus Actions," *Social Forces,* XIV (1934), 230–237.

37. B. Kutner, Carol Wilkins, and Penny R. Yarrow, "Verbal Attitudes and Overt Behavior Involving Racial Prejudice," *Journal of Abnormal and Social Psychology,* XLVII (1952), 647–652.

38. Leslie T. Wilkins, *Prediction of the Demand for Campaign Stars and Medals* (London: Central Office of Information, 1948).

One of the few successful attempts at deriving predictions from measured attitudes.

39. Kurt Lewin, *Principles of Topological Psychology* (New York: McGraw-Hill, 1936).

Lewin's definition of behavior as $B = f(P, E)$ and its implications.

40. George G. Stern, "$B = F(P, E)$," *Journal of Projective Techniques and Personality Assessment,* XXVIII (1964), 161–168.

An attempt at studying environmental influences on perception, attitudes, and behavior.

41. Gardner Murphy, Lois B. Murphy, and Theodore M. Newcomb, *Experimental Social Psychology* (New York: Harper, 1937).

See especially their comments on the relationship between attitudes and behavior on pp. 898–900.

7

Projective Techniques in Attitude Study

Attitude scales rely for their effectiveness on the cooperation and frankness of the respondent. This may have its disadvantages. For one reason or another, a respondent may try to fake or give a great many "Uncertain" responses. Fear, misunderstanding, the desire to place oneself in a more favorable light, social taboos, dislike for the research worker, and other motives may all play a part in distorting the results and may lead to outright refusal. This has led to the development of methods of attitude measurement whose purpose is less obvious to the respondent.

Sometimes, by means of indirect methods, we can approach a deeper level in the respondent than we can with attitude scales alone. For this reason, we may wish to use both methods in the same inquiry, to obtain data on the same attitude-complex at several different levels. It is important to plan such an investigation with great care, or the results will tend to be contradictory instead of complementary.

When to Use Projective Techniques

In planning our investigation one of the first things we will have to decide is how deeply we need to probe. If we can stay at a relatively superficial level, then direct techniques for attitude measurement, such as the various types of attitude scales, ratings and rankings, grids and indices can be used with advantage and will yield quantitative results. If, however, we have to penetrate deeper, perhaps below the level of conscious awareness or behind the individual's social façade, then indirect, projective techniques have to be used. Projective techniques can be particularly useful in evoking and outlining stereotypes, self-images and norm-percepts, for instance, ideas connected with "the good housewife."

The best way to find out whether or not we will need to probe in depth is to carry out a series of careful pilot interviews, to explore the origins, complexities, motivational links, and ramifications of the behavior and attitudes in question, so as to enable us to conceptualize them. Extended interviews will most likely yield a number of promising lines for investigation, which may be studied by means of attitude scales and other direct techniques, but which may also call for projective devices. Such techniques should be used as infrequently as possible in a purely exploratory way; as a rule, they should be built and utilized to test specific hypotheses emerging from the depth interviews. In other words, they should be used as part of a systematic plan.

What Projective Techniques Can Do

When suitably designed, projective techniques can help to penetrate some of the following barriers:

1. The barrier of awareness. People are frequently unaware of their own motives and attitudes and cannot give us the answers we need, even with the best will in the world. For instance, a very submissive man may keep a dog in order to exercise his desire for dominance and control; a lonely woman may keep cats as some kind of substitute for children; but these respondents might be quite unaware of such needs and motives.

2. The barrier of irrationality. Our society places a high premium on sensible, rational, and logical behavior. Most of us tend to rationalize a lot of the time; we stress, or invent, sound

logical reasons for actions whose origins are far from rational. For instance, if a sample of motorists are asked to rank the ten most important characteristics of a new car, they will generally put "reliability" and "safety" high on the list, with "styling" or "appearance" toward the bottom. However, if they are asked to state which characteristics their friends or neighbors regard as important, "styling" jumps to third or second place. The average motorist is not aware of the extent to which he actually is influenced by appearance—he likes to think that his choice is determined by such rational aspects as safety, performance, reliability, and economy.

In an experiment carried out at an exhibition, people were asked to choose between two cameras in terms of quality. A considerable majority chose camera B. Actually, the two cameras were identical, but camera B had a small weight concealed inside it. Feeling the extra weight, people tended, subconsciously, to think of that camera as a more "solid job," with "better materials," and so forth. Yet if they had been asked for their reasons, they would no doubt have spoken of shutter speeds, lens quality, or flash synchronization, and any suggestion that weight played a part in their decision would have been regarded as preposterous.

3. The barrier of inadmissibility. Our society sets many norms and expectations for all of us, and we find it difficult to admit to a stranger, or even to ourselves, that we sometimes fail to meet such standards. Ideally, we ought always to pay our fare on the bus, share our sweets or cigarettes with friends or workmates, tell only innocent jokes, and drop our litter in litter-baskets—yet we sometimes fall short of these ideals, and this produces guilt feelings and a desire to "cover up." For instance, when passing around a roll of assorted candies, many people have some kind of strategy that will prevent their favorite flavor from being picked by someone else—but one would need indirect techniques to find this out.

4. The barrier of self-incrimination. This is really a variant of inadmissibility. It concerns those aspects of behavior and feelings that might lower the respondent's self-esteem, such as racial prejudice, violation of sexual taboos, irrational fears, or alcoholic

overindulgence. For instance, when men's toiletries (such as after-shave lotions and deodorants) were first introduced, many men had the secret fear that they would be considered homosexuals if they used these products. People about to undergo an operation are sometimes extremely afraid that they will "say terrible things" while under the anesthetic. People do not admit such secret fears because they are afraid to make themselves look silly, childish, sinful, or prejudiced, but projective techniques can often help us to uncover such feelings, attitudes, or emotions.

5. The barrier of politeness. People often prefer *not* to say negative, unpleasant or critical things, unless they have specific complaints. They tend to say that most things are "all right," and present a rather bland façade. Thus, projective techniques could help to show us whether, say, a given newspaper was considered rather vulgar by certain groups of respondents.

It follows that whenever the pilot work shows us that any of these barriers exist with respect to the problem at hand, then the use of projective techniques should be considered in the survey that is being designed.

How Indirect Techniques Work

There are four commonly used approaches, which overlap to some extent:

1. Association. The "say-the-first-thing-that-comes-into-your-mind" approach is based on the assumption that a fast response to a stimulus word, picture, or question, will be less "guarded" and therefore more revealing of underlying attitudes and motives.

2. Fantasy. The respondent is asked to guess, or tell a story, or discuss a picture in imaginary terms. In doing so, he has to use his own attitudes and experience as "building blocks," and this will give us an insight into some of the deeper levels of his personality. For instance, we might show a rather vague picture of a man with a worried face leaving a bank. The respondent's task is to tell us what the man is feeling, and why, and what has taken place in the bank. In doing this, the respondent is likely to reveal

some of his own attitudes and feelings toward banks and his attitude to saving, borrowing, and financial problems generally.

3. Ambiguous stimuli. All perception involves a certain amount of projection and interpretation on the part of the respondent—the more so when the stimulus is indefinite and ambiguous. The term "projection" is not used here in the strict Freudian sense; rather, it refers to the fact that whenever a subject is asked to respond to a relatively ambiguous stimulus, he will reveal something about himself when making his response. Usually, the subject is not aware that the stimulus is ambiguous; to him, it has but one clear meaning, and he proceeds to respond accordingly. However, in imposing his particular connotation on the stimulus, he has already told us something about himself. For instance, we might ask a group of prison officers: "Why are uniforms worn?" Now, it is not at all clear whether the question refers to the uniforms of the wardens, or the uniforms of the prisoners, or any other uniforms. Nor is it always clear what is meant by a uniform; in some prisons, wardens wear ordinary clothes, made to a standard pattern inside the prison, and these may or may not be considered "uniforms." When a respondent begins to answer such a question, he will almost unwittingly assign a particular meaning to it, and in so doing he has revealed his particular way of looking at the issues involved.

4. Conceptualizing. We can find out something about respondents' attitudes by the way in which they name things, order things or group things. For instance, is Nescafé regarded as part of the concept "coffee"? Are Chinese regarded as "colored"? We can give respondents various labels or objects to "sort in whatever ways you think they belong together," and question them about the grouping afterward.

All these approaches have certain elements in common. They all rely on spontaneity of interpretation, on the fact that the respondent (and often the interviewer) must not know the purpose behind the task or the questions. They all rely on a greater or lesser degree of ambiguity in the task or in the stimulus, so that the respondent has to provide his own interpretations. They should always be as nondirective as possible, so as not to bias the responses. And they all require a certain amount of interpretation on the part of the research worker.

In dealing with projective material, we are almost inevitably involved in interpretation of the responses, that is to say, we do not necessarily take them at their face value but impose some significance or categorization of our own on them. For instance, a small boy of ten was given a set of incomplete sentences to finish, among them the sentence beginning "In the dark. . . ." This is what he wrote: "In the dark I am never, NEVER afraid!" Now it is clear that we should not simply accept this young man's doubly underlined assurances; indeed, we may well feel that he "doth protest too much" and that he is probably very fearful in the dark, though he denies this. We have here a problem in interpretation, and much depends on how far we are prepared to go. At the completely "objective" level, we should classify the response as "not afraid"—which would probably be nonsense; at a more interpretative level, we might classify it as "denial of fear"; at a deeper level still, we might simply classify it as "fear response." The deeper we go, and the more we indulge in such interpretations, the less objective we become—and probably reliability (consistency between interpreters) also suffers. In the construction and use of projective techniques we seek, therefore, some kind of half-way house: a system of coding, scoring, classifying, or interpreting that satisfies the demands of consistency and of objective scoring criteria, yet one that permits us to go some part of the way beneath the prima-facie value or meaning of the responses.

There is often a painful conflict between the demands of objectivity, scientific method and rigor, on the one hand, and the desire to get the fullest flavor of meaning and significance out of such self-revealing responses, on the other. We have not yet acquired methods that will allow us to do both. In making his choice of "level," the social scientist faces a difficult task requiring judgment and sophistication. Small wonder, then, that some of us build our half-way houses a little further down the slope than others.

Types of Techniques

Indirect or projective techniques have long been used in the field of clinical psychology, and some of the devices to be discussed in this chapter are simply applications or offshoots of well-known clinical tests. There was a time when projective techniques were greeted with great and somewhat undiscriminating enthusiasm and when almost every Ph.D. thesis in clinical psychology contained the development of yet another projective test. More recently, systematic attempts to make such tests valid, reliable, and scorable have met with such great difficulties that many of them have fallen into disuse. Some remain valuable in the clinical field where one is dealing with individual cases and where the test-material can be used to gain further insight into the patient's problems, even if it does not meet the demands of objectivity. In group situations, however, or where we have no supportive sources of information, such tests are found wanting.

The attractiveness of projective devices lies in the fact that they seem to go below the surface, that they can give us "insights," and provide us with "revealing" information. They do this primarily because they present the respondent with an ambiguous stimulus, which he has to interpret; in doing so, he reveals to us something of his perceptual world, his fantasies, his characteristic modes of responding, his frames of reference. Some stimuli, however, are more ambiguous than others. One could imagine a gradient, all the way from such highly ambiguous stimuli as a cloud, a blank page, or an inkblot, through rather more structured but still largely ambiguous stimuli such as incomplete sentences or uncaptioned cartoons, to highly structured stimuli that leave the respondent little latitude. It has been suggested that such a gradient would roughly correspond to greater or lesser "depth" within the person; the more ambiguous the stimulus, the deeper the level of personality that it reveals—but the interpretation also becomes more difficult and the problems of objectivity and validity are greater. In social research we have tended, therefore, to work with techniques of moderate degrees of ambiguity; many of our problems do not require the exploration of the deeper levels of personality, and by using stimuli that retain some of their structure we can usually devise ways of making them suitable for large-scale investigations.

Before discussing some of these techniques in detail, it may be necessary once more to stress the need to plan in advance what use will be made of them and the way the analysis is to take place. Will the results contradict other data? Will they be used to interpret the results of more direct methods of questioning? At what "level" do we want to explore our respondents? What relative importance do we intend to give to "rational" and "irrational" factors? Careful pilot work should make it possible to answer most of these questions; failure to plan in advance will often result in large quantities of unanalyzable or contradictory information.

Sentence Completion

As the name suggests, this device consists of a number of incomplete sentences—sometimes just a single word—that the subject is asked to complete, usually in writing, with the first thing that comes to his mind. In clinical psychology the use of sentence-completion tests is well known, and there are standard sets of sentence openings with standard scoring methods (see Holsopple[7]). In clinical work, we usually want to obtain some kind of character analysis (although we may compose a special set of sentence beginnings for an individual case to explore a particular problem), but in social research we tend more often to deal with general attitudes, values, beliefs, and feelings. For this reason, each investigator generally composes his own incomplete sentences tailored to the needs of his particular problem.

It should be realized that sentence beginnings can vary greatly in their ambiguity. Compare, for instance: "If only . . ." and "The nicest cigarette of the day. . . ." It is clear that responses to the first item could range very widely indeed, whereas responses to the second item are limited to smoking, and probably to the mention of a particular time or occasion during the day.

Sentence beginnings can also differ in subtlety. Some of them approach the problem in a highly predetermined way and obtain useful but rather narrow results. Others are more "open," and their aim is less obvious, so that the results may produce more spontaneous and more revealing information. Often it is best to have items of both types in a judicious mixture. Extensive pilot work is essential to make sure that the desired results are obtained.

In all social-research techniques and in sentence completion in particular, the effects of context should be kept in mind. For instance, if a respondent had been asked a lot of questions about his smoking habits and had been given a series of incomplete sentences dealing with cigarettes, he would be inclined to complete the sentence "If only . . ." with some comment about smoking. In this way, contextual influence can be a help or a hindrance, depending on our intent. If we had wanted to explore the respondent's more general worries and regrets, not only those with a relationship to smoking, then the context would have produced a rather misleading restriction, making it appear as if his chief concern was with cigarettes and smoking. On the other hand, we can sometimes utilize contextual influences of this kind to guide the responses into certain areas, but this will have to be taken into account when we interpret the results.

In sentence-completion techniques we are looking particularly for spontaneity. When we seek to test a particular hypothesis or explore a certain problem, we tend to have greater confidence in a set of responses given to items that do not reveal our purpose. For instance, suppose we were conducting an investigation into the fears and worries of hospital patients undergoing surgery and that one point at issue was the patients' attitudes to anesthetics. We might give them a sentence such as the following to complete: "When I see them coming to give me the anesthetic. . . ." Here are some of the responses

I would like to get under the bed
I get frightened
I was not conscious of them approaching me
I was a bit nervous
Glad I know I will be alright when I wake up
I think to myself: it won't be long now before I get rid of my pain

Relieved that the worst is over
I'm relieved
Ten horrible seconds of sheer panic
I twitch, become nervous, although I feel this unnecessary
I am very pleased
I feel very frightened and sick, and hope I may wake to see daylight again
I get butterflies in my tummy!
I just accept it
I hope to wake up again
I'm glad that the awaiting has expired
I feel afraid
A very good idea
I hope they give enough—and not operate before it has its effect
I feel a bit scared
I wonder if I will wake up again
I am glad.

It is obvious that these responses can be classified quite easily into such groupings as "fear," "extreme fear," "relief," "acceptance," "gladness," and so on. However, the item is highly directive, and its purpose is clear to the respondent. A skeptical surgeon would point out that the wording of the item is rather suggestive. We ourselves might feel that the results tell us little about the feelings or attitudes behind the fear or the acceptance of anesthetics and how such feelings compare to the respondents' attitudes to other frightening events in hospital. Preceding that, therefore, but within the same context, we might set a much "wider" item: "*My worst fear is. . . .*" with the following results for the same group of respondents:

"*My worst fear is . . . .*"
being treated roughly
mostly undressing in front of women
waking before the operation is finished
will I have to come back to have another operation?
injections

Arterialgram X-ray
bedpans
pain
what of the future?
being afraid without cause
when I have no-one to come and see me
that my graft does not take well
myself
to fall out of bed
to contract an incurable disease
in my present case: eating
injections
coming into hospital
death
no fears
when a patient dies
helplessness.

There are two references to "injections" (which may or may not refer to the anesthetic) and one interesting response concerning insufficient anesthesia ("waking before the operation is finished"), but, otherwise, there is no evidence that the fear of anesthetics runs high. If there had been many references to fear of anesthesia, it would have seemed more trustworthy, say, to our skeptical surgeon, because here the particular hypothesis being tested is not obvious to the respondent and the results are consequently more convincing.

In the same research, dealing with surgical patients in a hospital, we might wish to obtain some idea of the methods that patients favor in trying to cope with anxiety, in particular whether they find that talking to other patients is helpful or important. To begin with, we might use a fairly "open" item, as follows:

"The best way to overcome fear is. . . ."
say a prayer
don't think about it
ask for help from above

to forget it
pray
to try to face up to it
get to know your doctor
not to think of it
write down these fears and examine them
to admit to it. No-one is fearless
to keep up your heart
to try and believe that you will get better
to take a lesson from others
face it
to have faith
not to think of it
share it if possible
—I don't know
to try and help other people who are frightened
to screw up courage
don't think.

We note only three or four responses that concern communication with other patients. We can acquire a further understanding of people's feelings about this by setting a much more specific item:

"*Talking to others about your coming operation. . . .*"
I don't
you find things out
is not one of my pet subjects, better try and forget
doesn't worry me—I like to sympathize
is very good
helps one to feel happier about having them
no use
does not really appeal to me
a favorite theme after—a time for worry and speculation before
one can dispel fear
they cannot understand it

is quite an interesting pastime and surely one's own is more interesting than the other patients'
is objectionable, unless it helps to allay fear
is a bad thing
makes you a bore
would not interest me much unless it has a bearing on my type of operation
makes you feel as if you have some experience about it
is foolish
I don't love much
is a bit sickening
you should be careful never to suggest fearful odds and to make people hate it
trying to keep them from worrying.

Thus, each type of item has its function, and this has to be kept in mind when the sentence-beginnings are designed. Pilot work is most helpful here, for some items yield quite unexpectedly varied results, whereas others produce very stereotyped responses. After a time, one acquires a flair for writing good sentence-beginnings.

How is this type of data to be quantified? With the more direct type of item the results can usually be coded or classified much as one would code the results of an open-ended question. (See Chapter 9.) The same approach, in principle, is adopted with the subtler items, but a more "interpretative" coding frame is often required. For instance, suppose that we had given the following item (among others) to three groups of housewives—middle-class, working-class, and socially mobile women: "I feel embarrassed and uncomfortable when. . . ." Here are some of the results:

WORKING-CLASS

I am wrongly dressed
I have lost my temper
a visitor calls and I have an empty pantry
my child repeats something about somebody we have been discussing

my four-year-old daughter makes loud remarks about deformed persons

MIDDLE-CLASS

I can't hear properly

other people's children climb on my furniture

my husband introduces me to his female business associates

I am given gifts

my husband and my mother argue

I am complimented profusely

SOCIALLY-MOBILE

In the company of people of a higher wage group

I have to visit my children's school and talk with their teacher

my husband loses his temper in public

I am laughed at

I am asked to entertain strangers

my children misbehave in company.

Rather than have specific categories, such as "dress," "temper," "visits," "strangers," one might try a slightly more ambitious category such as "social defeats." From the few cases we have here, it would seem that embarrassment over "social defeats" is more common among the upwardly-mobile housewives.

As with open-ended questions here, too, one may be led to a particular form of categorization by the need to explore a particular hypothesis or by the data themselves—as in the above example. When developing such categories, usually on a small subsample or a pilot sample, it is often helpful to divide the respondents into the subgroups of concern. We can then start building the coding frame by asking: In what ways do these groups of people differ in their responses to this item?

Here are two further examples in which the results are more readily and more meaningfully classified after they have been subdivided according to the respondents' background. They were obtained in an inquiry carried out among psychiatric nurses in a mental hospital. Observe the nature of the differences between student nurses and nurses with twelve or more years of experience, to the following items (among others):

"I wish that doctors. . . ."

STUDENT NURSES

would sometimes be more understanding
had more time to teach and discuss with staff
were a little more unbending sometimes
were more considerate
had more time to discuss why they are doing certain kinds of treatment
would sometimes show more humor

NURSES WITH TWELVE OR MORE YEARS OF EXPERIENCE

would come to the ward on time
would have patience with their patients
were more ready to appreciate nursing experience
would occasionally discuss patients with staff
would find out from the nurses the condition of certain patients
would spend more time on the wards
took more notice of nurses' knowledge
would discuss more fully with staff.

There seems to be a general desire for more and better communication with the medical staff, but the tone of the younger nurses is more sad than angry and more eager than cross, whereas the older nurses feel passed by and are evidently critical of the doctors.

Our second example illustrates the difference between these two groups of nurses in attitude toward the patients. Here is how they responded to the following item:

"Patients who are incontinent. . . ."

STUDENT NURSES

need sympathetic handling
are often distressed by it

are difficult to prevent getting bed sores
are to be pitied
need careful nursing—I don't mind incontinence
require much help and understanding
present a nursing problem
just can't avoid this
invite examining the reason for this

NURSES WITH TWELVE OR MORE YEARS OF EXPERIENCE

need routine habit training
make hell of a mess
develop bed sores easily
need constant supervision
should not be rebuked but restrained
should be made clean again when incontinent
are prone to bed sores
should be changed frequently
can be trained over a time to be dry
should be changed every two hours.

It is quite clear that the whole attitude and approach differs between these two groups, the attitude of the younger nurses being much more "psychological" than that of the older ones, and the coding would have to take account of that.

Perhaps these examples also illustrate what we mean when we say that projective techniques can be revealing, without the respondents being aware of this, and also permit greater depth and subtlety. Here are some rich, though unselected, responses of university students to the item:

"If my father. . . ."

had more respect for others' intelligence, my mother would be happier
had received a better education, he might have got further than he has
had lived with us during the war, I would never have feared him

had a quieter temperament he would be happier
has many hobbies, he isn't able to look after his family
had not left home, things would have been easier
had loved me less, he would have disciplined me less
had not remarried a woman with a son of 19, life might have been less complicated
had been as much a friend as my mother, home would have been happier still
were not as he is, I would have disliked him
did not adore me so, I should not be so spoiled
had been a rational person, life would have been easier
had not been away in the war, life would have been still better
has any money he buys phonograph records.

This sentence-beginning was taken from the Kell-Hoeflin sentence-completion blank.[8] The authors offer the following scheme of classification, though no doubt different ones could be devised:

"If my father. . . ."

POSITIVE

Expresses feelings of warmth, closeness, love, understanding, pride.

(a) Extreme warmth, closeness, much pride in parent. . . . was a different person, I don't see how I could be happy. My father is a wonderful person and very understanding.

(b) Warmth, closeness, understanding: . . . was rich, he would still be a wonderful man; . . . was not considerate and concerned about his family, my statements would no doubt be different.

(c) Positive feelings toward parent: . . . weren't the way he was, I'd be unhappy; . . . had lived, life at home would be most complete; . . . would relax more from farming, he would be a great guy; . . . were living, I'd be happier in many respects; . . . is given a free hand in his new position, he will do very well; . . . were a custodian, I would respect him just as much; . . . would die, I would be almost lost in this world; . . . hadn't worked so hard, we wouldn't have all the things we do; . . . had not encouraged me, I would not be in college.

NEUTRAL OR MIXED FEELINGS

(d) Contradictory feelings toward father or his behavior: . . . wasn't both fun and strict, it wouldn't seem like home; . . . would just be serious, life would be different.

NEGATIVE

Expresses regret, blame for rigid, strict behavior, lack of understanding, warmth.

(e) Mild regret, lack of warmth, understanding: . . . did not believe in it I sometimes did it anyway because I thought I should; . . . had more education than he has, he would go farther in his work; . . . had been younger, he would have played ball with me; . . . worked entirely on the farm, it would improve; . . . had confided more in my mother, it would have made a happier home; . . . were less serious, I would be better acquainted with him; . . . would have stayed on in one of his earliest jobs, he would be a wealthy man today; . . . was able (health), we could have a very good and prosperous large farm; . . . were alive, things would be more settled at home; . . . had more capital, we could have a very satisfactory business partnership.

(f) Regret, blame, no understanding, rigid standards: . . . grew up, things would improve; . . . and mother hadn't gone on a trip out west, they wouldn't have separated; . . . and I had more nearly the same interests; . . . said no, he meant what he said; . . . had done more with me than for me, I believe we would get along better; . . . had been more considerate and interested, we might have been a family; . . . and I had been closer before his death, it would have been a good thing; . . . could understand what I want most; . . . were a Catholic, there would be more understanding at home.

(g) High degree of sternness, impossible standards demanded: . . . would only listen to reason, he might be less mean; . . . gave a command, we jumped to obey.

FACTUAL

(h) Facts, such as status of father, if no feelings implied, or irrelevant remarks: . . . had time, he would write another book (had crossed out "is a professor"); . . . had money enough, he would be raising more Poland Chinas; . . . had graduated from college, he would have been a teacher.

We have given a more extensive description of the design and the scoring of the incomplete-sentence technique because much of what has been said here applies also to the other projective techniques, which will be considered below.

Cartoons

Here the respondent is presented with a picture or a drawing such as one might find in comics or in cartoon strips, with "balloons" indicating speech. However, one of the balloons is empty and the respondent's task is to fill it. He will read and study the cartoon, then place himself in the situation of the character with the empty balloon and answer accordingly. This technique is analogous to another well-known clinical test, the Rozenzweig Picture Frustration Test,[10] but in social research its use is much wider.

Figures 7–1 and 7–2 are two examples that were used in a study with adolescents. The drawings have deliberately been left rather vague and schematic to facilitate self-identification. As with the sentence-completion technique so here, too, the answers can be classified "projectively," according to the attitudes, frames of reference, and role perceptions that they reflect. In our two examples, the results would show us a good deal about the respondents' attitude to authority, and there might well be social-class or other group differences in their reactions.

There is almost no limit to the types of problems that this technique can be made to explore, and it is readily adaptable to all kinds of consumer research. It can and has been used in ordinary field interviews.[11] A suspected disadvantage is that the respondent may occasionally fail to identify himself with the character in the cartoon, and therefore give an answer that tells us very little about his likely reactions in a similar situation.

Figure 7–1. Mother catches adolescent son smoking.

Careful pilot work, to make sure that the pictures are perceived as intended, is essential.

It is possible to apply this technique without the use of pictures or drawings. The respondent is asked to imagine the situation from the words of one of the characters (shopkeeper to lady customer, "I'm sorry you are returning this vacuum cleaner, madam, can you tell me what seems to be the matter?") and responds accordingly. Even multiple-choice answers may be provided.

As always, before deciding on the use of a specific technique,

Figure 7–2. Teacher catches adolescent boy arriving late for class.

it is necessary to anticipate what one hopes to find out by using it. Quite possibly, there are problems for which open-ended questions would be more successful than cartoon-filling. The cartoon technique is perhaps at its best when dealing with the perception of human relations, such as authority, social class, waiting in line, games, buying and selling.

It would be a mistake to assume that subjects would necessarily react to such situations in real life in the way that their responses might suggest. The responses reflect attitudes and feelings, but their behavioral expression will depend on the actual situation (see Chapter 6).

Picture Interpretation

This technique, too, has its origins in a clinical device, the well-known Thematic Apperception Test. The test consists of twenty cards, one blank and nineteen with various vague drawings on them. The drawings represent, for the most part, human figures in situations that the respondent is asked to describe and to interpret in the form of a story. The stories are subsequently analyzed according to a rather complex scheme of interpretation.[13, 14]

In social research, one or more TAT cards may be borrowed, or more likely some pictures or drawings will be used that relate to the problem at hand. Figures 7–3 to 7–6 are some pictures that were used by Caudill[16] to explore attitudes and social relationships in a mental hospital; the pictures were shown to both patients and staff.

In the original TAT and its various offshoots, the respondent is asked to make up a story about each picture. Since the pictures are ambiguous, to a greater or lesser extent, and since they depict various social situations, the respondent's story will tell us a good deal about himself, his attitude to the world, his chief preoccupations, his feelings toward the most important people in his life, and so on. With the aid of a scheme of analysis we may, on the basis of a dozen stories or more, arrive at a fairly good character description of the respondent, which can be used clinically and which could otherwise only have been obtained by means of lengthy interviews, if at all.

In social research our aims are likely to be less ambitious. We will probably want to gain an understanding of people's attitudes toward a particular problem or relationship, in large numbers. Therefore, we will probably use fewer pictures, and they will be focused on our specific research problem. Caudill, in his exploration of relationships inside a mental hospital, used pictures dealing with typical (though still ambiguous) mental-hospital scenes. His results did not enable him to do a character analysis of each of his respondents, but he learned a good deal about their attitudes and feelings from the way they perceived and interpreted the pictures. In an earlier investigation, Proshansky[18] used ambiguous pictures to measure attitudes to labor.

Figure 7–3. A patient at the front door of the hospital (either entering or leaving).

Figure 7–4. Evening on the open ward.

Figure 7–5. The night nurse making rounds on the open ward

Figure 7–6. A patient in seclusion.

The technique has been widely used to measure ethnic prejudice and achievement motivation. A typical example of its use in the commercial field might be some pictures showing a motorist at a garage or talking to a mechanic, which is a situation that could prompt various fears, frustrations, authority problems, and other attitudes. It has been shown, for instance, that some motorists regard the mechanic as a friend; others treat him more like a servant; and to a third group he is a mixture of a doctor and a magician.

As the purpose of the test becomes less broad and fundamental, so the type of analysis will become more specific. We may no longer require our respondents to tell a story but, instead, ask them to answer a number of questions about the picture or to rate it on a number of characteristics. Such questions or ratings need to be so designed that they will seem quite reasonable to the respondents, yet require them to interpret the picture and to use their imaginations, thereby revealing their own attitudes. For instance, we may show a picture of a baby with a rubber pacifier in its mouth, followed by a series of questions including some about the baby's mother (who is not shown in the picture). We may ask respondents to guess her age, her social background, the number of other children she has, and so on, in order to see whether the practice of giving a baby a pacifier to suck is thought of as something that is done in certain social classes, or only in large families where the mother is very busy, or only by young and inexperienced mothers. Such questions will need to be embedded in groups of other questions, and a control sample should be shown the same picture but without the pacifier.

People are surprisingly willing to guess. In an investigation of attitudes toward types of alcoholic drinks (beer, liquor, wines, cocktails) one can show respondents pictures of many kinds of people, and guesses about their favorite drinks will be readily forthcoming. A picture of a loaded shopping bag will produce "character sketches" of the good and the bad shopper, the bargain hunter, the buyer of convenience goods, the supermarket addict, and others, according to the type of goods displayed. The need for control samples and control pictures must be borne in mind, to find out which cues respondents are using to arrive at their guesses.[17]

Pictorial techniques are particularly useful with young children. For instance, a picture-inset test has been designed to test attitudes to skin color among three-year-old children.[12]

Stories

Stories are most commonly used when we wish to test one or more specific hypotheses. The respondent is presented with a brief account of some events, and at the end he is asked to make a choice, say, between two characters in the story, or to state which course of action he himself would have adopted, or how the motivation of one character in the story can be explained. Often, therefore, the story technique, though projective, resembles the "closed" type of question.

For instance, here is a story that has been used to examine the attitudes of adolescent boys toward saving:

> Jim uses his pocket money to go to the movies, to sports events, to buy candy, books, and so on. It gives him a lot of enjoyment now, but he hasn't got anything put away for the future. Jack saves as much of his pocket money as he can. He will have money if he needs it in the future, but he goes without many pleasures now.
>
> Which of the boys is using his money in a better way?
>
> 1. . . . Jim
> 2. . . . Jack

Note the care taken in the wording of the two alternatives so as to make neither choice overwhelmingly more attractive.

For a more complex and subtle example, we may turn to a study of the attitudes of doctors. General practitioners are sometimes asked to help with all kinds of social problems, which may or may not be regarded as part of a doctor's job. Some of these involve him in a semipsychiatric role. To find out how doctors feel about such problems, a sample of general practitioners was asked to respond to a set of case vignettes, from which the following examples are taken:[19]

A married woman complains that she cannot go on looking after her widowed mother who lives with her. The latter has a hemiplegia and obviously needs care but seems cheerful and fairly alert. The daughter however is tearful and agitated and insists that "something must be done."

1. I would not regard this as a medical problem.
2. I would treat the patient symptomatically (i.e., with sedatives and/or antidepressant drugs) but make it clear that I would not intervene in the social situation.
3. I would feel the most important thing here would be to give the patient some relief from her burden. I might try to get a geriatric bed for the old lady for a few weeks or alternatively arrange for a daily home-help.
4. I would spend some time with the patient trying to bring out the underlying emotional difficulties. If indicated, I should continue with psychotherapy.
5. I would refer this patient to a psychiatrist.

A ten-year-old boy, with no previous history of disturbed behavior, is brought to you by his mother because, since they moved to the district, he has been difficult about school attendance. He has taken to malingering and playing truant and seems generally "nervy." Physical examination is negative.

1. I would not regard this as a medical problem.
2. I would treat the boy symptomatically (e.g., with sedatives) but would make it clear that his school attendance was a matter for the school to deal with.
3. I would regard this as a case for firm reassurance and positive advice (e.g., I would counsel the mother on how she should handle the problem; in addition, I might get in touch with the school principal to ensure proper management of the boy at school).
4. I would spend some time with the boy and afterward his mother, trying to bring out the underlying emotional difficulties; if indicated I would continue with psychotherapy.
5. I would refer this patient to a child guidance clinic or psychiatrist.

Sometimes the story technique can be combined with the use of incomplete sentences. Here are some examples from a story that has been used successfully with adolescent boys, together with one set of responses:

THIS IS A STORY ABOUT A BOY CALLED JOHN

1. *John came to a new school. He had hardly been there a few days when he already made friends because* . . . he was the sort of boy who attracted everyone's attention for no reason.
2. *Coming home from school one day, he happened to hear his father and mother talk about him in the other room. His father said:* . . . "I wish John could do better at school."
3. *And his mother said* . . . "But you know that he is not very good at learning."
4. *In the evening, after he was in bed and the lights were out, he was thinking of girls. He thought:* . . . "There's that horrible Maisy down the road always running after me, can't she leave me alone?"
5. *John had a friend he liked very much. Next day he said to his friend: "I want to tell you something which you must not tell anybody. The secret is:* . . . You know that somebody put a drawing pin on Canary's chair, well, I did it."
6. *After tea, in the evening, the family was sitting together. John was looking at his mother and said to himself:* . . . I think she understands me more.
7. *John thought: I love my parents very much, but* . . . it isn't my fault if I don't do so good at school.
8. *John thought of his future. He said to himself: When I am a man I'll* . . . be blowed if I'm going to do the job Dad wants me to do.

Analysis of the results can take place in two stages: for each item separately and then, in a more thematic way, for the story as a whole.

Pseudofactual Questions

Under this heading comes a variety of techniques in which people are asked seemingly innocuous questions of knowledge or belief, which can be analyzed projectively. A very simple example might be the question: "What percentage of the people in this town are foreigners?" Here, the true percentage is probably quite small, yet there will be a wide variety of estimates, and the size of the estimate has been found to correlate positively with antiforeigner prejudice scores on attitude scales and similar overt techniques.

If people are asked to estimate the results of public-opinion polls, they will tend to show a bias in favor of their own opinions. Estimates of the average wages of bosses and workers or of profit percentages will reflect political attitudes. The analysis of the results need take no account of the true answer, if there is one; the distribution of the high and low scores within the sample can be used.

The inclusion of one or two fictitious items among objects to be rated can be very successful. Suppose we are holding an "immigration" survey asking respondents to say whether people from various other countries or of different races or religions should be allowed to come to this country, or should be kept out, or sometimes be kept out. We might insert among these the names of one or two fictitious groups ("Moldavians," for instance, has been used successfully). When a respondent comes to such a name, referring to a group of people of whom he has never heard, he will almost never admit this. He will feel that a response is expected of him, and he will proceed to engage in argument with himself, along some of the following lines: "Moldavians? Hmm, never heard of them. I suppose they are all right; I've not heard anything said against them. Let's have some in and see what they are like"; or else "Moldavians? Hmm, never heard of them. Who knows what they might be like? Better be safe than sorry, we'll keep them out." Unwittingly, therefore, the respondent tells us what his attitude is and what kind of world he lives in: a world in which other people are dangerous and potential enemies until proven to be friendly; or a world in which most people are probably all right, unless there is some evidence to the contrary. Such projective responses correlate well with other prejudice scores.[20]

The "Guess who" device is another seemingly factual approach that can be used projectively.[21] We may ask: "These are the people who have too much power in our community. Who are they?" or "These are the people you can never be sure of, you never know what they are thinking. Who are they?" And so on. The items may be suitably varied to fit our own particular problem, and they may deal with the more stereotypical level or with deeper feelings. The illusion of a "general knowledge test" can be kept up by having a few items at the beginning and at the end that are innocuous.

It is evident that in many of these techniques the respondents are under some degree of subtle pressure. The "rational" answer to many of these questions would be "I don't know," or "The question is meaningless to me," but since the question is part of a survey, printed on a form, presented by an obviously sane and competent interviewer, who apparently expects a simple answer to a simple question, the respondent feels that he must say something; and since there usually is no true, factual knowledge on which he can base himself, he delves into his attitudes, stereotypes, prejudices, and feelings. In interpreting the data later on, we must take into account the fact that the subjects have been "forced" to some extent.

Apparently simple questions asking for some obvious explanation—questions so simple that they provoke respondents a little—can be most fruitful. In the previously mentioned inquiry into the attitudes of mental-hospital staff, the nurses were asked to imagine that they were taking a visitor around the wards and had to answer a number of questions, for instance, "Why do patients sleep together in wards or dormitories?" Some nurses gave administrative or historical reasons; some mentioned ease of observation of a large number of patients by a small number of nurses; but some said that the patients were frightened to sleep alone or that it was "good for them" to be together, and one nurse simply said, "It is the correct way to sleep."

The nurses were also asked, "Why are uniforms worn?" As we noted in a previous case, this is a rather ambiguous question, since it is not clear whether the question refers to the wearing of uniforms by doctors, patients, nurses, or attendants and since it is not always clear whether, say, a suit of hospital clothes is a "uniform." Most nurses referred to the uniforms worn by hospital staff, but their attitudes were very different; some spoke of the practical side, keeping clothes clean and safeguarding hygiene; some said it helped confused patients to know whom to approach; some said it was a mark of distinction and ensured respect and authority; others thought the uniform was just "traditional" and created a psychological barrier between themselves and the patients; still others said that a uniform helped the nurse to feel secure. When such responses are classified, clear differences emerge in the attitudes of different grades of staff—yet to the nurse-respondents the question seemed not attitudinal but factual.

Play Techniques

With children, and even with adults on occasion, certain play techniques can be used. In an interview, various objects are shown to the respondent to get him talking; he may then be asked to do something with them, for instance build a miniature house with blocks and furniture, which may reveal his attitudes through different spatial relationships (such as the proximity of parents' and children's bedrooms, or the size of one's own room versus that of others). In the psychiatric clinic, doll-play techniques are used both for diagnosis and for therapy.

A useful device, which could easily be adapted to other purposes, is the Bene-Anthony Family Relations Test.[26, 27] The child is asked to state who are the members of his family, and for each person a cardboard cut-out figure and a "mail box" are provided. The child is then given (or has read aloud to him) a number of "messages," such as "I wish I could keep this person near me always," or "I want to do things just to annoy this person in the family," and his task is to "mail" these messages. Provision is made for messages that apply to more than one person and for a "Mr. Nobody," who receives messages that apply to no-one in the family. The test can readily be scored to show affection, ambivalence, and hostility to different family members and can be used with children up to the age of adolescence. Adults can be asked to complete the test in accordance with how they remember their childhood feelings.

Getting respondents to sort objects or cards with labels on them and questioning them nondirectively afterward can be immensely revealing. People can be asked to sort or group almost anything: various kinds of pets, children's misdemeanors, holiday resorts, or chocolate bars; first, spontaneously, in whatever way they like and in an unlimited number of groups and then, perhaps, with some direction, such as "Now put together all those that would not be suitable for young children." This may be repeated several times, with different directions. In this way, we obtain, first of all, the respondent's frame of reference, the way he sees things: for instance, does he group holiday resorts geographically or according to distance, according to the type of facilities they offer, according to prestige associations and likely cost, or in terms of their suitability for children? We also obtain some idea of the importance to him of specific points, such as the name of a product's manufacturer, the intention that may lie behind a child's misbehavior, or the small differences in price between chocolate bars. Nondirective sorting tests can show how often such criteria are used spontaneously as classificatory principles and by what kinds of respondents.

Experiments

Experimental procedures can sometimes be used to explore attitudes. A classic example is the study by Hartshorne and May[22] that dealt with children's honesty. A variety of ingenious procedures was employed in which children were given opportunities to cheat without (so they thought) the possibility of detection. Other experimental procedures have included the use of eye-movement cameras to study the subject's scanning habits of advertisements and pictorial material; a large variety of choice situations and judgment tests; and varieties of the "country-house week-end" methods to assess personality and attitudes.

The field of color preferences and their effects on consumer behavior is one where experimental procedures are often necessary. People cannot accurately forecast their own color preferences, so that verbal or pictorial tests are of little help. Nor are most people aware of the "halo effect" of color, the extent to which it affects our whole attitude to a particular object. It is best, therefore, to set up the experiment in such a way that the subject is preoccupied with some other task and is unaware of the real purpose of the experiment. We might wish to do a color study of detergent packaging, for instance, with housewives. Each housewife can be given two samples of detergent, in packages of different color, and asked to state which detergent is better and why. In fact, both detergents are identical; yet a large proportion of respondents will give higher ratings to one of the two, thus demonstrating their color preference and its impact on their judgment. Note that they were *not* asked to state which color they preferred but which detergent was better.

Sometimes, an experiment can lead the way in an interviewing situation. We may, for instance, make use of the "free-gift situation," which often arises at the end of group sessions. Respondents are under the impression that the session is "over," and that they have a free choice among the products set up in an adjacent room. In fact, their choice will be carefully watched (and the procedure suitably randomized); they will be interviewed again immediately, to see what has led them to make their particular choice. In this way we may bring some real-life attitudes and motives into play. We may discover, for instance, that some people like products packaged in tubes, whereas others dislike tubes, because they feel that tubes have to be gradually rolled up as they get empty; tubes seem to make "moral demands" on them, and so they prefer bottles, jars, or cans.

• *Selected Readings*

GENERAL REFERENCES TO PROJECTIVE TECHNIQUES

1. Donald T. Campbell, "The Indirect Assessment of Social Attitudes," *Psychological Bulletin,* XLVII (1950), 15–38.

   A very useful review of projective methods in attitude research; particularly thorough on "information" tests, guessing tasks, tests of critical thinking, and pictorial devices.

2. H. H. Anderson and Gladys L. Anderson, eds., *An Introduction to Projective Techniques* (New York: Prentice-Hall, 1951).

   A basic textbook.

3. J. E. Bell, *Projective Techniques* (New York: Longmans, Green, 1948).

   General textbook.

4. Claire Selltiz, Marie Jahoda, Morton Deutsch and Stuart W. Cook, *Research Methods in Social Relations* (New York: Holt, 1959).

   See chapter 8 on projective and other indirect methods.

5. H. Henry, *Motivation Research* (London: Crosby Lockwood & Son, 1958).

   Chapter 4 deals with the use of projective techniques in surveys.

6. G. H. Smith, *Motivation Research in Advertising and Marketing* (New York: McGraw-Hill, 1954).

   Includes a review of projective techniques used in market research.

SENTENCE-COMPLETION TECHNIQUES

7. J. Q. Holsopple, *Sentence Completion: A Projective Method for the Study of Personality* (Springfield, Ill.: C. C Thomas, 1955).

   Textbook on the clinical use of incomplete sentences.

8. Ruth Hoeflin and Leone Kell, "The Kell-Hoeflin Incomplete-Sentences Blank: Youth-Parent Relations," *Monographs of the Society for Research in Child Development*, XXIV (1959), No. 72.

   A sentence-completion method for the study of parent–child relations, with scoring system.

9. Eva Bene, "The Objective Use of a Projective Technique, Illustrated by a Study of the Differences in Attitudes be-

tween Pupils of Grammar Schools and of Secondary Modern Schools," *The British Journal of Educational Psychology,* XXVII (1957), 89–100.

Shows the use of a comprehensive scoring system for a sentence-completion test used with adolescent boys.

CARTOONS

10. S. Rosenzweig, "A Test for Types of Reaction to Frustration," *American Journal of Orthopsychiatry,* V (1935), 395–493.

    The well-known picture frustration test.

11. Fillmore H. Sanford and Irwin M. Rosenstock, "Projective Techniques on the Doorstep," *Journal of Abnormal and Social Psychology,* XLVII (1952), 3–16.

12. C. Landreth and B. C. Johnson, "Young Children's Responses to a Picture Inset Test Designed to Reveal Reactions to Persons of Different Skin Color," *Child Development,* XXIV (1953), 63–80.

PICTORIAL TECHNIQUES

13. Leopold Bellak, *The TAT and CAT in Clinical Use* (New York: Grune and Stratton, 1954).

    Clinical textbook.

14. W. E. Henry, *The Analysis of Fantasy* (New York: Wiley, 1956).

    With special reference to the TAT.

15. John W. Atkinson, ed., *Motives in Fantasy, Action, and Society* (New York: Van Nostrand, 1958).

    A series of studies using TAT measures of the needs for achievement, affiliation, and power, complete with scoring systems.

16. W. Caudill, *The Psychiatric Hospital as a Small Society* (Cambridge, Mass.: Harvard University Press, 1958).

    See especially the use of drawings of hospital scenes as projective devices (Figures 7–3 to 7–6).

17. M. Haire, "Projective Techniques in Marketing Research," *Journal of Marketing*, XIV (1950), 649–656.

Shows the use of shopping lists as a projective device, to obtain the "image" of the housewife who buys instant coffee.

18. H. Proshansky, "A Projective Method for the Study of Attitudes." *Journal of Abnormal and Social Psychology*, XXXVIII (1943), 383–395.

A pictorial method for studying attitude to labor.

19. M. Shepherd, A. A. Cooper, A. C. Brown, and G. W. Kalton, *Psychiatric Illness in General Practice* (New York: Oxford University Press, 1966).

PSEUDOFACTUAL QUESTIONS

20. E. L. Hartley, *Problems in Prejudice* (New York: Kings Crown Press, 1946).

See especially the use of "none-such" groups in attitude research, e.g., Wallonians, Danireans, and Pireneans.

21. Theodore M. Newcomb, *Personality and Social Change* (New York: Dryden Press, 1943).

An early use of the "Guess-Who" technique.

PLAY TECHNIQUES

22. Hugh Hartshorne and Mark A. May, *Studies in Deceit* (New York: Macmillan, 1928).

Experimental studies of children's attitudes.

23. L. E. Ucko and Terence Moore, "Parental Roles as Seen by Young Children in Doll Play," *Vita Humana*, VI (1963), 213–242.

24. R. E. Horowitz and E. L. Horowitz, "The Development of Social Attitudes in Children," *Sociometry*, I (1938), 301–338.

Play techniques for measuring attitudes in very young children.

25. C. W. Garber, Jr., "Play Techniques for Interviewing on Durable Goods," *Public Opinion Quarterly,* XV (1951), 139–146.

26. Eva Bene and E. J. Anthony, *The Family Relations Test,* Manual (London: National Foundation for Educational Research, 1959).

    A projective test for use with children (see text).

27. Mortimer M. Meyer, "Family Relations Test," *Journal of Projective Techniques,* XXVII (1963), 309–314.

    An account of the Bene-Anthony Family Relations Test.

ON PROBLEMS OF INTERPRETATION

28. Paul Meehl, *Clinical vs. Statistical Prediction: A Theoretical Analysis and Review of the Evidence* (University of Minnesota Press, 1954).

29. Leon H. Levy, *Psychological Interpretation* (New York: Holt, Rinehart and Winston, Inc., 1963).

8

Miscellaneous Techniques

In this chapter we will briefly discuss a number of other techniques, that may find application in social research.

Sociometry

The sociometric technique permits us to obtain a visual picture of the pattern of likes and dislikes between people in a group. The name J. L. Moreno[1, 2] has long been associated with the development of this technique and with its application in many now classic investigations. One of his earliest researches dealt with a community of adolescent girls; the girls lived in fourteen cottages, and there was a good deal of squabbling and uncooperative behavior both among girls sharing the same cottage and between girls in different cottages. Moreno asked each of the girls to state, on a short, confidential questionnaire, the names of the girls in the camp with whom she would most like to share a cottage and the names of those with whom she would least like to share. By sorting the names into groups of individuals who were mutually attracted and gradually rehousing the girls accordingly, the disharmony in the camp was greatly reduced.

This early application of the technique contains its most important ingredients, though a good deal has been added subsequently. Let us examine it in some detail. First of all, the technique can only be applied to a group and not to single individuals, although we may ultimately arrive at scores or descriptions for each individual in a group. The group should be closed, in the sense that each member of the group can both make and receive nominations, that each member knows at least some others in the group, and that nominations outside the group are not permitted. The nominations express positive feelings of some kind (liking, admiration, utility, wish-fulfillment), and the technique is often elaborated by asking also for nominations expressing negative feelings (with whom would you least like to be?). The number of nominations is usually limited (three is a common number) and is the same for every respondent. The questionnaire should specify a situation or criterion that the respondents should bear in mind when making their nominations; a criterion could be, as we have seen, sharing the same dwelling, or doing homework together, or belonging to the same club, and so on. It is often suggested that better validity is obtained if the criterion is real, so that the respondents know that some social action will follow the analysis of the choice patterns, such as the reassignment of campers to different tents. It is also important that the responses be given privately. (See Chapter 2.)

In its original form the technique is extremely simple. All that is required from each respondent is a slip of paper giving his name and the names of his choices. The situation to which the choices refer should also appear on each slip. If these data are available for each member of the group, and no choices have gone to persons outside the group by mistake, then the investigator is in a position to draw a visual representation of the pattern of likes and dislikes within that group. Probably the easiest way to start doing this is to draw as many small circles as there are members in the group, and arrange these in the form of an oval; now, taking each completed questionnaire in turn, we may draw arrows from the chooser to the chosen—using only first preferences, for a start. (See Figure 8–1.) Such a first attempt will not be very satisfactory, since it will show too many lines criss-crossing each other. The next step will require us to break the oval pattern and to rearrange the results in a more meaningful way. For instance, we might start with the most popular individual—the one receiving the largest number of choices. We may put him down in the center and arrange around him the little circles of all the respondents who have chosen him and also the person he (or she) has chosen. Next, we take another very popular individual and plot his choosers. After that, we

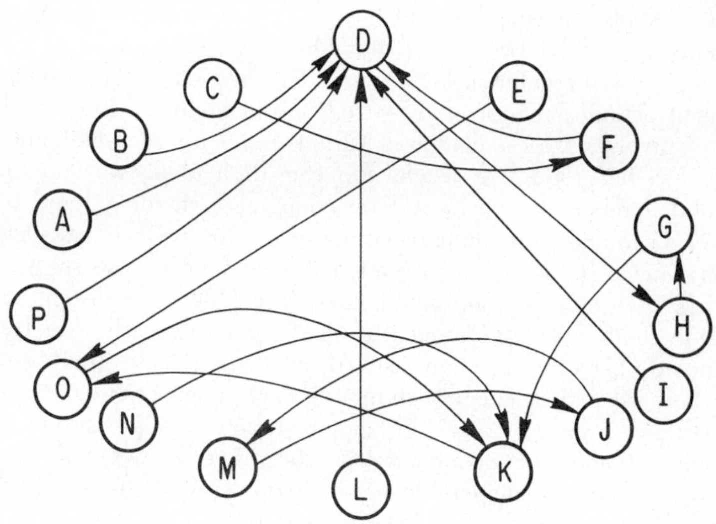

Figure 8–1.

might draw around the periphery those who have chosen one of the individuals surrounding these very popular persons, and so on. Not surprisingly, a specialized terminology has grown up around these sociometric configurations; for instance, very popular group members are often referred to as "stars." In any group, we are likely to find a few individuals who are chosen by no-one or by hardly anyone; they are referred to as "isolates." Then we may find "pairs," two persons who have given each other's names, whose choices have been reciprocal. There may be gangs or subgroups or "chains," as they are called in sociometry—groups of perhaps half-a-dozen respondents who give only each other's names. Of course, there may be all kinds of other patterns.

We will now make the picture more elaborate by bringing in the second and third choices, or as many as have been allowed, and further, by bringing in the negative choices. It will soon become obvious that, even with the aid of numerous attempts at redrawing and even with the help of colored inks and a variety of symbols, the complexity of the data obtained from a group of more than, say, two dozen individuals is too great to permit pictorial representation in this way. This has led to the development of index-analysis and matrix-analysis methods. Index-analysis involves the calculation of various ratios for each individual or for the group as a whole. For each individual, we find the total number of choices and rejections and, dividing these by (N–1) to allow for comparisons across groups, we may calculate his choice status and his rejection status; we may also subtract these two indices from one another, to enable us to distinguish individuals who are frequently liked from those who are frequently liked by some and disliked by others. For the group as a whole, we may calculate such indices as group cohesion (the proportion of mutual pairs), group integration (the proportion of isolates), and other common-sense ratios; there are ways of making such indices comparable across groups (see [3]). If more than one choice per person has been permitted, then the indices have to take this into account as well.

Matrix-analysis starts by setting up a square of rows and columns, with the names or numbers of the group members both across the top and down the side. Customarily, the latter represent the choosers; in the row opposite each name we may now plot this person's choices and rejections in the relevant columns. First, second, and third choice may be indicated by entering the numbers 3, 2, and 1 in the appropriate cells (or some other weighting or notation may be employed); rejections may be similarly entered, preceded by a minus sign, or a separate rejection matrix may be composed. Some of the data for index-construction may be readily compiled by adding up the entries in each column representing the incoming choice-patterns. For some purposes, we now proceed to rearrange the matrix, by changing the order of the individuals simultaneously and in the same way both in the rows and columns, aiming to bring as many positive choices as possible near the diagonal, while moving rejections away from the diagonal. (See example in Table 8–1.) This will reveal cliques, leadership patterns, and group cleavages, but the clerical work involved is tedious unless punch-card machinery is available.

Table 8–1.

		CHOSEN															
		Middle Class								Working Class							
		A	B	C	D	E	F	G	H	I	J	K	L	M	N	O	P
CHOOSING: Middle Class	A				X												
	B				X												
	C						X										
	D								X								
	E															X	
	F				X												
	G											X					
	H							X									
CHOOSING: Working Class	I				X												
	J													X			
	K															X	
	L				X												
	M										X						
	N											X					
	O											X					
	P				X												
		—	—	—	6	—	1	1	1	—	1	3	—	1	—	2	—

The x's represent the first choices of a group of schoolboys, divided according to their social background. Although we have not yet plotted their second and third choices nor their rejections, we can already see the beginnings of certain trends. For instance, eleven out of the sixteen choices are "within class" and only five are "across class"; this suggests that social background might be important to these boys in deciding with whom to make friends.

We also note that boy D is outstandingly popular; interestingly enough, all the "across-class" choices of the working-class boys go to him (although his own best friend H is a middle-class boy). Could this mean that working-class boys are basically more inclined to stick to their own class, unless an outstandingly attractive middle-class person, such as boy D, happened to be in the same group? We note further, that there are eight boys who have received no first choices; are these boys, in fact, isolated or rejected? Obviously, to answer such questions we shall need to plot the second and third choices and the patterns of rejection, and the study will have to be repeated in a number of groups before more general conclusions can be drawn.

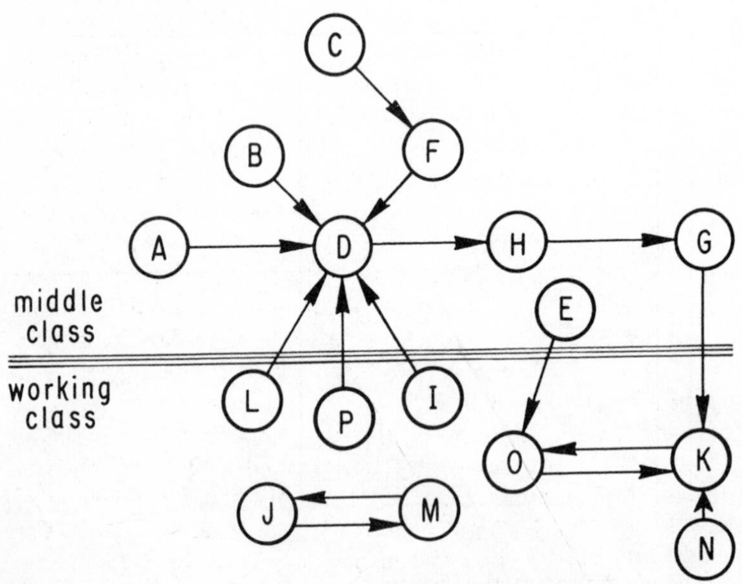

Figure 8–2.

In Figure 8–2, we see the same pattern of first choices drawn as a diagram. The "class-barrier" runs across the page. As we have seen, boy D is very popular, and there are five choices across the "class-barrier." We now also note another interesting phenomenon, namely, that among the working-class boys there are two "pairs" (reciprocated choices). This might, if repeated in further analysis, strengthen the evidence for the greater group cohesion of the working-class boys.

In many investigations we have other information available to us about each individual, besides the sociometric choice data. For instance, we may have his social class, sex, age, ethnic group, and so on. This will enable us to group the respondents in a meaningful fashion and to study the extent to which such a grouping accounts for the choice/rejection patterns, with the aid of matrix-analysis. We can distinguish various kinds of in-groups and out-groups, and we can calculate the extent to which choices are restricted to the in-group and rejections to the out-group and how many choices take place across subgroup-barriers. For instance, very young children in a mixed group will choose each other without regard to sex; later on, boys and girls will only choose their own sex, but toward adolescence there will be some choices across the sex line. Likewise, the degree of integration of minority-group members can be studied and compared.

The sociometric technique can also be used to focus attention on certain individuals. Thus, we may wish to identify the qualities that make for popularity or leadership in certain groups or the effects of isolation or rejection; sociometry will enable us to pick such individuals for more intensive questioning. In industry or in the armed forces, "buddy ratings" have been used to study the relationship between leadership and popularity or to identify people who are powerful and influential.[5]

It is possible to construct a sociogram on the basis, not of questionnaire responses, but of observations of frequency and duration of contact between members of a group. It is also possible to use the sociometric approach projectively: the respondent has to answer such questions as "Who do you think would choose to work with Mr. A?" and "Whom do you think Mr. A would choose?" thus giving us a consensual percept of relations existing between members of the group.

Sometimes, no limit is placed on the number of names permitted; this enables us to calculate a measure of social expansiveness of each individual. We can also vary the criterion, for instance by asking first, "Who are your best friends?" then, "With whom would you rather be, if you had to join the army?" and next, "Whom would you like to take home to tea?" This may tell us something about the qualities that our respondent considers necessary in a friend, in a fellow soldier, and in a visitor to his home and family.

This last elaboration raises the question of validity. Some investigators have suggested that sociometric questionnaires are of doubtful validity unless the respondent knows that the results will be used for a restructuring of the group. Many others, however, have freely used hypothetical criteria, in ways analogous to an attitude questionnaire. An excellent discussion will be found in Lindzey.[4]

The Semantic-Differential and the Repertory-Grid Techniques

The semantic-differential technique was originally developed by Charles E. Osgood and his colleagues[6] as part of their quantitative study of meaning. It consists essentially of a number of seven-point rating scales that are bipolar, with each extreme defined by an adjective; examples might be wise/foolish, strong/weak, excitable/calm. The respondent is given a set of such scales, and his task is to rate each of a number of objects or concepts on every scale in turn. It is possible to submit sets of such ratings to factor-analysis, in a search for the basic dimensions of meaning; Osgood has shown the importance of three factors (evaluation, potency, and activity), though other factors (such as tautness, novelty, and receptivity) may also play a part.

As we saw in Chapter 4, there are risks in using rating scales; for instance, are we justified in basing our calculations on the assumption of equality of intervals, both within each scale and between different scales? Osgood offers valuable evidence on the validity, reliability, and sensitivity of his scales, and, in any case, some of the most interesting types of analysis permitted by this technique refer not to objective assessments by groups of respondents but to the subjective semantic world of single individuals.

It is obvious that, if the semantic differential is simply regarded as a set of rating scales, it can be used to obtain the percepts of various political personages, different national or ethnic groups, or any other subject matter. If we are willing to average sets of ratings given by groups of respondents, then we can compare the results produced by different groups for the same concept or object. Thus, we can show that women, on the average, regard a given brand of cigarettes as less mild (stronger) than men do. If we put the rating scales one below the other and plot the means of the groups of raters for one particular object, we shall be able to compare their profiles.

Table 8–2, for instance, is part of a set of rating scales used to study and compare different brands of cigarettes; it illustrates a simplified use of the semantic-differential technique:

Table 8–2.

Cool	: ____ : ____ : ____ : ____ : ____ : ____ : ____	Hot
Thick	: ____ : ____ : ____ : ____ : ____ : ____ : ____	Thin
Leaves a clean taste	: ____ : ____ : ____ : ____ : ____ : ____ : ____	Leaves an unpleasant aftertaste
Burns the back of your throat	: ____ : ____ : ____ : ____ : ____ : ____ : ____	Doesn't burn your throat
Poor man's cigarette	: ____ : ____ : ____ : ____ : ____ : ____ : ____	Rich man's cigarette
Mild	: ____ : ____ : ____ : ____ : ____ : ____ : ____	Strong
Masculine	: ____ : ____ : ____ : ____ : ____ : ____ : ____	Feminine
Cigarette for smoking at work	: ____ : ____ : ____ : ____ : ____ : ____ : ____	Cigarette for smoking when going out
A quick smoke	: ____ : ____ : ____ : ____ : ____ : ____ : ____	A long smoke
Makes you cough	: ____ : ____ : ____ : ____ : ____ : ____ : ____	Doesn't make you cough

Note that the ratings deal not only with "factual" aspects such as mild/strong or thick/thin (which are often very much a matter of opinion anyway) but that such scales can be built up and used to explore the "images" of certain brands or products ("poor man's cigarette"/"rich man's cigarette"), or of the companies that produce them, describing the latter on such dimensions as "modern/old-fashioned," "weak/powerful," "responsible/irresponsible," and so on. Some investigators prefer to use five-point or three-point rating scales.

Employed in this way, the technique really boils down to a selection of rating scales made up for the particular purpose at hand, on the basis of pilot interviews. In setting up these scales, the location of the positive end should be randomized, so as to try to counteract response set due to position. If several concepts have to be rated, it is best to have a separate rating sheet for each one; thus, the same set of scales can be given over and over again, each time with a different concept at the top of the page. Care should be taken that the two adjectives at the extremes really are opposed and do define some kind of scale or dimension between them. Some extremes have more than one opposite (for instance, sweet/bitter or sweet/sour), while others have none (for instance, burning), so that instead of having two extremes we really have but one extreme and a neutral end (in terms of our example, burning/not burning). It is possible and often useful to obtain responses to rating scales that hardly seem appropriate to the concept under consideration, such as masculine/feminine (with respect to a brand of cigarettes), or rough/smooth (with respect to Socialism). Such scales, by their more imaginative approach, can be used to cover aspects that respondents can hardly put into words, though they do reflect an attitude or feeling tone.

Osgood's work has led to the development of twenty rating scales that among them define the five basic factors involved in the analysis of meaning and have a very wide range of application. These are:

cruel/kind
curved/straight
masculine/feminine
untimely/timely
active/passive
savory/tasteless

unsuccessful/successful
hard/soft
wise/foolish
new/old
good/bad
weak/strong
important/unimportant
angular/rounded
calm/excitable
false/true
colorless/colorful
usual/unusual
beautiful/ugly
slow/fast

Norms have been collected on these twenty scales for 360 words;[7] they should be helpful to any investigator who is choosing sets of scales or concepts.

One of the most interesting aspects of this technique is the way in which it can be used to show the "semantic space" of a respondent or of a group. Simple profile-analysis can show us the different ways in which several objects or concepts are rated on the same set of scales and how two or more groups differ in these respects. The next problem is to show how the concepts are related to one another, if not in all their semantic and attitudinal patterns of associations, then, at least, in terms of similarity or difference. To this end, Osgood uses sets of "D-scores," which summarize the degree of difference between concepts. Let us assume that we have obtained ratings from a single respondent for a number of concepts. Next, we take any two concepts and calculate the differences between them on every scale, then square these differences, add the squares for the entire set of scales, and take the square root of the sum; this is the D- or distance-score for those two concepts. Now we repeat the operation for all possible comparisons between the concepts used. This will result in a triangular table or D-matrix, showing the distance score of every concept against all the other concepts used. Inspection of such a matrix can be illuminating, and if it can be shown to consist essentially of not more than three factors, then we can go further; we can draw the D-values in a diagram, showing concepts that are separated by small D-values closely together, and others at a greater distance. (See Osgood.[6]) A diagram of this kind makes it much easier to study the relative similarity of different concepts to the respondent. We can also study changes over time (for instance, after psychotherapy); if we wish to deal not with a single individual but with a group, then the ratings should be added and averaged, after which the D-values can be calculated as before.

It must be understood that the value of the technique depends largely on the suitable choice of concepts and rating scales. Since the scales will be applied to all the concepts, clearly the problem of relevance or applicability must be considered: can we, for instance, apply calm/excitable to certain foods? Another issue is the scale's factorial composition, which is often not available. We are somewhat less restricted in our choice of objects, which may well be largely determined by the nature of the investigation. However, the pilot work will show whether more imaginative objects, such as "My Ideal Self" or "The Good Housewife" can fruitfully be used.

As part of his broader theoretical framework, Kelly[8] has proposed the repertory-grid technique, which has been taken further by Bannister and others in several investigations and a very clear explanatory paper.[9] The technique is essentially an individual approach, though it can be adapted for group sessions. Its purpose is to supply a "map" of the respondent's "personal constructs" and their interrelationships or changes over time—it is an attempt to find out how each person "sees" the world around him, or at least that part of his world with which the investigation is concerned, such as his family members, certain objects or abstractions, brand names, other nations or groups, consumer durables, and so forth. Repertory-grid testing is not a single test, but a highly flexible technique which can be evolved afresh for each new investigation.

To begin with, it is probably best to let the respondent supply his own constructs. In accordance with Kelly's theoretical approach, *a construct is a way in which two things are alike and in the same way different from a third;* we therefore start by getting the respondent to look at sets of three objects, photographs, persons, and so on and ask him to say in what way two of these are alike and in that way different from a third. For instance, the respondent may be shown pictures of three men, and he may say that two of them are "Jewish-looking," while the third is not. This is how we find out what are, to him, meaningful attributes of the stimulus material; these are his "constructs." Such constructs are incorporated in a grid, down the left-hand side; across the top will appear the "objects," the things, persons, photographs, nationalities, or other stimulus material, to each of which the construct is to be applied, now that it has been produced. Each construct is regarded, not as a matter of degree, but as a dichotomy: as an attribute, it is either present or absent. Thus, in the above example, the respondent may now be shown a series of photographs of men, and in each case he has to say whether or not the person is "Jewish-looking." The investigator takes the respondent through the grid step by step, in each case placing a check underneath each object that is said to possess the construct in question. (See Table 8–3 for an example of this.) Inspection now allows us to make certain inferences; for example, two constructs that go together (both being checked, or left unchecked, all along the two rows) have similar or subsumed meanings to our respondent; in the example below, "intelligent" and "Jewish-looking" go together in this way. Likewise, we may infer that two objects, in whose columns the patterns of checks and blanks are closely matched, are perceived as similar by the respondent.

The most important aspects of the repertory-grid technique are the constructs (attributes) and the objects (cards, persons, photographs) to be included. These depend entirely on the purpose of the investigation and should flow directly from it. Such purposes can, in turn, be classified as being concerned with *objects* (to find out which person, things, photographs, and so on

Table 8–3.

	Photo A	Photo B	Photo C	Photo D	Photo E
Constructs					
Intelligent	—	√	—	√	√
Tough	√	—	√	—	—
Jewish-looking	—	√	—	√	√
Likable	—	√	—	√	—
Selfish	√	—	√	—	—

are seen as similar or in what ways objects are said to differ), with *structure* (to find out how the meaning of different constructs hangs together, to study the individual respondent's "construct map"), or with *change* (for instance, due to psychotherapy or due to advertising). Variations in the technique are often introduced. We may, for instance, ask the respondent to produce his own objects, such as "my best friend," "the most intelligent person I know," "my favorite uncle." Or we may offer certain constructs to the respondent, rather than letting him suggest them; this latter procedure has the advantage that it turns the repertory grid into a group technique, so that many respondents can be asked to fill in the same grid, and factor-analysis[11] as well as other statistical techniques can be applied. Osgood's main semantic dimensions can, of course, be incorporated by offering one end of every scale as constructs to the respondent. When using the grid as a group technique we can simplify the analysis by instructing respondents that they must give checks to half the number of objects on each construct. If the objects are put on cards, the respondent simply has to sort these into two equal groups: those that do, and those that do not, possess the construct in question.

The repertory-grid technique is extremely flexible, allowing studies at the personal level (for instance, of schizophrenic thought[10]) as well as at the group level. It has been employed in such diverse inquiries as the study of social-class differences in language and thinking habits, group differences in value systems, and the perception of different kinds of houses. The assumption underlying each variant of the technique is that we can usefully infer the way a person "sees" the world from patterns of associations between constructs and objects. Kelly's theoretical framework is not strictly necessary in order to make use of the technique but for studies of change, in particular, it would well repay a detailed consideration.

Stereotypes and Brand Images

Stereotypes[12, 13, 14] are verbal labels, used as shorthand in thinking; they are like "pictures in the mind," with ready-made associations that are generalized. Stereotypes usually refer to human groups, such as parsons, plumbers, Germans, Negroes, or mothers-in-law; it is typical of stereotypes that they lead to overgeneralization, so that every member of such a group is expected to have the alleged group characteristics. We all need stereotypes to some extent, and no great harm is done so long as we are ready to alter them or drop them when we are confronted by new evidence. Some people, however, use stereotypes as a realistic guide to action, and this can be very dangerous.

When stereotypes refer to commercial products they are more often called "images" (for instance, the "image" of margarine, or of Scotch whisky) or "brand images" (when they refer to a specific, branded product). Well-known organizations or large firms may also be said to have images.

Stereotypes often reflect an attitude, either favorable or unfavorable. When we are faced, therefore, with the problem of obtaining and studying stereotypes, almost any technique of attitude measurement may be usefully employed.

Among the techniques used to elicit stereotypes are incomplete sentences, grids, adjective checklists, varieties of the semantic differential (see preceding section), photographs, voice recordings, and rating scales. For instance, in the study of national character stereotypes we may use the grid in Table 8–4. Note the last line: "Impossible to characterize." It is useful to have this category, to avoid the criticism that the responses have been "forced." Even so, such techniques can only show us which stereotypes respondents will choose; these may or may not cor-

Table 8–4.

	Americans	French	Germans	Russians	British
Hardworking					
Intelligent					
Peace-loving					
Practical					
Domineering					
Cruel					
Progressive					
Conceited					
Self-controlled					
Impossible to characterize					

respond with their normal thinking habits. As an alternative approach respondents are sometimes presented with the results of a public-opinion poll and asked to guess in which country the poll was taken.

Several investigators have used photographs to elicit stereotypes. In a typical procedure the respondent is shown a series of photographs of faces and is asked to complete a set of rating scales dealing with personal characteristics about each photograph; some time later, he is shown these same photographs again, but this time a label (say, an ethnic group) has been attached to each of them. The photographs are mixed with others, to make it unlikely that the respondent will remember having seen them, and the change in response after adding the label is evaluated. This is a before-and-after design; this type of design can also be used to study changes in stereotypes or brand images, after an advertising campaign or a major political event.

Items resembling attitude statements can be used to elicit generalizations about particular groups. Table 8–5, for instance, is part of an old people questionnaire:[15]

Table 8–5.

	Agree	Disagree
CONSERVATISM		
They are set in their ways		
They are old-fashioned		
They are conservative		
They are out of step with the times		
They like old songs on the radio		
They respect tradition They hold on to their opinions		
They object to women smoking in public		
They like to think about the good old days		
They prefer old friends rather than make new ones		
They would like to live their lives over again		
They are critical of the younger generation		
They dislike any changes or interference with established ways of doing things		
They feel that young parents do not know how to bring up children properly		
ACTIVITIES AND INTERESTS		
They vote for the political candidate who promises the largest old-age pensions		
They are more interested in religion		

ACTIVITIES AND INTERESTS	Agree	Disagree
They like religious programs on the radio		
They collect many useless things like string, paper, and old shoes		
They like to play checkers or dominoes		
They spend most of their time reading or listening to the radio		
They take a keen interest in politics		
They prefer to read newspapers rather than books		
They do not take part in sports		

A similar aim can be reached by employing verbal labels in a coding frame with a free-response type of question. In an inquiry concerning the impact of television on young people,[17] groups of school children were given a list of people (such as scientists, Russians, old people, rich people, Negroes, and so on) preceded by the following instruction: "Here is a list of different kinds of people. How would you describe them to a friend? Finish each sentence to show how you would tell your friend something about them—not what they look like, but what sort of people they really are." For the item "old people" the responses were classified as follows:

The defective: crippled, bedridden, physically handicapped, can hardly walk, not good at climbing stairs, can't move quickly, incapable of earning a living.

Benign and heart of gold: despite grumpiness are very nice, sweet, old souls, generous, kindhearted, sentimental.

The forgotten: lonely, forgotten, finished with, not remembered, never visited, only their memories.

The crusty old soul: crusty, strict, domineering, irritable, pick younger generation to bits, always criticizing, a nuisance, always want attention.

The wicked: miserly, greedy, grasping.

Miscellaneous.

Lambert and his colleagues[16] in Canada used four bilingual speakers to read French and English versions of a brief passage of prose onto tape. These tapes were subsequently presented to groups of English- and French-speaking Montreal students, who completed ratings on fourteen personality traits for each voice. The students were unaware that the French and the English version were read by the same persons. Statistical comparisons of the ratings showed the stereotypes that each group had of the other and of its own group. The technique is adaptable to the study of subtle differences in accent and dialect and of the stereotypes which they evoke.

Variations of the semantic-differential technique (see example in preceding section of this chapter) can also be used to build up an image of a specific product or a brand.

Diaries

The diary technique refers to a daily record kept by the respondent at the research worker's request—not to a document containing intimate personal confidences. The function of the diary is to obtain, as accurately as possible, a daily or even hourly record of certain of the respondent's activities. Since the technique is expensive, difficult to design and to place, and hard to analyze, it should only be used when the necessary estimates cannot be obtained in any other way. Moreover, there is the danger that the respondent's interest in filling up the diary will cause him to modify the very behavior we wish him to record. If, for instance, he is completing a week's diary of his television-viewing behavior, this may cause him to engage in "duty viewing" in order to "have something to record," or he may view "better" types of programs in order to create a more favorable impression.

Most commonly, diaries deal with behavior rather than with

attitudes, interests, or emotions. Mass-media consumption patterns are a frequent topic, along with many other spare-time activities, illnesses, visiting and being visited, the use of various forms of transport, and so on. Diaries cover a given time span, such as a week or a fortnight, or sometimes a much longer period. The limited time span is then regarded as a sample, from which weekly, monthly, or annual rates can be calculated. This raises the question of the representativeness of such a time sample; how "typical" was the respondent's behavior in that particular week? Will the typical and the atypical "iron out" when we collect large numbers of diary records? Is the activity with which we are concerned subject to fluctuations? (Compare, for instance, newspaper reading, which shows fluctuations between weekdays and the weekends but is fairly stable over the year, with gardening, which will show wide seasonal variations as well.) Much depends on the degree of generalization required; the figures may be typical for a given week or month but not for the year as a whole. It is obvious from these considerations that the dates or spread of dates for diary placement should be chosen with great care.

As we have seen, there are various types of questions from which we may derive estimates of respondent's behavior. Here are some examples: "Within the past seven days, how often have you. . . ." "Within the past seven days, have you done any of the following: (Check all that are right for you) (a) (b) (c) (d) (e) (f) ." "How long ago is it since you last . . . ." "How many times a week do you usually . . . ." The type of question used will depend on the purpose of the research; for instance, the second question enables one to conceal the purpose of the study, while the last one asks the respondent himself, in effect, to ensure that his answer is "typical." All these questions present problems with regard to validity and selective recall and tend to yield *under*estimates. Daily checklists, on the other hand, may yield *over*estimates; here the respondent is daily given or sent a list of magazines, radio programs, social activities or other relevant material, with a request to fill out such a list for that day. The diary technique, used with proper safeguards, can yield results that are probably nearest the "true" frequency for a given period, but a good deal of comparative research is needed to make sure of this.

The diary technique is attended by so many difficulties that it will only be used when our requirements can be met in no other way. What are some of these requirements? One of them might be the timing of activities within the day, when an hourly record is needed. Another is the summing of certain activities over a period of a week or longer for the same respondent, such as the amount of outdoor leisure activities, weekday/weekend contrasts, or the reciprocity of visiting behavior. A third requirement might concern such unobservable behavior as dream records. Sometimes one has seriously to consider whether better data would not be obtained by specially stationed observers or by mechanical means, for instance, the daily tasks of nurses, or television channel-switching habits, but of course observational or mechanical methods present their own difficulties. Diaries come into their own particularly when we are dealing with information that is not likely to be remembered accurately for a period of time and needs to be recorded immediately.

The design of a diary form will follow along the same lines as any other self-completion device. We will have to pay a good deal of attention to definitions (for instance in a health diary, what things pertaining to disease, malaise, self-medication or medical consultation are to be recorded), and to the problem of time intervals (daily, hourly, minute-by-minute). In setting out the form, even more attention than usual must be given to making it clear, providing adequate space, and making it look interesting and important. As always, careful pilot work using alternate diary layouts is vital; it is, for instance, not at all easy to find out if the diary form is *failing* to obtain certain information. A frequent problem is the difference between weekdays and weekends in the patterning of many activities.

A diary will need to be accompanied by written instructions. These should generally cover the need for accuracy and frankness, the danger of allowing the diary to influence one's own behavior, and the importance of filling out the diary at the requested intervals and not at the end of the period. Among other topics, we may also deal with the respondent's feeling that a given diary period may be atypical.

Next, there are the problems of placement and collection, and the sampling problems allied to these. Diary samples are often much smaller than usual, while at the same time the difficulties in placement increase the danger of volunteer bias. Many investigators stress the need for a personal touch, suggesting that an interviewer should spend time persuading the respondent, instructing him or her in the details of the recording process, perhaps calling in or telephoning once or twice during the diary period, and personally collecting the diary and thanking the respondent. If co-operation can be obtained, school children can be asked to fill out diaries about their previous day's activities for a week, under the (nondirective) supervision of their class teacher, during the first period of every school day.[17] They can even be asked to keep notes of their activities over the weekend, for entry in Monday morning's diary. Some schools regard this as very useful practice for their pupils. It is important, in such cases, to brief the teacher personally, to maintain interest in the children by means of letters or visits, and to make it very obvious to the children that their diary records are being collected by the research worker and will not be seen by the school.

In some studies it is possible to have one informant in a family who keeps a diary for the whole household, for instance, in respect of leisure activities in the home, or in respect of illnesses and medical needs. Care must be taken, however, that the chosen informant really is in a position to give full information on others and is not absent from the home for crucial periods or unaware of the activities of some persons in the family. Other members of the family should also be warned against letting the diary-keeping affect their behavior.

Since diaries often continue for periods of a week or longer, we have the problem of sustaining motivation. It often happens that, as the diary period wears on, less and less information is recorded. One way of preventing or reducing this "falling off" effect is, as we have seen, by means of encouraging letters, personal visits, or telephone calls, where possible. Another is by varying the colors of the daily pages or by adding extra questions now and then, on separate slips of paper. The important thing is that whatever the method of encouragement, we make the respondent feel that we realize how much work we are asking for, that we are very grateful for his assistance, and that the data really are important for the purpose of our research. Perhaps, in the final analysis, how the respondent feels about the stated purpose of our study will be more important than personal encouragement or financial inducements.

It happens quite often that we cannot tell the respondent the true purpose of our investigation, for fear of biasing his behavior. We may in such cases have to ask for rather more information than we need, in order to "cover up" our real purpose. Suppose, for instance, that we need to know how television is affecting leisure-time activities, especially social ones; this is a subject on which many people have strong views, and so we may obtain biased data if the respondents are aware of our interest. It would be better, therefore, if they were not told that the study has anything to do with television but instead, say, it were presented as a cross-cultural study of leisure. And further, we will want to ask for *everything* the respondents do in their spare time, so as not to reveal our special interest in social activities. This raises ethical questions and inevitably adds to our practical difficulties.

Diaries are among the most arduous techniques to code and process. They provide rich illustrative material but, in addition, we usually need to abstract certain data for tabulation. Let us take a very simple example: bedtimes. If we have a week's diaries for each respondent, then we have seven bedtimes available. We may code and process each of these separately, to show mean differences of bedtimes between different days of the week, and between weekdays and weekends. However, we shall also want to develop codes covering seven days together, for each respondent. For instance, we may want to develop a "regularity" code to show how much the bedtimes fluctuate in the course of a week. These are simple tally codes; things become more complex if we have to assess, say, the "sociability" of a family on the basis of a week's diaries, or their tendency toward self-medication, or the "richness" of a person's dreams. We must bear in mind also that the diary is often part of a larger survey and that the diary results must be linked to other data. Considering, then, the difficulties of design, placement, completion and processing, it is not surprising that diaries are often given to only part of our sample.

• *Selected Readings*

SOCIOMETRY

1. J. L. Moreno, *Who Shall Survive?* (Beacon, N.Y.: Beacon House, 1953).

   First published in 1934 as a monograph, this has long been the chief source book of the sociometric movement and a recognized classic, covering also the origins of psychodrama and sociodrama. See especially pp. 92–104, 284–407, 459–527, and 566–587.

2. J. L. Moreno, *The Sociometry Reader* (Glencoe, Illinois: The Free Press, 1960).

   A major source book of sociometric research. See especially pp. 133–387 and pp. 534–547 on methodological problems.

3. Charles H. Proctor and Charles P. Loomis, "Analysis of Sociometric Data," in Marie Jahoda, Morton Deutsch, and Stuart W. Cook, *Research Methods in Social Relations* (New York: The Dryden Press, 1952) Part II, chap. 17.

   A clear textbook reference showing how sociometric data can be analyzed.

4. Gardner Lindzey and Edgar F. Borgatta, "Sociometric Measurement," in Gardner Lindzey, ed., *Handbook of Social Psychology* (Cambridge, Mass.: Addison-Wesley, 1954).

   An excellent textbook reference on the whole field of sociometry.

5. Robert J. Wherry and Douglas H. Fryer, "Buddy Ratings: Popularity Contest or Leadership Criteria?" in J. L. Moreno, ed., *The Sociometry Reader* (Glencoe, Ill.: The Free Press, 1960).

SEMANTIC DIFFERENTIAL

6. Charles E. Osgood, George J. Suci, and Percy H. Tannenbaum, *The Measurement of Meaning* (Urbana, Ill.: University of Illinois Press, 1957).

Introduces the technique of the semantic differential. See especially chapter 3 "The Semantic Differential as a Measuring Instrument," and chapter 6 "Semantic Measurement in Personality and Psychotherapy Research."

7. J. J. Jenkins, W. A. Russell, and J. Suci, "An Atlas of Semantic Profiles for 360 Words," *American Journal of Psychology,* LXXI (1958), 688–699.

REPERTORY GRID

8. George A. Kelly, *The Psychology of Personal Constructs* (New York: W. W. Norton, 1955).

Volume I contains the basic theory, and the development of the repertory test (see especially chapters 2, 3, and 5).

9. D. Bannister, "Personal Construct Theory: A Summary and Experimental Paradigm," *Acta Psychologica,* XX (1962), 104–120.

A clear, expository paper.

10. D. Bannister, "The Nature and Measurement of Schizophrenic Thought Disorder," *Journal of Mental Science,* C VIII (1962), 825–842.

11. L. M. Levy and R. D. Dugan, "A Factorial Study of Personal Constructs," *Journal of Consulting Psychology,* XX (1956), 53–57.

STEREOTYPES

12. W. Buchanan and H. Cantril, *How Nations See Each Other* (Urbana, Ill.: University of Illinois Press, 1953).

Studies of the role of stereotypes in international attitudes.

13. Henri Tajfel, "Social Perception," in George Humphrey and Michael Argyle, eds., *Social Psychology through Experiment* (London: Methuen, 1962).

14. A. N. Oppenheim, "Communication," in George Humphrey and M. Argyle, eds., *Social Psychology through Experiment* (London: Methuen, 1962).
15. Jacob Tuckman and Irving Lorge, "Attitudes Toward Old People,' *The Journal of Social Psychology,* XXXVII (1953), 249–260.
16. W. E. Lambert, R. C. Hodgson, R. C. Gardner, and S. Fillenbaum, "Evaluational Reactions to Spoken Language," *Journal of Abnormal and Social Psychology,* LX (1960), 44–52.

DIARIES

17. H. T. Himmelweit, A. N. Oppenheim, and P. Vince, *Television and the Child* (London: Oxford University Press, 1958).

For stereotypes, see pp. 253–255; for diary technique, see pp. 72–75 and pp. 417–419.

9

The Quantification of Questionnaire Data

The purpose of the questionnaire and of the survey as a whole is measurement. The final product is likely to consist of a series of tabulations and statistical analyses, together with a few selected quotations from the raw data, and these will be turned into a report showing in what way our findings bear on the hypotheses with which we set out. During the quantification stage of a survey the words and phrases spoken or written by the respondent will be processed; they will be turned into figures and symbols that can be counted and added up. In this way we obtain the entries for the tables that we need in order to draw conclusions.

In the case of precoded questions, attitude scales, grids, indexes, and other "closed" techniques there is little difficulty: we assign, or have assigned beforehand, numerical symbols to the various answer categories, and as soon as the questionnaires return from the field they can be made ready for punch-card analysis or other forms of processing. In precoded questions each answer will usually carry a number, and that number can be used in the analysis. With scales and other devices, some simple scoring operations may have to be carried out, but, essentially, the nature of the techniques will determine the process of analysis in a routine fashion.

This is not so in the case of free-answer or "open" questions, probes, and some projective techniques. Here, the data reach the office in the form of words and sentences written down either by the interviewer, or by the respondent, or perhaps in the form of tape recordings, and before we can start any kind of statistical analysis we first have to convert the data into numerical form. Usually we do this with the aid of a classification system, and the process of classifying responses in this way is known as coding, followed by punching.

Punched Cards

Punched cards are small, rectangular cards into which holes can be punched that can be read or sensed electrically by machines. (See Figure 9–1.) In this way we convert the responses to our questionnaire into electrical impulses, which can be counted or used in other ways by sorters, tabulators, and computers. The holes in each card are meaningless unless we know how each hole is related to a particular questionnaire response or code. Each punch card is therefore divided into as many as eighty columns, and each column contains up to twelve positions. Now, if we have some scheme of card allocation, we will know that a hole in position 3 on column 34 indicates, say, the possession of a telephone.

In small surveys, all the data can probably be accommodated by using one punch card per respondent, since each card may contain up to 12×80 items of information. In larger studies, more than one card per respondent will be needed, and the cards will be numbered, colored, or identified in some other way; in addition, each card must always carry the case number of the particular respondent, which will be repeated on the second and on all subsequent cards relating to that respondent. It becomes extremely important to adhere strictly to the particular card-allocation scheme designed for our survey, since, without it, the holes in the punch cards become meaningless.

Punch-card analysis requires a number of machines and operations, and these will vary with the particular type of installation available. The holes in the card are made by a card punch, a

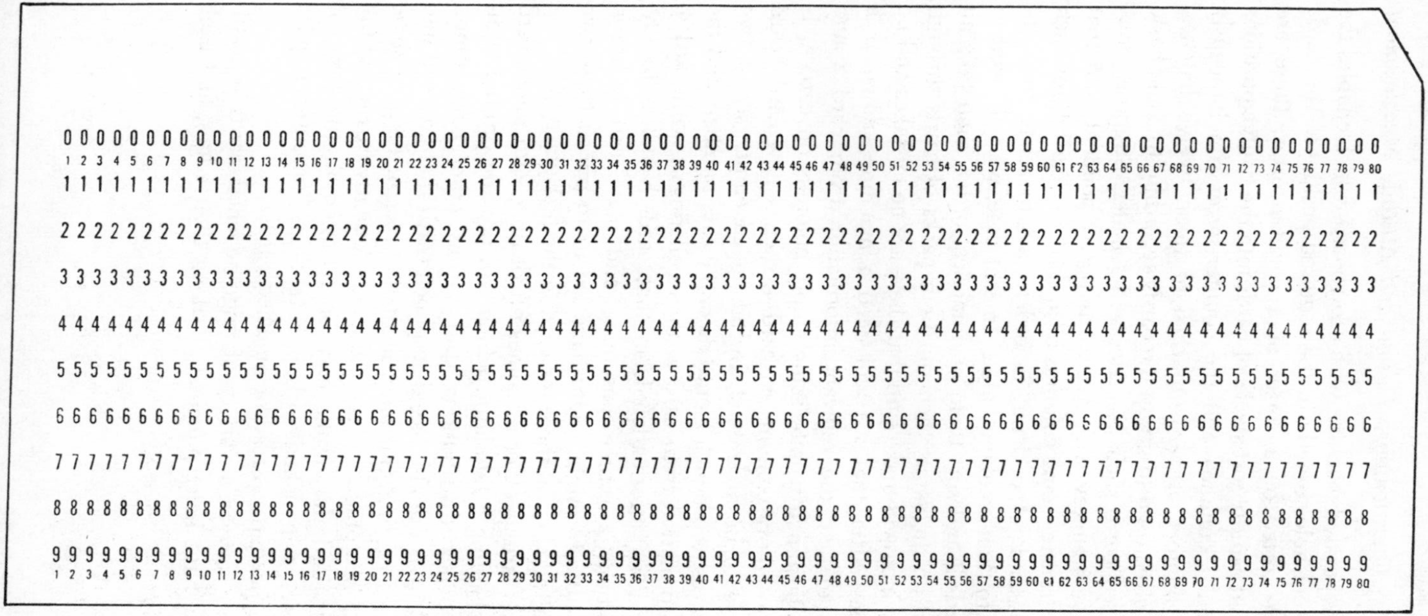

Figure 9–1. Example of a punch card.

small, hand-operated machine with a keyboard, which enables the operator to cut holes exactly in the required positions. The cards can then be sorted on a sorter or a counter-sorter; these are machines that rapidly sort stacks of cards into the twelve positions on a particular column—and the counter-sorter simultaneously counts the number of cards in each of these twelve batches. Sorters are often used to group the cards according to some basic variable of concern, such as males and females. Suppose, now, that we have a survey with five cards per respondent, and that we need to transfer some columns from card 2 to card 4, for each of two thousand respondents, in order, say, to relate their income level to their smoking habits. In that case, we will want to take all cards 2 and sort them in numerical order, then take all cards 4 and do the same, then run both packs of cards through a collator, which will make sure that there are no mistakes and no discrepancies; after that we will need a machine known as a reproducer to take the relevant information from card 2 and automatically punch it onto some empty columns on card 4. If there are no empty columns on card 4, then a new card (card 6) will have to be assembled, by taking an empty set of two thousand cards, reproducing onto them the case numbers and the relevant information from card 2, then collating it with card 4, and reproducing information from that card. Needless to say, such operations are time-consuming and may lead to error, whereas a little foresight might have led us to punch these two sets of data together on the same card in the first place.

There are various other machines for dealing with punch-card analysis, including a tabulator, which will provide printed additions, frequency distributions, and varous other calculations. Many computers are also based on punch cards that are read into the machine and then put onto magnetic tapes or discs or some other means of storage; the computer subsequently carries out the calculations, and the results may be returned in the form of printed tables, or punched cards, or both. Some computers require punched paper tape instead of punched cards.

For small surveys a variety of edge-punched cards is available. These have holes punched all along their edges, and each hole is numbered and allocated to a particular question response. When a particular response has to be indicated, a channel is cut with a pair of clippers between the hole and the edge of the card. In the subsequent analysis a needle, rather like a knitting needle, is stuck through that particular hole in all the cards, and the cards of those respondents who have given this particular answer will drop out. By counting these cards, a frequency table can be composed. We may find it convenient to weigh the cards rather than count them; we may use two or more needles to establish correlations; we may use complex procedures of coding and card allocation; but, essentially, this technique tends to be limited to surveys with only a few items of information per case and with not more than a few hundred respondents. It comes into its own, say, in the analysis of abbreviated medical records; a general practitioner may clip a card for every patient he has seen during a given period and do the analysis himself without the need of costly equipment and with the help of the additional information written on the body of the card itself. Students doing pilot studies may also find edge-punched cards helpful.

Anyone contemplating the use of some kind of punch cards for survey analysis would be well advised to find out what facilities are available to him for analysis, and to seek expert assistance, well before starting the process of coding and card allocation.

Coding Frames

Each free-answer question, probe, sentence-completion item, or other "open" technique in our questionnaire will require its own classification scheme. Only rarely can we use a scheme devised for some other inquiry. Our first task will therefore be the design of all the classification schemes, usually known as "codes" or "coding frames," required for our particular study. Quite possibly we have already given this matter some thought during the pilot stages, and perhaps we have produced some tentative drafts for coding frames. However, the coding frames proposed during the pilot stage will have been based on the raw data obtained from pilot samples, and since the responses of such samples may differ markedly from those of the main sample, we must always construct our coding frame with the aid of responses from the main sample.

It is very tempting to start the design of our coding frames as soon as the first returns from the field work arrive back at the office. However, since these are likely to be unrepresentative, it is advisable to wait until all the returns or a substantial part of them are in. Otherwise, we run the risk that the coding frames will turn out to be a poor fit, so that they may have to be amended, perhaps several times, in the course of the coding operation. It is always undesirable to have to amend a coding frame in midstream, as it were, because amendments produce errors and are wasteful in that they require re-coding of questionnaires that have been coded already.

How do we set about designing a coding frame?

Probably the first step should be the examination of a representative sample of responses. In practice, we select a convenient number of questionnaires (say, fifty or sixty cases) on a representative basis and copy all the responses to a particular question onto sheets of paper. At the top of each sheet will be the text of the question as it appeared in the questionnaire, and below that will be copied all the various answers given to that question by our subsample of fifty or sixty cases, each answer preceded by the case number. Where answers are few, for instance if the question applied to only part of the sample, more cases will be needed, until we have a sufficiently large and varied selection of answers. When we come to design the coding frame of the next free-answer question, we go through the entire batch of selected questionnaires again, copying all the responses to that particular question together, so that we can look at them.

From this point on we must bear in mind very clearly what it is that we are trying to do. By imposing a set of classificatory categories, perhaps eight or ten in number, on a very much larger and probably very varied set of responses, we are inevitably going to *lose information* (see Chapter 2). Bearing in mind the aims and hypotheses of the survey and the particular purpose of the question under consideration, we must so design the coding frame that this loss of information will occur where it matters least, enabling us to run our comparisons or test our hypotheses with the greatest accuracy. This means that our set of categories will not necessarily be designed simply "to do justice to the responses"; other considerations may apply, and compromises often have to be made.

For a start, how many categories should we have? If there were no constraints, and we were anxious not to cause any distortion, we might like to have almost as many categories as there are responses, grouping under one heading only those responses that are identical. This is obviously not a practical proposition. Even if we could afford to follow so elaborate a coding scheme, we would probably find during the statistical analysis that each category contained only one case or a very few cases. Therefore, *the number of categories we can afford to have will in part be determined by the number of cases in the sample and the number of statistical breakdowns we shall use;* a category that will, in the final analysis and after subdivision of the sample, hold fewer than two or three dozen cases must usually be regarded as a luxury. However much it offends our semantic sensibilities or philosophical finesse, we must realize that it is pointless to retain a category that is used by too few people.

There is one exception to this argument. It sometimes happens that we have a hypothesis about a certain type of response being absent or very rare. In that case we might reserve a category for it in order to show just how rare it is. For instance, suppose we had asked people why they had changed from one brand of cigarettes to another, and suppose, further, that we wished to test the specific hypothesis that people very rarely admit to reasons of economy in answering such a question. In such a case we would make up a coding frame suitable to the distribution of the answers we get but, come what may, we should reserve one category for "economic reasons," or something like that.

There are also purely technical considerations that are likely to reduce the number of categories. Most surveys will be analyzed by means of punch-card equipment. These cards consist, as we have seen, of 40, 60, or 80 columns, each containing twelve categories (running from 0 to 9, V and X), and a "blank" position. It is technically feasible to run on into a second column if we wish to use more than twelve categories, or we can use two columns to make 99 or 144 categories (by using the first column for the tens, the second column for the units); we could continue in this way with three or more columns, or we could even multi-punch within the same column so as to produce dozens of different categories within one column—but such steps are not undertaken lightly, because they add to the complexity and reduce the speed of the analysis and often result in errors. Most survey practitioners try to keep their coding frames down to twelve categories for this reason, though they may go beyond this number occasionally. Since we will require categories for "miscellaneous," "don't know," and "no answer," this would leave us effectively with nine possible categories. This number may, at first sight, seem impossibly small when the variety of responses is being considered, yet it is surprising how often one starts off with a much more ambitious scheme only to find that eight or nine categories will suffice after all, with the added advantage of increased frequencies in each category.

These limitations may apply differently when we use a computer, especially one that has a punched-tape input; but card space is even more at a premium when we use edge-punched cards, which are sorted by hand or with a needle.

Thus we see how it has come about that the typical coding frame in many surveys will have fewer than a dozen categories. This means inevitably that the coding frame is relatively crude (entailing loss of information), and it becomes something of a challenge to devise a code that will do its job without too much sacrifice, within such limits.

What other considerations guide us in the composition of coding frames? Let us take, for example, a question asking for the respondent's favorite film star. Let us assume that we have copied the replies of five dozen people, and that we are now faced with the problem of classifying these responses. One approach might simply be by frequency. We allot, say, seven categories to the seven names occurring most often and lump the remaining names in one or two other categories. Or perhaps we wish to expand the frame; we could have dozens of categories, each with one film star's name, if we chose. Or we might decide to group the names under different labels, such as "romantic," "Western," "musical," and so on, according to the type of role with which such film stars are associated. Then again, we may decide to have two coding frames, one for male and one for female film stars. Or we may wish to group together those stars who also appear on other mass media and those who do not. We may classify stars by their ages, or by their ethnic background, or by the number of divorces they have had. So we see that it is often not a simple matter to design a coding frame that will "do justice to the data," and that, moreover, the type of coding frame we need will depend on what we wish to find out. Suppose, for instance, that we wish to examine the hypothesis that men will most often admire female film stars, whereas women will more often mention male film stars. In that case, all we need to do, strictly speaking, is to classify the responses by sex into just two categories, male stars and female stars. This would tell us all we needed to know—though it would not enable us to go very much further. On the other hand, suppose we had the hypothesis that a lot depends on the star's age in relation to one's own age, with younger respondents admiring a somewhat older and more mature person, while middle-aged respondents prefer a younger star. In that case we would need a fairly complex coding frame giving categories of age differentials, up or down from one's own age, and to do the coding we would need to know both the respondent's age and that of his most admired film star.

When we copy out the responses, it is helpful to group the respondents in terms of one or more variables of concern, such as sex, age, social mobility, and so on. This often suggests differences in content, flavor, or expression between subgroups, and a coding frame can be designed to highlight these. For this reason, the copied responses must not merely be regarded as a try-out; they should be most carefully studied and perused.

Usually, the order of the categories is unimportant, and the categories are quite independent of one another. Sometimes, however, we may need a coding frame that is more like a rating scale. For instance, we may use some of our categories to indicate the degree of favorableness with which the respondent views a certain person or object; some responses would be classified as "Highly favorable," others as "Moderately favorable" or as "Favorable with reservations," and so on. Sometimes the coding frame requires a logical structure; the classification of one's favorite subject at school might be an example. Here we would perhaps wish to use two linked frames, analogous to two punch-card columns: the first frame would have the broad categories, such as (1) "languages," (2) "numerical subjects," (3) "natural history," and so forth, while the second frame would be different for each of the broader categories, and would contain the subcategories, so that, say, code 14 might be French, code 26 might be Trigonometry, and code 36 could stand for Geology. When the question is somewhat more projective, we may require a frame-of-reference code. Suppose we had asked a sample of the general population the question: "Why are caps worn?" and that our objective was to find out with what kind of role or group the wearing of caps was most readily associated. In that case our coding frame would not contain categories such as "in order to command respect and obedience" or "to protect the wearer's head"; but rather such categories as "school," "prison services," "police and fire brigades," "scout cubs and other youth groups," "nurses and ambulance men," and so on. This means that the coder has to infer from the contents of the response what context was in the respondent's mind—if possible.

It should also be mentioned that for some questions, typically those used for classificatory purposes, there are probably some well-designed and elaborate coding frames available ready-made. A classification of occupational prestige (see Appendix I) might be one example. When using prepared coding frames one should follow the coding instructions most carefully, and, of course, the original question(s) should be the same, if comparability is desired with the results of other investigations using the same coding frame. Occasionally, too, we may have asked the same question in "open" and in "closed" form; in that case there may be something to be said for using at least some of the pre-codes of the "closed" question as categories in the coding frame of the "open" question.

Every coding frame is likely to need two or three categories that are standard, namely "miscellaneous," "don't know," and "no answer" or "not ascertained." When we are pressed for space, the latter two categories are frequently grouped together. On the other hand, sometimes it is important to know how many respondents said that they did not know the answer, or which ones refused to commit themselves; these two categories may not be just "waste categories." Into "miscellaneous" go all those responses that cannot readily be fitted into one of our prepared categories. In cases of doubt, it is better practice to classify a response as "Miscellaneous" than to force it into another category. One reason for this is that it is best not to blur the limits of the categories. Another is that if such doubtful responses occur with unexpected frequency, then at some point they can be "rescued," by making the decision to amend the coding frame and introducing a new category; in that case we merely have to look again at the responses coded "Miscellaneous" with a view to reclassification, instead of having to recode every response category. Such a course of action should be seriously considered if the frequency of "Miscellaneous" responses rises above, say, 15 per cent or so.

It should be realized that code categories can always be combined, putting together all the male film stars, or all the favorable plus moderately favorable responses, or all the respondents doing manual labor of any kind. This is sometimes necessary when we are dealing with small subanalyses, where the lack of cases is making itself felt.

Each category in a coding frame should be designated in the clearest possible way. It should be described in words, or given a label, and it is always helpful to give many illustrative examples taken from actual responses. Suppose we have asked people a question about the platform of a given political party and that we wish to classify the answers in terms of the amount of knowledge revealed by the respondents. In such a case it would not be enough, to set up a coding frame with categories such as "very good," "adequate," "poor," and so forth. Obviously, this would lead to inconsistencies among the coders and might not be clear to our readers. We have to set up definite criteria, such as: "Very good: gives at least three different items of party policy correctly" together with some examples of actual responses. This is particularly important when numerous coders will be engaged on the same survey, in order to ensure consistency and reliability, but even where the investigator does all his own coding the categories should be as clear and as unambiguous as possible, for it is only too easy to change one's standards as one goes on. It is also necessary that the future reader know what is the precise meaning of each category; often verbal labels are ambiguous, but examples can make the meaning clear.

In the entire coding operation it is necessary to introduce frequent checks, both with others and with oneself, for statistics based on inconsistent coding can be very misleading. Some coding frames are relatively objective and merely require consistency and attention to detail on the part of the coder, for instance the coding of favorite school subjects. Other coding frames, however, require a certain amount of interpretation on the part of the coder, for instance coding the job dissatisfactions of teachers or the reasons people give for not saving more than they do. We then have to face the delicate problem of designing a coding frame that goes "deep" enough, yet one that can be used consistently by the coding staff available, bearing in mind their training and experience. In some investigations it is necessary to check every coded response or to have two coders working independently on the same data and then discussing and resolving the differences between them. The primary aim must be consistency and the elimination of ambiguities; a coder who "stretches" a category in order not to have to classify a response under "Miscellaneous," or one who "improves" a category from one day to the next, or who finds that he "knows" what the respondent "really meant," merely does the study a disservice. The better and clearer the coding frame, the fewer such occasions will arise.

We may now turn to some examples of coding frames.

Here, for a start, is a very simple code that enables us to classify a man's army service:

V don't know, can't remember, etc.
X no answer, not ascertained
0 no military service
1 private
2 noncommissioned ranks, below sergeant
3 noncommissioned ranks, sergeant and above
4 commissioned ranks up to and including captain
5 commissioned ranks, major and above
6 special service troops
7 Navy or air force, merchant navy
8 in service, rank not specified

Obviously this is a fairly crude code, designed for a particular purpose—chiefly, that of ascertaining the highest army rank attained by the respondent. Most of the categories are, therefore, prestige levels, and the categories are ordered, though this is not strictly necessary here. Note that, for special reasons, a separate category has been reserved for private. Also, that most of the other categories cover a range (from—to) of ranks, so that the highest and lowest rank have to be specified; thus, if we had worded category 2 as "noncommissioned ranks up to sergeant," this would not have made it clear whether the rank of sergeant was or was not to be included in that category. Clearly, for other purposes one would code the material differently, in terms of home service versus various overseas theaters of war, or in terms of army, navy, air force, or marines, and so on. For some purposes we can make use of what is known as an "over-punch," say, for all those with any kind of overseas service; such a double code would enable us quickly to extract those respondents who had served abroad. Note, finally, that this is also an example of a logical code, which could largely have been anticipated except for the cut-off points for each category.

Next, we look at a somewhat similar example. Here is a coding frame for the answers to the question "During the past seven days, how many hours have you spent reading newspapers?" in a student survey:

V don't know, can't remember, etc.
X no answer, not ascertained
0 none
1 less than 1 hour
2 1 hour to 2 hours 59 minutes
3 3 hours to 4 hours 59 minutes
4 5 hours to 6 hours 59 minutes
5 7 hours to 8 hours 59 minutes
6 9 hours to 10 hours 59 minutes
7 11 hours and over

Here we have another ordinal code, going up in regular steps of two hours. Obviously, the actual categories have been determined from a sample of responses; how else would we know that intervals of two hours would be the most appropriate or that very few students read newspapers for more than eleven hours a week? A "miscellaneous" category is not, of course, required, but note that "None" has been given a separate category on its own—to show which students had not read any newspapers at all.

In the same survey of student reading habits, some questions were asked about the most recent textbook that the student had read in the college library; one of the questions was "What system did you follow in reading this book?" to which the following coding frame was applied:

V don't know, no answer, not ascertained
X miscellaneous
0 chapter headings
1 skim chapter by chapter, then make notes
2 read from cover to cover
3 skim and make notes
4 concentrate on one section only
5 use index, look up pages
6 read chapter summaries
7 just read conclusions
8 introduction only
9 read various sections thoroughly

We observe right away that the categories for "don't know" and for "no answer; not ascertained" have been grouped together in order to allow sufficient space for the other categories. We also notice that the categories are described in somewhat abbreviated style; this is liable to lead to misunderstandings. Likewise, it is not clear how categories 1 and 3 differ from each other; this kind of ambiguity should be avoided, and it should certainly be one of the points to be discussed with the coders before they start. The code is obviously based on the study of a sample of responses; it is neither ordinal nor logical, in our sense. To some extent, the makers of the frame were also guided by the knowledge of what the teaching staff regarded as good practice in getting the most out of one's time in the library. Last but not least important, this is a multiple-mention code: a student can obviously use two or more of these systems in reading a book, and we must so devise our code that we can cope with multiple answers (see below).

Also in the same study of student reading habits were questions about the most recent extracurricular book read. These books were coded as follows:

V no answer, not ascertained, don't know
X miscellaneous
0 biography, autobiography
1 travel and geography
2 crime, detection, Westerns, mysteries
3 poetry
4 essays and short stories
5 humor
6 plays
7 books about art, music, ballet, theater, etc.
8 theology, religious books
9 novels (see next column also)

NOVELS CODE

V modern, romantic
X modern, historical
0 modern, novel of ideas (social message)
1 modern, other

2 between wars, romantic
3 between wars, historical
4 between wars, novel of ideas (social message)
5 between wars, other
6 classical, romantic
7 classical, historical
8 classical, novel of ideas (social message)
9 classical, other

(N.B.: Classical meant that the book was published before 1914.)

This is an example of a double code and an example of a grouped code as well. To begin with, a relatively crude classification was made of the main types of books mentioned by students—a classification that cannot bear comparison to the elaborate systems of classification employed by librarians but that sufficed for the purpose at hand. It then became evident from the study of a sample of responses that novels were by far the most popular type of extracurricular reading, and so it was decided to do a more detailed, but separate, classification of this kind of fiction. If a respondent mentioned a novel, he was given a 9 on the first coding frame, and coded once more on the second frame. In the second frame we have, first, three broad groupings (modern, between wars, and classical [pre-1914]), and then, within each of these, four categories (romantic, historical, novel of ideas, and other). This fits quite neatly within the confines of one punch-card column; if the student had not read a novel, this second column would remain blank. The relative crudeness of both these frames illustrates once again the inevitable compromise between the degree of refinement in which one can indulge, and the constraints of sample size, number of statistical breakdowns, quality of coders, punch-card space available, and so on. Both frames also illustrate the need for examples; in the actual coding operation lists were kept of names of books that occurred frequently, together with their date of publication and agreed classification by content. Even so, there would obviously be much room for discussion and need for checking and cross-checking. In the end, if it seemed as if a particular book could fit into more than one category, it would be necessary to lay down a ruling, however arbitrary, in order to maintain consistency among the coders.

We now come to a more difficult kind of code. In an attitude study of teachers, the following question was put: "In these days, what qualities in children do you think a teacher should encourage most?" This question is obviously very wide indeed, and the answers covered a considerable range. Here is the frame that was finally developed:

V religion
X ambition, striving
0 no answer, not ascertained, don't know
1 *self-development and happiness:* spontaneity, happiness, curiosity, creativity, self-reliance, active and open personality, originality
2 *rational use of energies for the attainment of educational and work goals:* industry, efficiency, perseverance
3 *active adjustment to social situations:* sociability, cooperativeness, comradeship
4 *inhibitory adjustment to social situations:* self-control, self-discipline, correct manners, cleanliness, orderliness
5 *inhibitory adjustment to authority figures:* respect for authority, deference to teachers and elders, obedience
6 *self-assertive adjustment to social situation:* competitiveness, toughness
7 *goodness, kindness, love, tolerance, generosity*
8 *adherence to enduring values, personal integrity:* truthfulness, honesty, sense of justice, sincerity, sense of honor, dignity, courage
9 other

This coding frame requires a good deal of interpretation of the responses, before they can be classified. The coders would have to think and discuss quite carefully; inevitably, coding this kind of material is slow. Note that often a broad verbal label has been given, followed by some examples. We observe that this, too, must be a multiple-mention code.

Finally, here is an example of a frame-of-reference code. The question asked was: "Taking all things into account, what would be the most likely cause for another world war? I don't mean just the things that happen before a war, like Pearl Harbor, but the real cause." Here is the coding frame:

- V no answer; there will be no war
- X don't know
- 0 military preparations as such
- 1 a specific nation or group of nations is mentioned as responsible
- 2 conflicting economic interests
- 3 power conflicts, tendencies for nations to want to expand, get more control
- 4 economic and social needs of underprivileged peoples
- 5 ideological conflicts, differences in political belief and systems
- 6 human nature in general, man's aggressive tendencies, reference to "instincts," etc.
- 7 moral-ethical problems, breakdown of values, loss of religious influence
- 8 people's mistrust of each other, misunderstandings due to different social traditions and experiences, cultural differences
- 9 other

As we see, here we do not code the contents of the responses, but rather the framework within which the respondent seems to be thinking, his frame of reference. This kind of code places quite a heavy burden of interpretation on the coder and requires a special effort to ensure reliability. The results, however, can be quite revealing and may make the effort worthwhile.

It is worth mentioning that the analysis of sentence-completion items and other projective devices proceeds in much the same way as that outlined above.

For the content-analysis methods applied to written documents, radio broadcasts, case histories, propaganda, etc., the reader may be referred to Festinger & Katz.[5]

The Coding and Punching Process

Perhaps the first thing we should do after designing all the coding frames is to draw a second small sample of completed questionnaires and try out the new codes. After making any necessary amendments the coding frames may now be finally typed or duplicated and, where necessary, assembled in a *code book* that is distributed to every coder, together with coding instructions. The coding instructions should lay down some general principles, such as the way to deal with queries, the case-numbering system, the method of coding multiple-answer questions, and even such details as the type and color of the pen or pencil to be used. In large survey organizations there may be a separate coding department dealing, perhaps, with several surveys at a time, and obviously some hierarchical arrangements have to be made in order to regulate the various responsibilities and the flow of work. In particular, there should be a standard procedure for keeping track of each questionnaire from the moment it comes into the coding section, for it is very easy for questionnaires to get lost, if they happen to become query cases, or part of a try-out sample, or if they get mixed up with a batch of questionnaires from another survey.

Usually, it is best to let each coder work right through each questionnaire, going from question to question and from code to code until he comes to the final page, because he gains an overall picture of the respondent and can check on any apparent inconsistencies. Sometimes, however, there may be a good reason for allotting one question or one batch of questions to one particular coder, who will code those questions and nothing else. This may happen, for instance, if a particularly elaborate socio-economic class code is used, in which case it saves time and reduces inconsistencies if one coder becomes thoroughly familiar with the coding frame and codes no other questions.

Suppose, now, that a coder has read a response, has studied the coding frame, and has decided into which category the answer falls; how should he indicate that classification? There are, broadly speaking, only two possibilities, each with its variations: the coder will put the number indicating the classification either on the questionnaire itself or on a separate sheet of paper, usually known as a punch sheet. To decide which is most appropriate in a given survey, we must consider both the proportion of free-answer questions and the work of the punch operators who will put the data on tape, punch cards, or edge-punched cards. The punch operators work fastest and with the least amount of error when they can work more or less automatically. Any disturbance, such as poorly written or illegible figures, entries left out, many pages to turn, and so on will break the smooth rhythm of their work and will cause delays and rising costs. From the punch operators' point of view, punch sheets are probably ideal: they never see the original questionnaires, there is no text to read, no pages to turn, just long rows of figures to punch, and an easy check at the end of each case. A punch sheet might consist of a sheet or a set of sheets of vertically and horizontally lined paper with the variables across the top and the case numbers down the side, as is illustrated by Table 9–1.

Table 9–1.

Questions:	Q1	Q2a	Q2b	Q3	Q4	Q5i	Q5ii	Q5iii	
Col.	6	7	8	9	10	11	12/13	14	etc.
Case Numbers:									
62700									
62701									
62702									
62703									
etc.									

Each question is given its own column or columns (in the case of analysis by punch-card machines) or its own variable number (in the case of analysis by computer), and the first few places are allocated to the case number. The job of the coder is to fill in all the entries for each case; the job of the punch girl is to punch each row (across the page) of the punch sheet onto cards or tape. If the questionnaire requires more than eighty columns, a second punch sheet is started for each case, and so on. It is most important that no empty spaces be left on a punch sheet unless the "blank" position has a specific meaning on that column; the punch sheet should not be passed on to the punch operators until all the queries have been resolved. Some survey organizations prefer punch sheets of a different design.

This procedure is, as we have remarked, ideal from the punch operators' point of view, but how does it affect the coders? This will depend largely on the number of closed or precoded questions in the survey. If the survey consists entirely of precoded questions then it is usually wasteful to have the responses copied specially onto punch sheets, and in any case, no coding will be required, so that after checking, the completed questionnaires are sent straight on to the punching section, and the punching takes place from the original questionnaires. If only a handful of free-answer questions have been asked, while the large majority are precoded, then most likely the coders will be instructed to put the coding entries directly onto the questionnaires, probably in the right-hand margin in line with the written answer. The punch operators will then punch the precoded questions as before and will insert the code entries where they arise. If there are large numbers of free-answer questions in the survey, then the decision whether or not to have punch sheets becomes more difficult, since their use involves the coder not merely in putting his code entries in the correct place on the punch sheet (instead of in the margin of the questionnaire) but also in the copying of all the precoded responses onto the punch sheets—a tedious operation, which can cause errors. If we decide not to use a punch sheet in these circumstances then it would be as well to take this into account in the layout of the questionnaire itself. Otherwise, the punchers will have to search through a maze of printed questions in order to "pick up" circled or checked precodes, interspersed with entries made by the coders. A well-planned layout, for instance by having all precodes down the right-hand side, can make this work easier, faster, and, above all, more accurate; remember, for instance, that if a punch operator misses one figure all the remaining figures for that case will be one place "out." For this reason also it is important to check all questionnaires as they come in, especially if they have been filled in by respondents and not by interviewers, to make sure that no questions have been left out. Once in a while, usually when time presses, it may be best to have the questionnaires punched twice: once in order to punch only the precoded questions, and a second (later) time to punch only the free-answer (coded) questions, perhaps from a punch sheet; the two sets of data can be amalgamated by the machines subsequently, if that is desired, since both sets will carry the identifying case numbers.

We may remark in passing that use can be made of the identifying case numbers for classification purposes. Suppose, for instance, that we have a sample of children selected through their schools. We may, for example, decide to give each child a six-figure number: the first digit to indicate sex (1 or 2, meaning boy or girl); the second digit to indicate district or area (assuming there are not more than ten districts represented in our sample); the third digit will indicate the school that the child attends (assuming there are not more than ten schools in each district); the fourth digit might be used to indicate the grade or level within the particular school; and the last two digits will identify any given child within his or her class. Thus, case number 279513 would mean, to the initiated, a fifth-grade girl in school 9 in district 7, identifiable as No. 13 on the list of names for her class. Likewise, we can quickly bring together all the third graders, or all the children from district 4, or all the boys from school 81 (meaning school 1 in district 8), and so forth. There is no need to insist on numbering all cases consecutively; if there are only three school districts represented in the sample, then the remaining numbers in that column will remain unused.

In most coding operations, the first hundred or so cases will be the slowest and will give rise to the largest proportion of queries. The coders, though they have been carefully briefed and though the codes have been made as explicit as possible, will inevitably differ in their coding of certain responses, and there are also likely to be weaknesses in the coding frame. From the start, therefore, we must organize a procedure for dealing with queries, a procedure for regular discussion of difficult cases, a procedure for making amendments in the codes or the establishment of special rulings, and a checking procedure. In any but the smallest surveys there should be a coding supervisor, whose job it is to organize and implement these procedures, to do some of the check coding, and to decide whether or not a code will be amended. Earlier, when we discussed the "miscellaneous" category, we saw that amending a code is something that is not to be done lightly, since it will involve recoding; by resisting the temptation to "stretch" categories and by classifying all doubtful responses under "miscellaneous," we can reduce the work of recoding if, at a later stage, we should decide to make a new category for some of the cases hitherto classified as miscellaneous. In any case, it is always best to keep the meaning of each category as clear as possible; this will cause fewer doubts when we come to interpret the findings.

The life of the coder is greatly eased if, throughout the survey, we keep to certain consistencies in designing the coding frames. For instance, we may decide always to code "miscellaneous" or "other" as category 9, "no answer" or "not ascertained" as category 0, and so on. If we use gradings or ratings, we should try to make them all follow the same direction, from positive to negative.

One useful refinement in the coding process is the instruction "record," in the case of certain questions. The instruction means that the coder is to copy out verbatim what the respondent or the interviewer has written, together with the identifying case number. For instance, in an election study we may ask our coders to "record" any references to the Communist party, in order to study their particular flavor more closely. Sometimes, we may give this instruction because we wish to look more closely at certain selected cases or to use their answers as illustrative quotations in our report.

Multiple-Mention Codes

We have several times made reference to multiple-mention codes. This is one solution to the problem that arises when the respondent gives or is asked to give more than one answer to a question. Suppose we have asked: "What do you mostly do in your spare time?" and let us assume that we have developed a broad set of nine categories. We can arbitrarily decide to allot, say, three punch-card columns to this question, one each for the first, second, and third answer. We may even wish to assume that the order of the answers indicates the importance they have for the respondent, so that the first column will contain the most important answers—though many would question this assumption. We will also have to ignore all fourth and subsequent answers, while having to cope at the same time with the problem that not everyone has given three answers, or even two. Moreover, when it comes to the statistical analysis, we will have to treat each set of answers independently, and since the frequency distribution of the first answers may well be very different from that of the second and the third answers, how are we to interpret these results? In questions such as these it may be better to have a different wording, for instance: "What are the three things you most enjoy doing in your spare time? Please put them in order of their importance to you." Now that we have a reasonable assurance that most respondents will produce the same number of answers, we have done away with any possible fourth or fifth answers, and we can feel fairly sure that the first answer really is the most important one. Furthermore, if we find that the frequency distribution of this answer differs from that of the other two, then we can make use of their relative importance to say, for example, that photography usually rates first place among middle-class men, whereas working-class men only mention it as a second or third choice.

There is, however, another solution to this problem that can be applied when phrasing the question in the above way is not suitable or would "force" the answers too much. Let us consider again the example given earlier from a student-readership survey, concerning the different systems used in reading a textbook in the college library. We saw then that many students might use more than one system while working from the same book. What would happen if we coded these responses all on the same column? Technically speaking, there would be no difficulty in the case of punch-card analysis, since it is possible to punch up to twelve holes in the same column, and since the machines can produce frequency distributions for each position on every column. The only difficulty that may arise is the sorting problem: if we wished to classify respondents into a dozen broad groups in accordance with their reading systems, how would we classify a respondent who has used more than one system? Perhaps we could first sort him in with those who have used his first system, and then re-sort him in with those who have used his second system, and so on, though this does become rather tedious. For this reason, multiple-mention codes are best avoided for questions that will be used to group respondents into subsamples. From the statistical point of view, we must find a way of coping with the problem of having more answers than we have respondents. There are no difficulties in tabulating such data and turning them into percentages, even though such percentages will add up to more than 100 per cent. Similarly, if we wish to study group differences we can compare such percentages—but the problem of assessing statistical significance presents a difficulty, because the data are not independent.

Let us take this problem a little further. Suppose that we had obtained, in the above example, the data contained in Table 9–2 for two hundred men and fifty women students:

Table 9–2.

	Men (N = 200)	Women (N = 50)
V don't know, no answer	8 %	8 %
X miscellaneous	10	8
0 chapter headings	11	14
1 skim chapter by chapter, then make notes	18	16
2 read from cover to cover	10	36
3 skim and make notes, skim and make notes	25	30
4 concentrate on one section only	3	12
5 use index, look up pages	30	30
6 read chapter summaries	3	2
7 just read conclusions	36	34
8 introduction only	10	10
9 read various sections thoroughly	10	14

We might be tempted to raise the general question: Are reading systems related to the respondent's sex? However, this would require us to calculate a 12 × 2 chi-squared test of significance on the raw frequencies from which these percentages are derived, and this is not possible since chi-squared assumes that the entries in the cells are independent—an assumption that is not justified where more than one answer comes from the same individual. What we might do, however, is to test each category against all the others put together, in a series of 2 × 2 chi-squared tests. (See under statistical comments, page 257.) If we look again at these percentages we notice a substantial sex difference on category 2 ("read from cover to cover"): 10 per cent for men versus 36 per cent for the women (or, in raw frequencies: 20 out of 200 men and 18 out of 50 women). We can now test all those who responded in terms of category 2 against all those who did not (all non-2 responses), i.e., 180 men and 32 women, with the aid of an ordinary 2 × 2 chi-squared test. This reduces the problem of lack of independence. It allows the respondent to give as many answers as he likes, which can all be coded and used, and it makes no assumptions about their relative importance to the respondent. Note that we do the chi-squared tests on the total number of *cases* in each sample, not the total number of responses. This, then, is a way in which we can deal with the statistical analysis of multiple-mention codes.

Punching Errors

All survey processes require built-in checking procedures, but none more so than the punching operation. This work is usually done by semiskilled girls who have no interest in the survey contents and who work more or less automatically and at very high speeds. Inevitably, errors creep in, and often there are substantial differences in the quality of work from different agencies or other bureaus. Where exactitude is of prime importance, say, for calculating a payroll, it is best to have each set of raw data punched twice, by two different operators, and have the results compared mechanically. Any discrepancies can then be spotted and removed. Since this procedure is expensive and time-consuming, social surveys that can tolerate a small margin of error frequently use a sampling procedure for checking. Every tenth case, say, will be checked, to keep an eye on the amount of punching error that creeps in, and this may show that all is well, or that a more intensive check is needed, or even that 100 per cent checking is required, as above. The checking is done by means of a procedure known as "verifying"; in this, a second punch operator runs each already punched card through a machine just like a card punch, except that it does not cut holes in the card. She will press the keys in accordance with the codes on the documents, and if the holes in the card are in the correct places, the card will pass through unhindered. If, however, there is a discrepancy, the machine will stop and show a red light; the second operator will then have to check whether she herself or the first punch operator has been in error and deal with the card accordingly. By their very nature most punching errors are random, and, therefore, the likelihood of a particular category in a particular code being seriously affected is small. The really serious punching errors are those which are systematic; perhaps a particular question tends to be overlooked more frequently due to poor layout, or perhaps the 1's and 7's of a particular coder look too much alike, or there has been a misunderstanding about questions with multiple answers.

Before the start of the statistical analysis, especially if this is to take place on a computer, a series of checking operations should be performed on the completed tape or pack of cards, to pick up such obvious inconsistencies as a housewife classified as a chartered accountant aged four years.

Card Layout

In describing the various stages of questionnaire processing it will have become evident that they are to a considerable extent interlocked and related to the preceding stages of questionnaire design, as well as to the following stages of statistical analysis. It is no good asking questions which cannot be analyzed, nor can we ask for tabulations of data that are not there or that have been coded in a different way. Through all the stages of a survey we have to engage in a good deal of intelligent anticipation. We cannot, for instance, design a coding frame in isolation; we must consider exactly what we will want to do with the data when they have been coded: how small will the statistical breakdown groups be? How will we cope with multiple answers? Must we keep the code in parallel with the codes of other related questions? Will the code allow us to decide unambiguously for or against the hypothesis that gave rise to the question? Will the code allow us to say something concerning other hypotheses, too? Is the code unnecessarily refined—or not sufficiently so?

One procedure that will help us in making correct anticipations at this stage will be the planning of the card layout, in the case of punch-card analysis, or its equivalent, in the case of analysis by computer. We have to decide where, in a limited space, each variable will go, keeping in mind both the work of the coders and punch operators and the problems of machine analysis. With short questionnaires there is really no problem. We take the questions in the order in which they come on the questionnaire; we allocate as many punch-card columns to each question as its coding frame requires; we add a few columns at the start of the card for the case number; and that is virtually all that is needed. Even then, however, there is something to be said for not starting at column 1 and working methodically through to, say, column 68; it might be better to start at column 13 and work right through to column 80, for, by organizing the card layout in this way, the punch girl has an automatic check that she has neither overlooked a figure, nor accidentally added an extra one—she knows that the end of the questionnaire and the end of the punch card should coincide.

When we come to longer or multiple questionnaires that will require three, four, or perhaps two dozen punch cards, the problems of card layout become more complex. We now have to keep in mind that data from card 1 may have to be related to data from card 3, for instance. We may reproduce mechanically onto card 1 those few columns from card 3 that we require, but to do that we must plan to leave some blank columns on card 1. To do the reproduction correctly, cards 1 and 3 for each case will have to be matched mechanically; so we must make sure that every set of cards carries the identifying case numbers. But how can we tell which is card 1 and which is card 3? We must give each of these a card number, which can be gang-punched on collectively. (Often, column 80 is used for the card number throughout.) Or else cards with different colored edges can be used. But what if we wish to calculate some kind of index on the basis of data that are spread over several cards? To do this, we may have to make up a summary card of some kind; or we may decide to calculate the index by hand, as part of the coding operation.

These illustrations have been taken from work with punch cards, but similar principles apply to any other form of analysis. We have to decide where the data ought to be placed, and to do that we have to think not only of the capacities of the machines but also of the whole plan of analysis.

When both the card-layout plans and all the codes have definitely been finalized, it is most useful to prepare a combined document containing the code content and card layout in full detail. Otherwise, during this and subsequent phases, we will always be dealing with at least three different and probably amended documents: the coding book, the card layout, and the original questionnaire—and very likely with punch sheets and various checking sheets, as well. Such a combined code-content and card-layout document should make it unnecessary to consult any of the preceding ones; on it should appear the original wording of every question in the questionnaire, together with its precodes or coding frame and the location it has been given on card or tape. It might further contain a notation for multiple-mention questions, matched control cases or other points relevant to the analysis, and, of course, it will show the location of the case number and, where necessary, the card number or tape identification. Such a document is tedious to prepare and must be free of errors, but once it has been duplicated and distributed it will repay its cost many times over in easing the work of all those concerned with the analysis of the survey: machine operators, programmers, statistical clerks, various advisers, and those concerned with interpretation and report writing.

The Plan of Analysis

Once the data are in numerical form, we can start with the tabulations. But what tables do we need? In the smaller and simpler surveys, where we can proceed step by step, the first tabulations we want will usually be the "straight runs," the simple frequency distributions of the answers of the entire sample to each question in the questionnaire. If the sample is a representative one, considerable interest may attach to these over-all tabulations, while any further tables will merely be in the nature of elaborations. But if we are dealing with a more complex sampling design then the real interest of the survey analyst will lie in the interrelations between the variables, and the over-all distributions will merely enable him to plan the study of these interrelationships more carefully. At this stage, we can see for the first time how often a much-discussed code category has actually been used, or how many twins there are in the sample, or whether it contains enough users of Product X to make comparisons possible with the users of other products. Some floating errors will also be detected.

We must now turn to our design, reminding ourselves which are our experimental variables, and set up some kind of grouping within the sample. We shall essentially be engaged in making comparisons between fairly stable sets of subgroups on a number of dependent variables. In the case of punch-card analysis we may well decide on some fairly complex grouping, using data from several columns, and then punch this grouping on a separate column on all cards. In the case of computer analysis using punched tape, it may be best to decide on the basic groupings beforehand and punch separate tapes for each subgroup. However, it is clear that from here on a carefully devised basic plan is needed for the "production runs." Of course, the better and tighter our design is, the more the analysis will "run itself"; if, for instance, we have utilized a factorial design then the main classifying variables are known from the start. If we have employed control groups, then a matching operation (which may first have to be checked by tabulation) will have preceded the analysis, and the comparisons will be between experimental and control groups. The same applies to the before-and-after type of design.

After this stage, there is usually a third one, which is much more difficult to plan. It comes after the main results of the survey have been tabulated and digested and have begun to give rise to new problems. At this point, we will very likely want to undertake a series of "cross-breaks," to study the relationships between certain subsidiary variables that were not part of the main analysis. Often such cross-breaks require that certain other variables be held constant, so that we either have to carry out a "within-within" tabulation (for instance, studying the relationship between family size and maternal strictness within each social class in turn) or else engage in the compilation of matched subsamples. This part of the analysis is both interesting and time-consuming, and in a sense there is no end to it, for there always seem to be further interesting possibilities just beyond the horizon. Most surveys are never "analyzed-out" completely; the analysis stops for lack of money or lack of time.

As we have seen in Chapter 1, unless this kind of detailed cross-analysis is planned for from the beginning and the sample collected accordingly, we tend very soon to run out of cases. Perhaps this is just as well, for there are distinct disadvantages in going on a "fishing expedition." The chances are that we will end up with a great many wasted tables, with a few substantial and interesting differences that we will be unable to interpret, and with a large number of small trends that may whet our curiosity; the latter are still more difficult to interpret and are not likely to emerge again in similar surveys. Quite possibly, we will obtain a finding that shows, for example, that men who marry women older than themselves also like their children to learn Latin at school, or that people with strong beliefs in the hereafter look at television less often—but unless we can say how these findings have come about and thus derive a new explanatory variable that might have wider applications, such results are of doubtful value. Up to a point, cross-breaks are useful and may yield important findings, but we must learn to curb our urge to do too many.

Sometimes there may be a fourth stage, which may be contrasted with the previous one in that it tries to "build up" rather than "break down" the data. Carrying out a principal-components analysis or developing a new composite index would come under this heading. Quite often such new variables will then require us to undertake new "production runs," to show how they are linked with our questionnaire data. This stage, too, is likely to present serious problems of interpretation, but at least we can hope to replicate these new measures in subsequent studies.

It is, perhaps, worth mentioning that only a small fraction of all the tabulations are eventually published, perhaps less than 5 per cent. This kind of "wastage" is inevitable; many results can be summed up in a few words, quoting perhaps one or two figures for illustrative purposes without publishing the entire table. This is especially true if the results are negative; if we have a questionnaire with 114 questions, and we wish to find out which of these are related to the respondent's religion, then this will require 114 tables, none of which will be published if the results are altogether negative. When writing a report it is important to ask ourselves constantly: "Is this table really necessary?" Otherwise, the reader will not be able to see the forest for the trees. In some cases, a number of tables can be accommodated in appendixes.

Statistical Comments

Competence in statistics is a necessary requirement for the research worker in any field; readers who are uncertain of their skill in this respect may try the test in Appendix II. There is no shortage of textbooks in this field covering sampling, tests of significance, and correlational and multivariate techniques, and computer programs are available for many of these calculations.

One way of approaching this entire field is to distinguish between quantitative and qualitative data. Quantitative data have additive properties, equal intervals, and usually a zero point; in social surveys age, family size, income, savings, and number of cigarettes smoked per day are all examples of quantitative variables. The statistical techniques applicable to them are means and standard deviations, t-tests and F-tests, analysis of variance, product-moment correlation coefficients, and so on. Qualitative data are not measured along a continuum; they lack additive or even ordinal properties and can best be thought of as frequencies in discrete categories. Qualitative data in social surveys might be the answers to the question "Who is your favorite film star?" or the reasons for not liking frozen peas, or a person's religious beliefs. Applicable statistical techniques are percentages, chi-squared tests and most other nonparametric devices, tetrachoric correlation coefficients (sometimes), and so on. It is very much worth bearing this fundamental distinction in mind, since the entire pattern of further analysis will be determined by it. If we are dealing with a variable which is quantitative, then we must ask the machines to produce sums, sums of squares, means, medians, standard deviations, t-tests, sums of cross-products, correlation coefficients, and perhaps analyses of variance or of principal components; if the variable is qualitative, then we must ask, first of all, for percentages and then find some way of applying nonparametric and multivariate techniques. In most surveys, the majority of the data will be of the latter kind.

It is worth pointing out that quantitative data can readily be turned into qualitative ones (albeit with some loss of information), by arranging them into frequency distributions. Thus, instead of giving the average age of a subsample, we say that 24 per cent were over 45 years old. However, qualitative data cannot be turned into quantitative data except in a very few instances and then only with the aid of certain assumptions. Social class is one such variable, which, though qualitative in the strict sense, is often used as a quantitative variable by making the necessary assumptions about equality of intervals and additive properties—a procedure that some regard as rather dubious. Measures of IQ or any other psychological test results, attitude scale scores, and index scores are all examples where such assumptions can, perhaps, be made with more justification.

In between the quantitative and the qualitative extremes lie variables that have ordinal properties, such as sociometric results, rating and ranking data, measures of relative interest, worry or liking, orderings of prestige or priority, and others. Here we can use Kendall's Tau[3] and sometimes other rank correlation coefficients or, with some loss of information, the usual techniques applicable to qualitative data (percentages and chi-squared tests). This latter approach is often resorted to, for the sake of uniformity and simplicity, though it takes no account of the ordering of the classes.

Many types of experimental design, including the factorial design, have been developed in relation to quantitative techniques of analysis, in particular analysis of variance, and to employ these designs in relation to the usual survey data, which tend to be qualitative, requires some ingenuity. Fortunately, a great deal can be done with the aid of simple percentages. For many surveys it is worthwhile obtaining or calculating percentage conversion tables for the subsamples that occur most frequently (for instance, for a cell and all possible combinations of cells of a factorial design) and designing special analysis sheets showing the percentages within the various subsamples—unless, of course, all this can be obtained directly in the form of a computer printout. Suppose we require breakdowns by sex, age, and social class; we might set up the following analysis sheet shown in Figure 9–2.

We start by filling in the cells, showing the frequency with which each subsample has given response x to question q (say, voting preference for a particular party). Since we know the total number of cases for each cell, we can calculate percentages within each cell. We next proceed to compute the various marginal percentages (each time by recalculating the percentages to the new base and not by averaging them). Now we have a set of figures from which we can, by inspection, derive some tentative conclusions, for instance that voting preference for this party seems to be associated with lower social class for males, but not for females; or that younger women tend to prefer this party in every social class. Note that we have here the analysis of just one category from a coding frame; for a code with twelve categories we must do this analysis twelve times over, in order to understand the pattern of response to a single question. Obviously, such analysis sheets will vary from survey to survey;

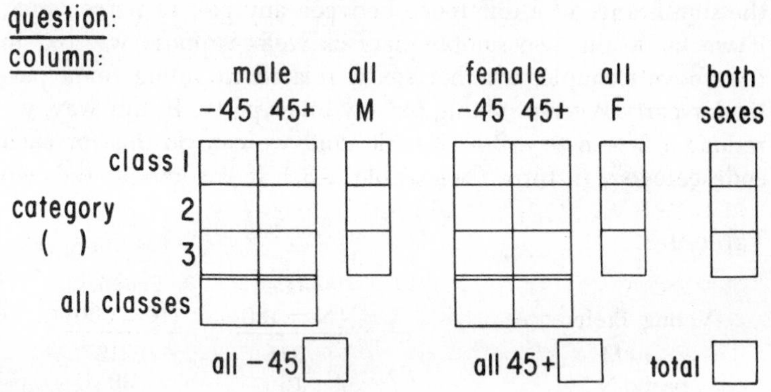

Figure 9–2.

a before-and-after design, for instance, would need quite a different pattern.

The most readily applicable test of statistical significance to data of this kind is the chi-squared test, which has been most helpfully discussed by Maxwell[2] but is usually outlined in almost any textbook of elementary statistics. This test is applicable to 2×2, $2 \times n$, or $m \times n$ tables, any of which may be used in the above example, depending on the issue to which we seek an answer. If we are interested in the over-all relationship between voting and sex, voting and age, voting and class, or voting and any combination of these three variables, then we should calculate $m \times n$ or $2 \times n$ chi-squared tests (assuming that we are dealing with categories that are mutually exclusive and that do not contain multiple-mention responses). If the particular over-all relationship that we have tested is statistically significant, then we may wish to go further and test for significance in relation to a particular category or party, for instance the relationship between age and voting for a particular party M. The reasoning here is analogous to the use of t-tests within an analysis of variance.

This kind of internal chi-squared analysis usually amounts to testing the differences between two percentages. Chi-squared is not normally applicable to percentages; however, with the aid of a nomograph (see Appendix III) it becomes possible to test the significance of a difference between any pair of percentages, if we know the two sample sizes as well. Suppose we ask, in the above example, whether sex is related to voting for a particular party P versus voting for any other party. In this way, we reduce a 2 × n to a 2 × 2 table, and we can do this for each code category in turn. (See Table 9–3.) If we look at the two

Table 9–3.

Voting Preference	Males (N = 180)	Females (N = 300)
party M	34%	31%
party N	16	30
party O	25	19
party P	10	5
party Q	8	8
no answer	4	3
don't know	3	4
	100%	100%

percentages for party N (16 per cent and 30 per cent) we are, by implication, also considering their complements up to 100 per cent (see Table 9–4), and since we know the two sample sizes,

Table 9–4.

	Males	Females
party N	16%	30%
non-N voters	84%	70%
	100%	100%

we can convert these figures into the usual 2 × 2 contingency table (see Table 9–5), though if we have the aid of the Zubin nomograph this will not be necessary. We can proceed in this way, testing the pairs of percentages for any of the parties against all those who do not vote for that party or, more generally, all those who have not given that particular response category. We can also amalgamate two or more categories; in the above example, if we assume that party M and party O are left-wing

Table 9–5.

	Males	Females
party N	29	90
non-N voters	151	210
	180	300

parties, then we can add the percentages for these two parties together, to test the hypothesis that men more often vote for left-wing parties (59 per cent versus 50 per cent). If we now return to the analysis sheet previously outlined, we can see that most of the percentage entries will be so set out that they can be compared and their significance indicated against all the remaining categories combined. Any analysis sheet will have four or five such sets of cells on one page, covering four or five code categories, so that the combining of adjacent categories is quite easy. Such combined percentages can be set out and tested for significance in the same way. Finney[4] has brought out a set of tables for chi-squared tests of small frequencies.

One other general point first mentioned in Chapter 3 is worth making here. Suppose that we have asked a number of questions in an effort to measure attitude to saving, and suppose further that we now find 22 per cent of middle-class respondents to be "in favor" of saving on our first question. This figure, by itself, is very nearly meaningless. It only acquires meaning when we can compare it, say, to a response of 32 per cent "in favor" among working-class respondents. But perhaps, if we look at a differently worded question on attitude to savings we will find a different result. Perhaps now we will find 28 per cent, or 50 per cent, of our middle-class respondents giving a favorable reply. Again, let us look at the working-class figures; quite likely we will find them running at around 40 per cent, or 60 per cent, for that question. In other words, it is often impossible to say, in absolute terms, how many respondents have a particular attitude to a given extent, because so much depends on the wording of the question; nevertheless, the *relative* differences (in terms of class, age, sex, or some other variable of concern) may well be quite stable and consistent, no matter how the question is phrased. In social research we have few absolute measures, but relative differences are well worth having if they are consistent, since they can give us an indication of relationships between variables.

• *Selected Readings*

1. Claire Selltiz, Marie Jahoda, Morton Deutsch, and Stuart W. Cook, eds., *Research Methods in Social Relations* (New York: Holt, 1959).

   See chapter 11 on coding and statistical analysis.

2. A. E. Maxwell, *Analyzing Qualitative Data* (London: Methuen, 1961).

   See especially chapters 1 to 7 on chi-squared tests and chapter 8 on rank correlations.

3. M. G. Kendall, *Rank Correlation Methods* (London: Griffin, 1948).

4. D. J. Finney, "The Fisher-Yates Test of Significance in 2 × 2 Contingency Tables," *Biometrika,* XXXV (1948), 145–156.

   For small numbers of cases.

5. Leon Festinger and David Katz, eds., *Research Methods in the Behavioral Sciences* (New York: Dryden Press, 1953).

   See chapter 10 for content analysis methods.

ELEMENTARY STATISTICAL TEXTS

6. Quinn McNemar, *Psychological Statistics* (New York: Wiley, 1955).

7. J. P. Guilford, *Psychomatic Methods* (New York: McGraw-Hill, 1954).

8. Palmer O. Johnson, *Statistical Methods in Research* (New York: Prentice-Hall, 1949).

9. E. F. Lindquist, *Statistical Analysis in Educational Research* (New York: Houghton Mifflin, 1940).

10. Celeste McCollough and Loche Van Atta, *Statistical Concepts* (New York: McGraw-Hill, 1963).

    A useful programmed learning text.

APPENDICES

I

Scales of Occupational Prestige

Since a man's occupation is, in Westernized societies, the most important single determinant of his social status, social-research workers often use it as an index of social class or prestige level. It becomes important, therefore, to have a widely accepted scheme by means of which most, if not all, jobs can be classified according to their status in the community. There are many such schemes using different classes and subdivisions and finding favor among some research workers rather than others. They raise some difficult problems concerning the nature and origins of occupational prestige and its relation to social class.

The first example presented here is a socioeconomic index for occupation based on research work done by NORC on part of the American census classification. For details of the construction of the scale see A. J. Reiss, *Occupations and Social Status* (New York: The Free Press of Glencoe, 1961). The occupations are grouped under various headings and the index figures indicate their respective prestige ratings. Anyone proposing to use the scale should read it through first to note the various headings (e.g., the various types of apprentices), the various occupational groupings (e.g., "operatives and kindred workers"), and the form which the nomenclature takes (e.g., launderesses, private household, living out). Further details, including the proportion of the working population in each occupational group, can be found in Reiss's book.

Socioeconomic Index for Occupations in the Detailed Classification of the Bureau of the Census: 1950[1]

Occupations, by Major Occupation Group	Socio-economic Index	Occupations, by Major Occupation Group	Socio-economic Index
Professional, Technical, and Kindred Workers			
Accountants and auditors	78	Entertainers	31
Actors and actresses	60	Farm- and home-management advisors	83
Airplane pilots and navigators	79	Foresters and conservationists	48
Architects	90	Funeral directors and embalmers	59
Artists and art teachers	67	Lawyers and judges	93
Athletes	52	Librarians	60
Authors	76	Musicians and music teachers	52
Chemists	79	Natural scientists	80
Chiropractors	75	Nurses, professional	46
Clergymen	52	Nurses, student professional	51
College presidents, professors, and instructors	84	Optometrists	79
Dancers and dancing teachers	45	Osteopaths	96
Dentists	96	Personnel and labor-relations workers	84
Designers	73	Pharmacists	82
Dieticians and nutritionists	39	Photographers	50
Draftsmen	67	Physicians and surgeons	92
Editors and reporters	82	Radio operators	69
Engineers, technical	85	Recreation and group workers	67
Aeronautical	87	Religious workers	56
Chemical	90	Social and welfare workers, except group	64
Civil	84	Social scientists	81
Electrical	84	Sports instructors and officials	64
Industrial	86		
Mechanical	82		
Metallurgical, and metallurgists	82		
Mining	85		
Not elsewhere classified	87		

[1] Reprinted with permission of The Free Press from *Occupations and Social Status* by A. J. Reiss. Copyright © 1961, The Free Press of Glencoe, Inc.

Occupations, by Major Occupation Group	Socio-economic Index
Surveyors	48
Teachers	72
Technicians, medical and dental	48
Technicians, testing	53
Technicians	62
Therapists and healers	58
Veterinarians	78
Professional, technical, and kindred workers	65
Farmers and Farm Managers	
Farmers (owners and tenants)	14
Farm managers	36
Managers, Officials, and Proprietors, Exc. Farm	
Buyers and department heads, store	72
Buyers and shippers, farm products	33
Conductors, railroad	58
Credit men	74
Floormen and floor managers, store	50
Inspectors, public administration	63
Federal public administration and postal service	72
State public administration	54
Local public administration	56
Managers and superintendents, building	32
Officers, pilots, pursers, and engineers, ship	54
Officials and administrators public administration	66
Federal public administration and postal service	84
State public administration	66
Local public administration	54
Officials, lodge, society, union, etc.	58
Postmasters	60
Purchasing agents and buyers	77
Managers, officials, and proprietors—salaried	68
Construction	60
Manufacturing	79
Transportation	71
Telecommunications, and utilities and sanitary services	76
Wholesale trade	70
Retail trade	56
Food- and dairy-products stores, and milk retailing	50
General merchandise and five- and ten-cent stores	68
Apparel and accessories stores	69
Furniture, home furnishings, and equipment stores	68
Motor vehicles and accessories retailing	65
Gasoline service stations	31
Eating and drinking places	39

Occupations, by Major Occupation Group	Socio-economic Index
Hardware, farm implement, and building material, retail	64
Other retail trade	59
Banking and other finance	85
Insurance and real estate	84
Business services	80
Automobile repair services and garages	47
Miscellaneous repair services	53
Personal services	50
All other industries (incl. not reported)	62
Managers, officials, and proprietors—self-employed	48
Construction	51
Manufacturing	61
Transportation	43
Telecommunications and utilities and sanitary services	44
Wholesale trade	59
Retail trade	43
Food- and dairy-products stores, and milk retailing	33
General merchandise and five- and ten-cent stores	47
Apparel and accessories stores	65
Furniture, home furnishings, and equipment stores	59
Motor vehicles and accessories retailing	70
Gasoline service stations	33
Eating and drinking places	37
Hardware, farm implement, and building material, retail	61
Other retail trade	49
Banking and other finance	85
Insurance and real estate	76
Business services	67
Automobile repair services and garages	36
Miscellaneous repair services	34
Personal services	41
All other industries (incl. not reported)	49
Clerical and Kindred Workers	
Agents	68
Attendants and assistants, library	44
Attendants, physician's and dentist's office	38
Baggagemen, transportation	25
Bank tellers	52
Bookkeepers	51
Cashiers	44
Collectors, bill and account	39
Dispatchers and starters, vehicle	40
Express messengers and railway mail clerks	67
Mail-carriers	53
Messengers and office boys	28
Office-machine operators	45
Shipping and receiving clerks	22
Stenographers, typists, and secretaries	61

Occupations, by Major Occupation Group	Socio-economic Index
Telegraph messengers	22
Telegraph operators	47
Telephone operators	45
Ticket, station, and express agents	60
Clerical and kindred workers	44
Sales Workers	
Advertising agents and salesmen	66
Auctioneers	40
Demonstrators	35
Hucksters and peddlers	8
Insurance agents and brokers	66
Newsboys	27
Real-estate agents and brokers	62
Stock and bond salesmen	73
Salesmen and clerks	47
Manufacturing	65
Wholesale trade	61
Retail trade	39
Other industries (incl. not reported)	50
Craftsmen, Foremen, and Kindred Workers	
Bakers	22
Blacksmiths	16
Boilermakers	33
Bookbinders	39
Brickmasons, stonemasons, and tile-setters	27
Cabinetmakers	23
Carpenters	19
Cement and concrete finishers	19
Compositors and typesetters	52
Cranemen, derickmen, and hoistmen	21

Occupations, by Major Occupation Group	Socio-economic Index
Decorators and window-dressers	40
Electricians	44
Electrotypers and stereotypers	55
Engravers, except photoengravers	47
Excavating, grading, and road-machinery operators	24
Foremen	49
Construction	40
Manufacturing	53
Metal industries	54
Machinery, including electrical	60
Transportation equipment	66
Other durable goods	41
Textiles, textile products, and apparel	39
Other nondurable goods (incl. not specified mfg.)	53
Railroads and railway express service	36
Transportation, except railroad	45
Telecommunications, and utilities and sanitary services	56
Other industries (incl. not reported)	44
Forgemen and hammermen	23
Furriers	39
Glaziers	26
Heat treaters, annealers, and temperers	22
Inspectors, scalers, and graders, log and lumber	23

Occupations, by Major Occupation Group	Socio-economic Index
Inspectors	41
Construction	46
Railroads and railway express service	41
Transport, exc. r.r., communication, and other public util.	45
Other industries (incl. not reported)	38
Jewelers, watchmakers, goldsmiths, and silversmiths	36
Job-setters, metal	28
Linemen and servicemen, telegraph, telephone, and power	49
Locomotive engineers	58
Locomotive firemen	45
Loom fixers	10
Machinists	33
Mechanics and repairmen	25
Airplane	48
Automobile	19
Office machine	36
Radio and television	36
Railroad and car shop	23
Not elsewhere classified	27
Millers, grain, flour, feed, etc.	19
Millwrights	31
Molders, metal	12
Motion-picture projectionists	43
Opticians, and lens grinders and polishers	39
Painters, construction and maintenance	16
Paperhangers	10
Pattern- and model-makers, except paper	44
Photoengravers and lithographers	64
Piano and organ tuners and repairmen	38
Plasterers	25
Plumbers and steam-fitters	34
Pressmen and plate printers, printing	49
Rollers and roll hands, metal	22
Roofers and slaters	15
Shoemakers and repairers, except factory	12
Stationary engineers	47
Stone-cutters and stone-carvers	25
Structural-metal workers	34
Tailors and tailoresses	23
Tinsmiths, coppersmiths, and sheet-metal workers	33
Toolmakers, and die-makers and setters	50
Upholsterers	22
Craftsmen and kindred workers	32
Members of the armed forces	18
Operatives and Kindred Workers	
Apprentices	35
Auto mechanics	25
Bricklayers and masons	32
Carpenters	31
Electricians	37
Machinists and toolmakers	41
Mechanics, except auto	34
Plumbers and pipe-fitters	33
Building trades	29
Metalworking trades	33
Printing trades	40
Other specified trades	31
Trade not specified	39

Occupations, by Major Occupation Group	Socio-economic Index
Asbestos and insulation workers	32
Attendants, auto service and parking	19
Blasters and powdermen	11
Boatmen, canalmen, and lock-keepers	24
Brakemen, railroad	42
Bus-drivers	24
Chainmen, rodmen, and axmen, surveying	25
Conductors, bus and street railway	30
Deliverymen and routemen	32
Dressmakers and seamstresses, except factory	23
Dyers	12
Filers, grinders, and polishers, metal	22
Fruit, nut, and vegetable graders and packers, exc. factory	10
Furnacemen, smeltermen, and pourers	18
Heaters, metal	29
Laundry and dry-cleaning operatives	15
Meat-cutters, except slaughter and packing house	29
Milliners	46
Mine operatives and laborers	10
Coal mining	2
Crude petroleum and natural gas extraction	38
Mining and quarrying, except fuel	12
Motormen, mine, factory, logging camp, etc.	3
Motormen, street, subway, and elevated railway	34

Occupations, by Major Occupation Group	Socio-economic Index
Oilers and greasers, except auto	15
Painters, except construction and maintenance	18
Photographic-process workers	42
Power-station operators	50
Sailors and deck hands	16
Sawyers	5
Spinners, textile	5
Stationary firemen	17
Switchmen, railroad	44
Taxicab-drivers and chauffeurs	10
Truck- and tractor-drivers	15
Weavers, textile	6
Welders and flame-cutters	24
Operatives and Kindred Workers	
Manufacturing	17
Durable goods	
Sawmills, planing mills, and misc. wood products	7
Sawmills, planing mills, and mill work	7
Miscellaneous wood products	9
Furniture and fixtures	9
Stone, clay, and glass products	17
Glass and glass products	23
Cement; and concrete, gypsum; and plaster products	10
Structural clay products	10
Pottery and related products	21

Occupations, by Major Occupation Group	Socio-economic Index
Misc. nonmetallic mineral and stone products	15
Metal industries	16
Primary metal industries	15
Blast furnaces, steel works, and rolling mills	17
Other primary iron and steel industries	12
Primary nonferrous industries	15
Fabricated metal ind. (incl. not spec. metal)	16
Fabricated steel products	16
Fabricated nonferrous metal products	15
Not specified metal industries	14
Machinery, except electrical	22
Agricultural machinery and tractors	21
Office and store machines and devices	31
Miscellaneous machinery	22
Electrical machinery, equipment, and supplies	26
Transportation equipment	23
Motor vehicles and motor vehicle equipment	21
Aircraft and parts	34
Ship and boat building and repairing	16
Railroad and misc. transportation equipment	23
Professional and photographic equipment and watches	29
Professional equipment and supplies	23
Photographic equipment and supplies	40
Watches, clocks, and clockwork-operated devices	28
Miscellaneous manufacturing industries	16
Nondurable goods	
Food and kindred products	16
Meat products	16
Dairy products	22
Canning and preserving fruits, vegetables, and sea foods	9
Grain-mill products	14
Bakery products	15
Confectionery and related products	12
Beverage industries	19

Occupations, by Major Occupation Group	Socio-economic Index
Misc. food preparations and kindred products	11
Not specified food industries	19
Tobacco manufactures	2
Textile mill products	6
Knitting mills	21
Dyeing and finishing textiles, exc. knit goods	8
Carpets, rugs, and other floor coverings	14
Yarn, thread, and fabric mills	2
Miscellaneous textile mill products	10
Apparel and other fabricated textile products	21
Apparel and accessories	22
Miscellaneous fabricated textile products	17
Paper and allied products	19
Pulp, paper, and paperboard mills	19
Paperboard containtainers and boxes	17
Miscellaneous paper and pulp products	19
Printing, publishing, and allied industries	31
Chemicals and allied products	20
Synthetic fibers	9
Drugs and medicines	26
Paints, varnishes, and related products	15
Miscellaneous chemicals and allied products	23
Petroleum and coal products	51
Petroleum refining	56
Miscellaneous petroleum and coal products	14
Rubber products	22
Leather and leather products	16
Leather: tanned, curried, and finished	10
Footwear, except rubber	9
Leather products, except footwear	14
Not specified manufacturing industries	16
Nonmanufacturing industries (incl. not reported)	18
Construction	18
Railroads and railway express service	15
Transportation, except railroad	23
Telecommunications, and utilities and sanitary services	21
Wholesale and retail trade	17

Occupations, by Major Occupation Group	Socio-economic Index
Business and repair services	19
Personal services	11
Public administration	17
All other industries (incl. not reported)	20
Private Household Workers	
Housekeepers, private household	19
Living in	10
Living out	21
Laundresses, private household	12
Living in	—
Living out	12
Private-household workers	7
Living in	12
Living out	6
Service Workers, Except Private Household	
Attendants, hospital and other institution	13
Attendants, professional and personal service	26
Attendants, recreation and amusement	19
Barbers, beauticians, and manicurists	17
Bartenders	19
Boarding- and lodging-house keepers	30
Bootblacks	8
Charwomen and cleaners	10
Cooks, except private household	15
Counter and fountain workers	17
Elevator operators	10
Firemen, fire protection	37
Guards, watchmen, and doorkeepers	18
Housekeepers and stewards, except private household	31
Janitors and sextons	9
Marshals and constables	21
Midwives	37
Policemen and detectives	39
Government	40
Private	36
Porters	4
Practical nurses	22
Sheriffs and bailiffs	34
Ushers, recreation and amusement	25
Waiters and waitresses	16
Watchmen (crossing) and bridge-tenders	17
Service workers, except private household	11
Farm Laborers and Foremen	
Farm foremen	20
Farm laborers, wage workers	6
Farm laborers, unpaid family workers	17
Farm-service laborers, self-ployed	22
Laborers, Except Farm and Mine	
Fishermen and oystermen	10
Garage laborers, and car-washers and greasers	8
Gardeners, except farm, and groundskeepers	11
Longshoremen and stevedores	11
Lumbermen, raftsmen, and wood-choppers	4
Teamsters	8

Occupations, by Major Occupation Group	Socio-economic Index
Laborers	
Manufacturing	8
Durable goods	
Sawmills, planing mills, and misc. wood products	3
Sawmills, planing mills, and mill work	3
Miscellaneous wood products	2
Furniture and fixtures	5
Stone, clay, and glass products	7
Glass and glass products	14
Cement; and concrete, gypsum; and plaster prod.	5
Structural clay products	5
Pottery and related products	7
Misc. nonmetallic mineral and stone products	5
Metal industries	7
Primary metal industries	7
Blast furnaces, steel works, and rolling mills	9
Other primary iron and steel industries	4
Primary nonferrous industries	6

Occupations, by Major Occupation Group	Socio-economic Index
Fabricated metal ind. (incl. not spec. metal)	7
Fabricated steel products	7
Fabricated nonferrous metal products	10
Not specified metal industries	9
Machinery, except electrical	11
Agricultural machinery and tractors	14
Office and store machines and devices	17
Miscellaneous machinery	10
Electrical machinery, equipment, and supplies	14
Transportation equipment	11
Motor vehicles and motor vehicle equipment	13
Aircraft and parts	15
Ship and boat building and repairing	2
Railroad and misc. transportation equipment	8
Professional and photographic equipment, and watches	11

Occupations, by Major Occupation Group	Socio-economic Index
Professional equipment and supplies	10
Photographic equipment and supplies	16
Watches, clocks, and clockwork-operated devices	—
Miscellaneous manufacturing industries	12
Nondurable goods	
Food and kindred products	9
Meat products	8
Dairy products	13
Canning and preserving fruits, vegetables, and sea foods	6
Grain-mill products	6
Bakery products	10
Confectionery and related products	10
Beverage industries	16
Misc. food preparations and kindred products	5
Not specified food industries	14
Tobacco manufacturers	0
Textile mill products	3
Knitting mills	4
Dyeing and finishing textiles, exc. knit goods	9
Carpets, rugs, and other floor coverings	14
Yarn, thread, and fabric mills	1
Miscellaneous textile mill products	6
Apparel and other fabricated textile products	9
Apparel and accessories	11
Miscellaneous fabricated textile products	6
Paper and allied products	7
Pulp, paper, and paperboard mills	6
Paperboard containers and boxes	10
Miscellaneous paper and pulp products	8
Printing, publishing, and allied industries	23
Chemicals and allied products	8
Synthetic fibers	4
Drugs and medicines	22
Paints, varnishes, and related products	8
Miscellaneous chemicals and allied products	8
Petroleum and coal products	22
Petroleum refining	26
Miscellaneous petroleum and coal products	3

Occupations, by Major Occupation Group	Socio-economic Index	Occupations, by Major Occupation Group	Socio-economic Index
Rubber products	12	Railroads and railway express service	3
Leather and leather products	6	Transportation, except railroad	9
Leather: tanned, curried, and finished	2	Telecommunications, and utilities and sanitary services	6
Footwear, except rubber	10	Wholesale and retail trade	12
Leather products, except footwear	12	Business and repair services	9
Not specified manufacturing industries	8	Personal services	5
Nonmanufacturing industries (incl. not reported)	7	Public administration	7
Construction	7	All other industries (incl. not reported)	6
		Occupation not reported	19

The second example, the Hall-Jones Scale of Occupational Prestige for Males, has the unusual merit that it is partly based on the prestige ratings given by a representative British sample and filled out by the judgments of expert sociologists. For details of the scale's construction, see John Hall and D. Caradog Jones, "Social Grading of Occupations," *British Journal of Sociology,* I (1950), 31–55; and David V. Glass, ed., *Social Mobility in Britain* (London: Kegan Paul, 1954). Though it seems a long list, it contains only a fraction of the job names that exist, but an effort has been made to include most of the occupations that are encountered frequently in survey work. Note the special section at the end, beginning with actor, giving the names of occupations that cover a range of classes, depending on the number of persons employed, size of farm, and so on. In the body of the scale itself there are also occupations that occur in several classes, depending on the respondent's level in, for example, the army, the civil service, or the police. To help with the classification of jobs that are not listed, each class has been given a label, such as "skilled manual"; this is also helpful in the interpretation of results and when classes have to be combined. Usually, the white collar/blue collar line of demarcation is drawn between classes 5(a) and 5(b).

When using the scale, it is important that every coder thoroughly acquaint himself with its contents and divisions and not regard it merely as a general guide. Every effort should be made to look up and find the actual job in question, and to hold over for discussion the names of jobs that cannot be found on the scale. For instance, one might be tempted to classify a storekeeper, a waiter, or a hairdresser as "manual," whereas they are classified as "routine nonmanual" on the scale. Again, a lorry driver is classified as "skilled manual" or as "semi-skilled manual," depending on whether he is a long-distance or a short-distance driver. Beware of such vague job titles as "clerk" or "engineer"; more information is required to enable us to distinguish between a town clerk, a legal clerk, a bank clerk, or a clerk of works, and between a qualified engineer, a sanitary engineer, a construction engineer, a motor engineer and a craftsman engineer, before they can be classified.

The Hall-Jones Scale of Occupational Prestige for Males

Class 1: Professionally Qualified and High Administrative

Accountant
Analytical chemist
Architect
Army:
  Major and upwards
Auditor
Bank manager
Barrister
Civil Service:
  administrative,
  C.E.O.'s, chief inspector of taxes, inspector of schools
Colliery manager
Consultant (engineer, doctor, etc.)
Contractor (building, railway, etc.)
Dental surgeon
Dentist (qualified)
Designer, aircraft
Diplomat
Director of Education
Doctor
Editor
Engineer (qualified)
Geologist
Headmaster (sec. school or prep. school)
Insurance actuary
Land or farm agent or steward
Landowner
Marine surveyor
Medical officer of health
M.P.
Navy:
  Lt. Cmdr. upwards
Planter
Police:
  C/Suptd., D/Cdr., Cdr., Asst/Commr., Chief Constable

Procurator fiscal
Quantity Surveyor
Race horse owner
Research scientist
Royal Air Force: Wing/Cdr. and upwards
Sheriff's substitute
Shipowner
Solicitor
Stockbroker
Sugar refiner
Surveyor (qualified)
Town Clerk
Treasurer, local authority
Underwriter, Lloyds
University lecturer
Valuation officer
Veterinary Surgeon (qualified)

Class 2: Managerial and Executive (with Some Responsibility for Directing and Initiating Policy)

Air pilot
Army:
Captain and below (commissioned)
Articled clerk
Bank clerk (senior)
Chiropodist
Civil Service:
S.E.O.'s, inspector of taxes (higher grade), inspector of taxes
Commercial artist
Commercial scientist
Dentist (unqualified)
Divisional Education Officer
Headmaster (elem. school)
Headmaster (indust. school)
Head postmaster
House property manager
Minister (nonconformist)
Navy: Lieut. and below (commissioned)
Optician (qualified)
Patent agent
Personnel manager
Pharmacist
Police:
Chief Inspector, Suptd.
Psychiatric social worker
Restaurateur
Royal Air Force:
Squadron leader and below (commissioned)
Sanitary engineer
Sanitary surveyor
Settlement warden
Teacher (sec. sch. or public school)
Veterinary practitioner (unqualified)

Class 3: Inspectional, Supervisory, and Other Nonmanual (Higher grade)

Advertising agent
Army:
W.O.
Bank clerk (junior)
Boarding out officer
Branch manager
Catering officer
Canal boat proprietor
Civil Service:
E.O.'s, Technical Officer, exptl. officer,
collector, tax officer (higher grade)
Church worker
Clerk of works
Club master (warden)
Colliery engineer
Commercial traveller
Committee clerk
Contractor
Dispensing chemist (employed)
Dog breeder
Draughtsman (qualified)
Drug and food inspector (L.G.)
Entertainment organizer
Farm bailiff or grieve
Forwarding agent

Goods agent (railway)
Head clerk
Horse breeder
Hotel keeper or manager
Industrial chemist
Inspector (insurance, engineering)
Jockey
Journalist or reporter
Librarian (assistant, qualified)
Marine engineer
Mental health officer
Mental nurse (qualified)
Navy: W.O.
Overman, colliery
Permanent way inspector
Photographer
Physiotherapist
Police:
  Inspector
Postmaster
Probation officer
Radiographer
Royal Air Force:
  W.O.
Rate fixer
Rating officer
Royal Marines:
  Sgt. Major,
  Q.M. Sgt.
Salesman
Sanitary inspector
Shorthand writer
Station master
Stockbroker's clerk
Teacher (elem. sch., jnr. tech., etc.)
Technician (B.B.C.)
Undertaker
Youth employment officer
Youth organizer

Class 4: Inspectional, Supervisory, and Other Nonmanual (Lower Grade)

Accountant's clerk
Advertising copywriter
Advertisement drawer
Army:
  Sgt. and S./Sgt.
Architect's apprentice
Auctioneer
Bank detective
Book keeper
Butler
Chef or hotel cook
Chemical sampler
Civil Service:
  H.C.O.'s
  Assistance Officer
Club leader
Coast guard
Costing clerk
Cricketer (professional)
Customs officer
Deputy overman
Draughtsman (apprentice)
Erection engineer (unqualified)
Estimating clerk
Film cutter
Footballer (professional)
Furrier
Insurance agent (industrial)
Librarian (unqualified)
Licensed victualler
Market gardener
Masseur (employed)
Merchant Navy:
  Radio Operator
  Cadet
  Midshipman
Navy:
  P.O. and C.P.O.
Police:
  Sergeant
Publican (innkeeper)
Radio Officer (civil airways)
Royal Air Force:
  Sgt. and S/Sgt.
Road safety officer
Relieving officer

Religious brother
Sampler in brewery
School Attendance Officer
Shop supervisor
Shop walker
Signal inspector
Stationer
Sub-Postmaster
Surveyor's assistant
Toy designer

Class 5(a): Routine Grades of Nonmanual Work

Booking clerk
Caretaker
Cashier:
  Box Office, Shop,
  Undefined
Civil Service:
  C.O.'s and T.C.'s,
  Asst. Collector,
  Tax officer
Clerk (routine)
Commissionaire
Dance band musician
Draughtsman (tracer-unqualified)
Hairdresser
Head Porter
Librarian, assistant (unqualified)
Police:
  Constable, special
  Constable, cadet
Post Office clerk
Prison officer (Warder)
Provident collector
Railway detective
Rate collector
Rent collector
Sheriff's assistant
Shop assistant:
  Chemist, Confectioner, Draper, Florist, Grocer, Ironware, Furniture, Stationer, Tailor
Storekeeper
Telegraphist
Telephone operator
Waiter
Window dresser

Class 5(b): Skilled Manual

Ambulance Man
Annealer
Apprentice (skilled trade)
Army:
  Cpl. and L/Cpl.
Baker
Blacksmith
Boiler maker
Boiler smith
Book binder
Book maker
Boot maker
Boot repairer
Brass finisher
Brass moulder
Bricklayer
Builder (employed craftsman)
Bus driver
Butcher
Cab driver
Cabinet maker
Carpenter
Carpet weaver
Cap maker
Capstan setter
Caster (dies)
Chain maker
Charge hand
Chauffeur
Checker
Chimney sweep
Clicker
Cloth lapper
Coach builder

Coachman
Colliery electrician
Colliery engineer
Colour mixer (if skilled)
Compositor
Concrete fencer
Cook
Cooper
Copper smith
Cord wainer
Cotton weaver
Cowman
Crane driver
Currier
Cutler
Decorator
Dental mechanic
Donkeyman (sea)
Dock gateman
Die-setter
Electrician (employed craftsman)
Engine driver
Engine stoker
Engineer (employed craftsman)
Engraver
Excavator driver
Farm worker (skilled)
Fitter
Forester
French Polisher
Fur finisher
Furnaceman (chemicals)
Galvanizer
Gamekeeper
Ganger
Gardener
Gasfitter
Glass blower
Glazier
Grainweigher
Groom
Gunsmith
Harness weaver
Head gardener
Horse dealer
Horseman
Hosiery trimmer
Inspector (Gas Co., transport etc.)
Instrument Maker
Ironmoulder
Iron or steel dresser
Iron driller
Jewel cast maker
Joiner
Laboratory assistant
Landscape gardener
Lathe setter
Leather dresser
Leather Splitter
Lock gateman
Lodge keeper
Lorry driver (long distance)
Machine repairer
Maintenance fitter
Maltster
Marble polisher
Mason
Mechanic (skilled)
Medical glass engraver
Merchant Navy:
  Apprentice
Miller
Millwright
Mole catcher
Motorman
Motor engineer
Motor mechanic
Moulder
Musical instrument repairer
Navy:
  Ldg. Seaman
Newsagent
Nurseryman
Operative (skilled)
Painter
Paint mixer
Paint sprayer
Panel beater
Paviour
Pattern maker

Pit repairer
Plasterer
Plater (iron and steel)
Plumber
Portmanteau maker
Potter
Printer's cutter
Printer
Puddler (metals)
Quarryman
Radio mechanic (skilled)
Railway crossing keeper
Railway guard
Railway signalman
Range fitter
Record maker
Retort builder
Rivetter
Ropemaker
Ropespinner
Royal Air Force:
  Cpl. and LAC.
Sailmaker
Seedsman
Shepherd
Ship's plater
Ship's carpenter
Ship's fireman
Ship's rigger
Shipwright
Signwriter
Silk weaver
Silversmith (skilled craftsman)
Slater
Slaughterer
Slinger
Spinner
Stage hand
Steel cutter
Steeple-Jack
Stillman
Studgroom
Sweep
Talleyman (checker)
Tailor
Tanner
Teazer (glass)
Telegraph linesman
Thatcher
Tilemaker
Tinsmith
Toolmaker
Toolsetter
Toymaker (skilled)
Tractor driver
Turn cock
Turner
Upholsterer
Valve tester
Vulcanizer
Waggon examiner
Waggon painter
Watchmaker and repairer
Waterproof coat maker
Weaver
Welder
Wheelwright
Woodman
Wool/worsted spinner

Class 6: Manual, Semi-skilled

Agricultural worker, farm servant
Armature winder
Army:
  Private
Artificial flowermaker
Assembler
Baker's assistant
Bargeman
Barman
Basketmaker
Billiard marker
Blacksmith's striker
Boilerman
Boot machinist
Brass bedstead maker
Brass wire worker

Brickmaker
Brushdrawer
Builder's scaffolder
Buttonhole cutter
Bus conductor
Butcher's assistant
Canvasser
Capstan operator
Carpenter's mate
Car park attendant
Carpet finisher
Carter
Catering assistant
Closer
Cloth finisher
Coal conveyor
Coal hewer
Coal trimmer
Core maker
Craneman (crane driver)
Darner
Deliveryman
Dental mechanic's assistant
Drayman
Driller (brush factory)
Dyer
Electrician's mate
Engineman
Farmworker (farm labourer)
File Setter
Finisher (laundry)
Fisherman
Fitter's mate
Furniture remover (employee)
Garage hand
Gasmantle maker
Gownpresser
Grain storeman
Grinder
Hall porter
Hammerman
Hand sewer
Holder-on
Hurdle maker
Ironer or clothes presser
Lathworker
Lighterman
Letter stamper
Lorry Driver (short distance)
Machine operator
Machinist
Maker (wooden-box)
Meter reader
Milkman
Muslin darner
Navy:
  A.B.
Office boy
Operative (semi-skilled)
Ostler
Packer
Packing case maker
Pearl stringer
Pirn winder
Pit headman
Plastic welder
Platelayer
Polisher
Porter (Town Hall)
Postman
Post Office sorter
Presser (tailor's)
Printer's feeder
Railway engine cleaner
Railway linesman
Railway porter
Roadsman
Rope slicer
Royal Air Force:
  A.C.2. and A.C.1.
Sawyer
Seaman
Serrator
Sexton
Sheet metal worker
Ship plater's helper
Shop Hand:
  Greengrocer, Butcher, Fishmonger
Shunter
Stableman

Stevedore
Stoker
Storeman
Surfaceman (railway or road)
Switchman
Telegraph Boy
Ticket collector
Tobacco spinner
Timber cutter
Tin pricker
Town porter
Traction engine driver
Trawlerman
Trimmer (coal, upholstery, etc.)
Van driver
Warehouseman
Warehouse worker
Wheeltapper
Wood machinist
Wool sorter
Worker:
Chemical, Leather, Starch, Steel, Rope, Rubber, etc.

Class 7: Manual, Routine

Bag sewer
Bath attendant
Bottler
Bottle washer
Boatman (canal)
Bolt screwer
Book folder
Boxmaker (cardboard)
Builder's labourer
Bundle maker
Cameraman (street)
Canteen assistant
Carman (shunter)
Carpet cleaner
Carpet factory worker
Cattle drover
Cellarman
Cleaner
Coal porter
Costermonger
Counterhand
Deal porter
Despatch labourer
Distillery worker
Docker
Drainer
Drain pipe layer
Errand Boy
Factory hand (routine)
Factory worker
Folder
Gasworker
Hawker (dealer)
Houseboy
Labourer
Lamp cleaner
Lamplighter
Lavatory attendant
Leather carrier
Lift attendant
Loader
Lorryman
Machine minder (routine)
Messenger
Navvy
Paper seller
Porter
Presshand
Publican's assistant
Quay labourer
Rabbit seller
Railway yardman
Refuse collector
Roadman
Roadsweeper
Scavenger
Showcard mounter
Sorter (not P.O.)
Stacker
Street trader
Tar sprayer
Vanman

Occupations whose allocation depends on criteria additional to the nature of the occupation itself, e.g., number of persons employed or supervised, size of farm, etc.

Watchman
Actor 1/4
Artist 1/2
Author 1/2
Bookie 4/5(a)
Business owner, director, secretary or manager: buyer:
- 100+ hands 1
- 10–99 hands 2
- 3–9 hands 3
- 1 or 2 man business, skilled trade 4
- 1 or 2 man business, other 5(a)

Clergyman 1/2
Clerk (local authority) 4/5(a)
Farmer:
- 250+ acres 1
- 100–249 acres 2
- 10–99 acres 3
- Up to 9 acres 4

Foreman:
- 20+ hands 3
- 3–19 hands 4
- 1 or 2 hands 5(b)

Haulage contractor 2/3
Hospital secretary 1/2
Librarian (head) 1/2
Maintenance engineer 3/4
Master mariner 1/3
Merchant (wholesale):
- Grading one higher than business owner throughout.

Merchant Navy:
- Captain 1/3
- Ship's engineer 3/4

Physical training teacher 3/4
Poultry farmer 3/4
Private tutor, coach, 2/3
Professional writer 1/3
Quarry master 1/2
Reader, publisher's 1/2
Registrar 2/3
Scaffolder 5(b)/6
Secretary of voluntary organization 1/3
Shopkeeper 1/5(a) (see business owner)
Statistician 1/2
Textile designer 2/3
Trade union official 3/4
Welfare officer 1/3

II

Statistics Test

If you get more than one answer wrong, you should not embark on social research without a refresher course in statistics.

1. Imagine that you had asked a group of men and a group of women: "Who is your favorite film star?" How would you find out whether there is a significant sex difference in the type of film star preferred?

2. Suppose you had IQ's available to you for a sample of delinquents and a sample of nondelinquents individually matched for sex and age. How would you find out: (a) whether delinquents tend to be duller than nondelinquents? (b) what is the degree of correlation between intelligence and delinquency?

3. A correlation of –0.29 has been observed, in a large sample, between intelligence and family size of completed families. What conclusions would you draw from this?

4

Go to church	Television Viewers	Nonviewers
regularly	23%	47%
occasionally	77%	53%
	100%	100%

Which of the following conclusions would you accept, on the basis of the evidence in the above table: (a) that irreligious people are among the first to buy television sets? (b) that television causes people to go to church less often? (c) that there is no significant difference between viewers and nonviewers, as far as church-going is concerned? (d) that regular church-going causes people to turn away from television?

ANSWERS

1. Construct two frequency distributions and apply the chi-squared test of statistical significance (*Not* means and standard deviations; these are qualitative data.)

2. (a) Calculate means and apply the formula for t-test of related means (these are matched samples).

(b) Either the biserial or possibly the tetrachoric correlation coefficients would be applicable (delinquent/nondelinquent is a dichotomy).

3. The correlation is relatively small, so the relationship is not very strong. However, it suggests that brighter parents have smaller families; that brighter children have fewer siblings; and that children from large families probably have parents who are not very bright; and vice-versa. We may add that brighter parents seem more motivated and/or more successful in limiting their families.

4. We can accept *none* of these conclusions, first, because we have no evidence of the *direction* of causality; moreover, there might be a third variable which affects both viewing television and churchgoing; and second, because we do not know the number of cases in the two samples, and therefore cannot test the strength of the relationship.

III

Nomographs for the Testing of Statistical Significance of Differences between Percentages

In order to facilitate the inspection of results, most surveys produce their findings in the form of large numbers of percentages. Eventually, we have to determine the statistical significance of differences between percentages, and usually this can only be done by going back to the raw frequencies and calculating chi-squared values. If we are dealing, for instance, with the differences between men and women in response to one particular multiple-mention question with, say, seven answer-categories, then we shall probably wish to test for the sex difference in respect of one or two specific answer-categories. In principle this means "collapsing" the 2×7 into a 2×2 table, or several 2×2 tables, testing for the statistical significance of one answer-category (or several answer-categories combined) against the remainder. The procedure has been outlined in Chapter 9.

In 1939, Joseph Zubin published a nomograph in Volume 34 of the *Journal of the American Statistical Association* (pp. 539–544), which has been recalculated and adapted for inclusion in the present text. It has the great advantage that we do not have to go back to the raw frequencies but can determine the significance of different proportions directly from the percentage figures. All we need is a ruler (preferably transparent), and the three charts that follow. All three nomographs are "read" in the same way, namely by placing the ruler at our two observed values on the left-hand line and right-hand line, and reading off on the middle line. The first chart enables us to find a "significant value," which will depend on the two sample sizes; if we place the ruler as accurately as we can against the two sample sizes (such as the number of men and the number of women, in the above example) on the left and on the right, then we shall be able to read off the significant value where the ruler crosses the center line. This value has to be *reached or exceeded* on one of the next two charts, or both, if the difference is to be statistically significant at one of the customary levels of probability. One chart has, on its center line, significance values for the 10 per cent and the 5 per cent levels; the next chart has the values for the 1 per cent and the 0.1 per cent levels. Thus, if we find that a difference between two percentages is significant at the 5 per cent level, it may be worthwhile checking on the next chart whether it will reach the 1 per cent or even the 0.1 per cent level.

It may be worth repeating that, ordinarily, chi-squared cannot be calculated from percentages, but only from the raw frequencies. In the case of the present nomograph, however, we can utilize percentages directly, because our first chart takes the respective sample sizes into account in establishing our "significant value." This is particularly helpful in survey work, where we often have to test large numbers of percentages for statistical significance but where such percentages are based on sample sizes that remain stable throughout the length of the questionnaire. Having once looked up our significant value on the first chart, we need henceforth concern ourselves only with the second and the third charts—unless we come to deal with a different set of subsamples.

Inevitably, nomographs are somewhat lacking in precision, so that for the more important differences, where these border on the limits of significance, the necessary calculations should also be carried out. The same applies to instances where the sample sizes are very low. Note also that a given difference (say, fifteen percentage points) may be significant at the extremes, where one of the percentages approaches zero or one hundred, but not in the middle ranges; if we merely observe the magnitude of the difference, without considering its place in the percentage range, we are likely to produce errors. Where one of the percentages is very small (say, below 5 per cent) or very large (say, above 95 per cent) the nomograph tends to give an overestimate of statistical significance, and calculations again become necessary.

Perhaps the most helpful way to use this nomograph is to think of it as an aid to inspection, a simple device that will enable us to focus attention on the more important differences and sort the grain from the chaff.

EXAMPLES

(1) $N_1 = 125$ $N_2 = 164$ significant value $= 0.119$
Percentages: 61 and 50, significant at the 10 per cent level.

(2) As above, percentages 81 and 70 significant at the 5 per cent level.
(NB: the difference between the two sets of percentages is the same, but the significance is greater when approaching extreme values 0 or 100.)

(3) $N_1 = 350$ $N_2 = 600$ significant value $= 0.068$
Percentages: 75 and 66, significant at the 1 per cent level.

(4) As above, percentages 12 and 5, significant at the 0.1 per cent level.

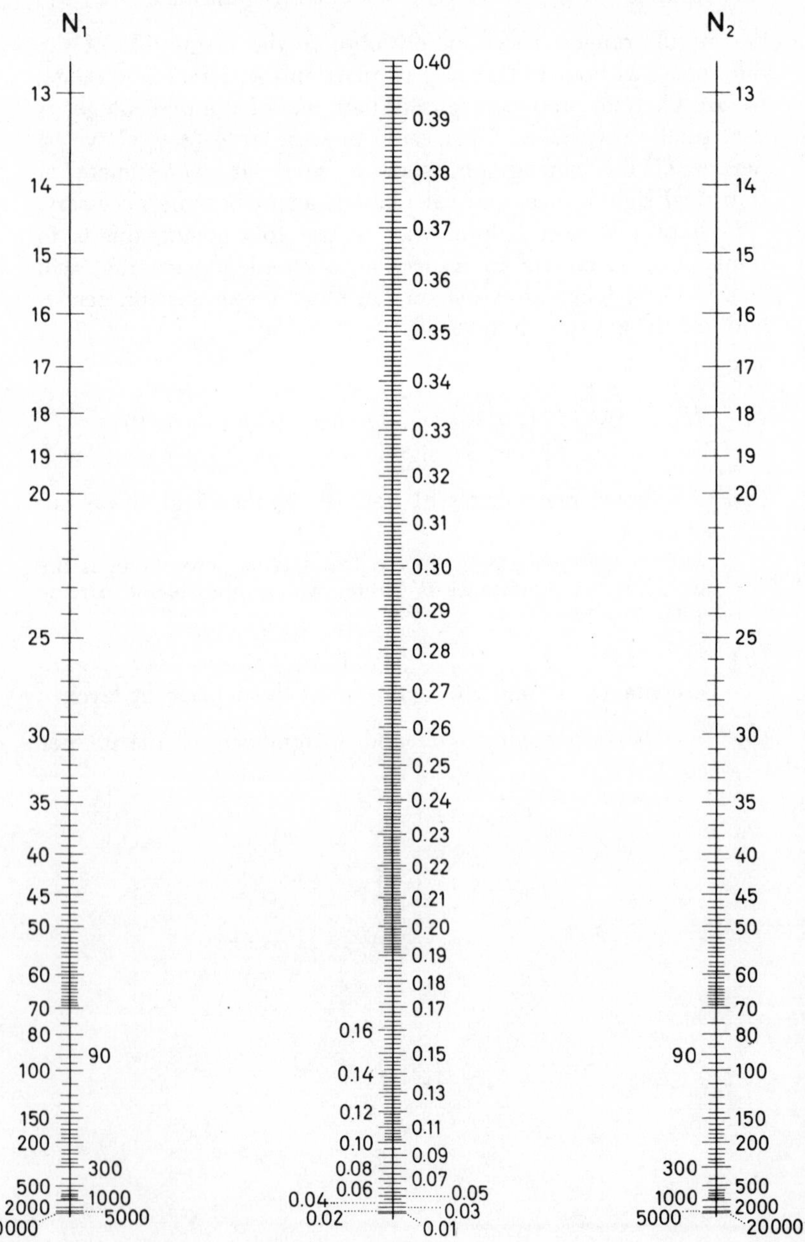

N1
N2
13
14
15
16
17
18
19
20
25
30
35
40
45
50
60
70
80
90
100
150
200
300
500
1000
2000
5000
20000
0.40
0.39
0.38
0.37
0.36
0.35
0.34
0.33
0.32
0.31
0.30
0.29
0.28
0.27
0.26
0.25
0.24
0.23
0.22
0.21
0.20
0.19
0.18
0.17
0.16
0.15
0.14
0.13
0.12
0.11
0.10
0.09
0.08
0.07
0.06
0.05
0.04
0.03
0.02
0.01

Chart 1

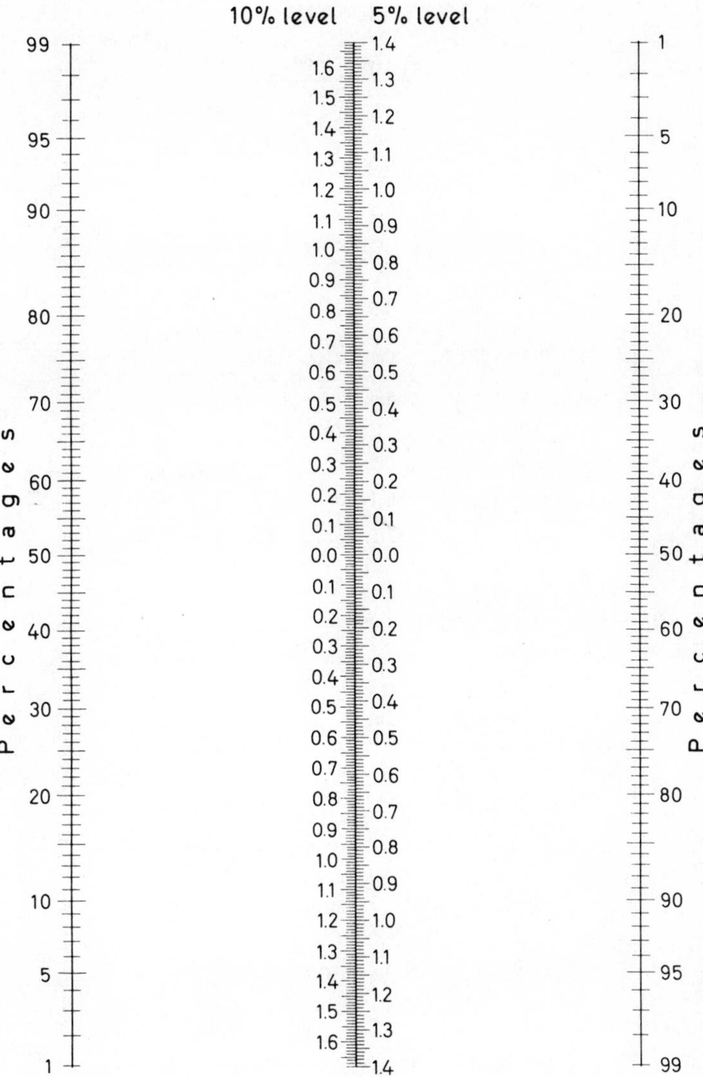

10% level
5% level
Percentages
99
95
90
80
70
60
50
40
30
20
10
5
1
1.6
1.5
1.4
1.3
1.2
1.1
1.0
0.9
0.8
0.7
0.6
0.5
0.4
0.3
0.2
0.1
0.0
Percentages

Chart 2

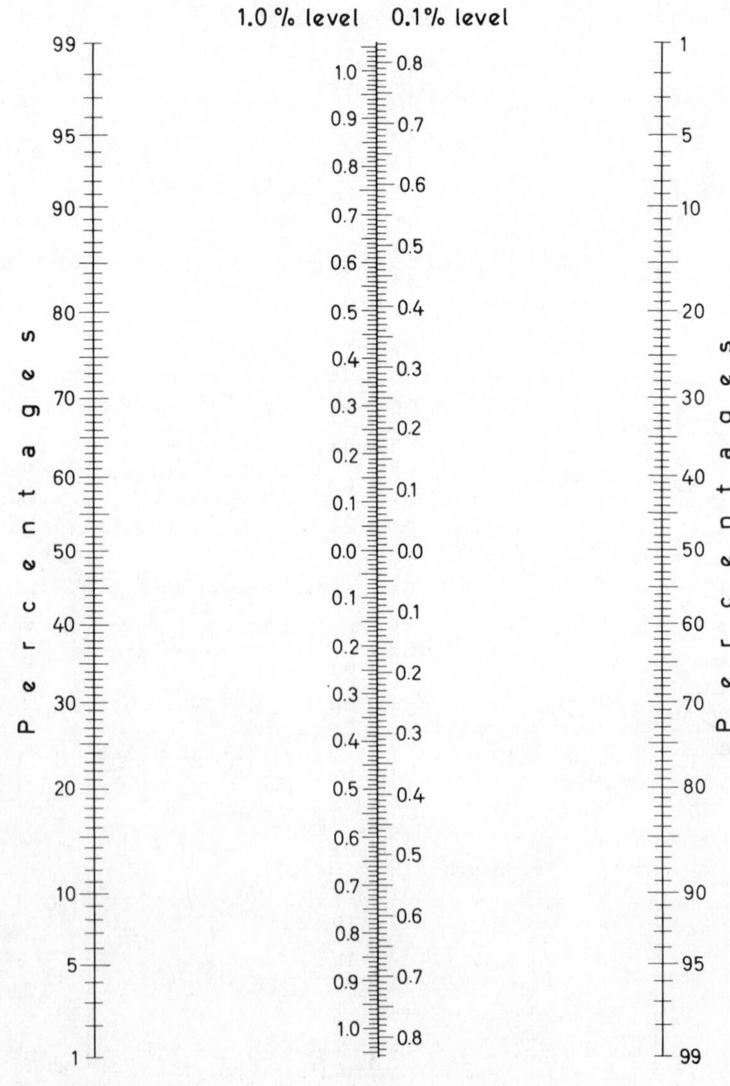
1.0 % level
0.1% level
Percentages
Percentages
99
95
90
80
70
60
50
40
30
20
10
5
1
1.0
0.9
0.8
0.7
0.6
0.5
0.4
0.3
0.2
0.1
0.0
0.8
0.7
0.6
0.5
0.4
0.3
0.2
0.1
0.0

Chart 3

Acknowledgments

I wish to thank a number of people for their kind permission to use material from their works, as follows:

A. L. Baldwin, J. Kalhorn, and F. H. Breese, "The Appraisal of Parent Behaviour," *Psychological Monographs,* XXIV (1949), No. 299.

E. S. Bogardus, "Measuring Social Distances," *Journal of Applied Psychology,* IX (1925) No. 4.

William Caudill, *The Psychiatric Hospital as a Small Society* (Harvard University Press, 1958).

John Hall and D. Caradog Jones, "The Hall-Jones Scale of Occupational Prestige for Males."

H. T. Himmelweit, A. N. Oppenheim, and P. Vince, *Television and the Child* (Oxford University Press, 1958).

R. Hoeflin and L. Kell, "The Kell-Hoeflin Incomplete Sentence Blank: Youth-Parent Relations," *Monographs of the Society for Research in Child Development,* XXIV (1959), Serial No. 72.

Jacob Tuckman and Irving Lorge, "Attitudes toward Old People," *Journal of Social Psychology,* XXXVII (1953).

A. J. Reiss, *Occupations and Social Status* (The Free Press of Glencoe, 1961).

Michael Shepherd, A. A. Cooper, A. C. Brown, and G. W. Kalton, *Psychiatric Illness in General Practice* (Oxford University Press, in press).

I also wish to thank International Computers and Tabulators, Ltd., for permission to reproduce the punch card I have used as Figure 9–1.

Index